The Mike Whitney Story

Foreword by Alan Davidson

IRONBARK

First published 1993, in Ironbark, by Pan Macmillan Publishers
Australia, a division of Pan Macmillan Australia Pty Limited 63-71
Balfour Street, Chippendale

Copyright © Mike Whitney 1993

All rights reserved. No part of this book may be reproduced or
transmitted in any form or by any means, electronic or mechanical,
including photocopying, recording or by any information storage
and retrieval system, without prior permission in writing from
the publisher

National Library of Australia cataloguing-in-publication data:
Whitney, Mike Quick Whit: the Mike Whitney story

ISBN 0 330 27467 8

1. Whitney, Micheal, 1959- 2. Cricket players – Australia –
Biography. I. Heads, Ian. II. Title.

796.358092

Typeset by Letter Perfect, 541 George St, Sydney
Printed in Australia by Australian Print Group

ACKNOWLEDGEMENTS

When looking back on the people who have supported my cricket career, the first person I will always acknowledge is my wife Debbie, for putting up with me over the past decade and being so understanding of the demands of life as a professional cricketer.

My mother and sister, Christine, have also been enormous supports, as has been "Dear" (my aunt June), all my in-laws, and all my other relatives, who, from day one, have been fantastic.

I also must acknowledge the surgeons — Dr Merv Cross, Dr Nathan Gibbs and Dr Kim Slater — and chiropractors Noel Patterson and Damien Treacy. And the physios, Elizabeth Steet, Errol Alcott and Pat Farhart, particularly Elizabeth, who has been my personal physio for 10 years. When I'm injured she will basically drop everything to try and get me back on the paddock. A thousand thanks are not enough for her.

And I must give a special mention to Kevin Dalton — the "Magnet Man".

Then there are my team-mates, particularly the guys from the NSW and Australian cricket teams, and my "brothers" from the Randwick Cricket Club. If it wasn't for Randwick I wouldn't have had the opportunity to go on and play at a higher level. I must mention Bob Radford, from the NSW Cricket Association, who has always backed me. And Alan Davidson, for being the patron of my testimonial year, for being kind enough to contribute the foreword to this book, and, most of all, for taking me under his wing and looking after me for the past 15 years.

I also must thank "Mardo" and the boys, who have always kept me level-headed.

I would like to mention all the guys involved in my testimonial year — it turned into something bigger than Debbie and I could have ever managed — but to list all the people and the sponsors would be impossible. However, I must acknowledge my major sponsors — Carlton and United Breweries, Reebok, Boswell Printing, Frontline Graphics and Subaru.

In relation to this book I must thank the people at Ironbark, particularly Ian Heads and Phil Tresidder, who have spent so many hours putting the book together. Ian has just been a dynamo, particularly in the latter stages. I also appreciate the assistance of Deborah Wood, the Ironbark publisher, Geoff Armstrong, who edited the book, Kylie Prats, who designed and produced the finished art, Scott Rigney for the front cover design, Ross Dundas, who provided the statistics section, and Ian Russell, who checked the manuscript to make sure my memory was always spot on.

Contents

Foreword by Alan Davidson, A.M., M.B.E.	vii
Introduction by Debbie Whitney	ix
Preface by Phil Tresidder	xiii
1. A Christmas Star	1
2. The Young Whit	7
3. Learning the Game	14
4. The Twists of Fate	18
5. How Do You Feel?	28
6. A Brush With Bacchus	30
7. The Lost Years	37
8. Bumpers, Batsmen, and One-Day Cricket	45
9. A Traveller's Tales	55
10. Proving The Critics Wrong	59
11. "How Can They Do This To You?"	64
12. Fire and Brimstone	67
13. Caribbean Magic	72
14. Indian Summer	86
15. The World Cup	94
16. True Blue	99
17. Hot Times in Sri Lanka	107
18. A Break in my Testimonial Year	116
19. Calling the Shots	130
20. Best of the Best	138
21. The Whitney Clan	144
22. The Bottom Line	147
Statistics	153

DEDICATION

To my mother, Beryl, for her ability to put up with me in my early years, and because she has been a great mother, raising two children on her own after my father died so early. She has passed on to me qualities that have helped enormously in my life.

And to the memory of the late Tim Towers, who was the first guy I opened the bowling with in first grade at Randwick. He was one of the nicest guys I ever met, and he was a left-armer — one of the brotherhood.

Foreword

By Alan Davidson, A.M., M.B.E.

I well remember receiving a phone call from noted cricket writer Phil Tresidder one day in 1977, regarding a young fourth-grade left-arm bowler he had seen that day playing for Randwick District Cricket Club. The following Sunday, I watched this young fellow and was suitably impressed — so much so as to offer my assistance to him should he so desire.

His talent, his determination and drive, and his desire for success were obvious to all. His approach to training and fitness was masochistic, surely a reflection of his childhood dream of playing with the legendary prop forward and captain, John Sattler, and the great South Sydney rugby league team.

All these attributes provided quick success, from grade cricket to the NSW Sheffield Shield team and then a contract in league cricket in England.

Who could believe what happened next? A dream became a reality. The story of his selection in the 1981 Australian Test team in England is like a fairy tale. All the more meritorious is that his Test appearance came in only his seventh first-class game.

Suffice to say his play has had its great moments. His bowling has always featured pure aggression more in keeping with the football field. This aggression often overtook his enthusiasm, but always his desire was to never say die. His humour and by-play have made him a popular player with crowds all over the world, and it is true to say that the affection was mutual.

Like all who give 100 per cent and more on every day, injuries can occur. Michael has had many such injuries, but nothing to match his disappointment over his non-selection to tour the UK in 1989, after he had been the leading wicket-taker for the Australian season. This was also after he had taken an incredible 7 for 89 in the final Test of the 1988-89 West Indies series, in Adelaide.

In 1991-92, however, the Australian selectors did chose him for the Perth Test against India, and he responded with his best-ever 7 for 27. Michael's description in this book of that performance in Perth is vivid, but pales into insignificance after his recollection of his famous last-over defiance of the great Richard Hadlee in Melbourne in December, 1987.

Mike's efforts for the Blues of NSW have been epic, not only in figures (he lies fifth in the all-time list of leading wicket-takers for the state) but also for his upholding of the traditions of cricket in NSW and his support and example to his fellow players.

Michael has put back into the game off the field also. His address to the various state under-17 teams at the National Carnival dinner in Sydney saw over 100 youngsters mesmerised by the words of wisdom from the "Pied Piper".

From surfer to player to entertainer and speaker, Michael has travelled the road, climbed the hill, and, by his presence, made the game richer.

Who will ever be able to forget the tug at the knee-guard and the hippity hop to start the run that meant a hard day at the crease for many a batsman?

Well played, Michael. May you by your example inspire others to achieve and reach the stars.

Introduction

by Debbie Whitney

We met at a New Year's Eve party, though the date itself is not so memorable for me (Michael's the best with dates). He was different from anyone I had gone out with before, and not in my wildest dreams would I have thought we'd eventually marry.

He was wild, loud and gregarious, but he had that glint in his eye, something mischievous which kept me remotely interested. Whoever said that opposites attract was certainly right in our case. That night was the start of our rocky road to romance. What was interesting was that even back in those days Michael was the centre of attention. Everyone gravitated towards him.

Michael had, and retains, such a passion for life. He lives for the moment, makes the most of every opportunity, and passes his experiences onto the next open ear. He is infectious and encouraging, loves people and does not like to be "alone" in his own company.

I never had the opportunity to meet his father (something I regret) but his mother, Beryl, was the strongest influence on his life. They are a matching pair. He certainly got his ability to talk easily from her, his "upfrontness" (if there is such a word), and his strength, courage and conviction. She is a woman of principle, fairness and equality, but tough, stubborn and unbending. Her viewpoint is "black or white", and so too is Michael's, in contrast to my varying "greys".

Part of the "Whitney" trait is the story-telling. My introduction to the family was one of warmth, friendship, and lots of stories starting from back in Beryl's youth, through Christine (Michael's sister) and Michael's baby years and adolescence, to present-day events. Everyone would have a turn at relating a story, and the next narrator would pick up from where the last left off. Nowadays, I can recall more of their family experiences than my own. Such is their ability to make a story from next to nothing, jazz it up a bit, do the actions, throw in voice impersonations and do a song and dance if required. If a new audience, then all the better. They were encouraged to entertain, which is the reason for Michael's confidence and self-esteem (one can only presume).

The bond that built up among the three of them, especially after Michael's father Roy's death (when Michael was 16), instilled in them a strong family loyalty. It is a trait that has passed to all levels of his life, such as his unfailing loyalty to Randwick Cricket Club (no money offer could convince him to leave). People who know Michael, and maybe even those who don't, know of his loyalty. I've yet to work out if this is really just a flow on from his hard-headedness ... or another of his many endearing qualities.

When I entered his life, another strong-willed female (perhaps softer dispositioned) became a major influence on him. I, too, had an upbringing dominated by a strong mother (a businesswoman, working in real estate in the days when women never worked, who raised four children whom she packed up to take with her). My twin sisters, just as dominant, were the reason for our (Michael and I) meeting. Jennifer is married to Peter Devlin (one of the captains of Randwick C.C. and now the curator at North Sydney Oval) and at their wedding, where I was bridesmaid and Michael the M.C., we were re-united.

Michael has always been surrounded by very strong females, all with their own opinions and each having a different influence on his life. The nature of such circumstances probably explains the fact that Michael is really a "man's man" and loves being with the boys. I suppose some balance has to be reached.

I've never met anyone who has the gift to relate to all levels in the way Michael can. This brings to mind a funny story.

In the dressing room prior to the Bicentennial Test, at the SCG in January, 1988, Bob Hawke, the then Australian Prime Minister, walked into the dressing room to wish all the boys in the squad good luck. Michael was lying on the rubbers' bench, having some work done on his back, as Hawke shook everyone's hand. The PM walked over to Michael, who exclaimed: "Hey Bob, I want to ask you something!"

Apparently a hush came over the dressing room (I'm sure they were all thinking: "What's he going to say?"), before Michael continued: "I've just bought a flat in Clovelly and I'm wondering if you can do anything about my stamp duty?"

Everyone broke up, and Mr Hawke answered: "Well, Michael, that's a matter for (the then NSW Premier, Barrie) Unsworth."

No-one could believe their ears. I'm sure only Michael would have the guts or gall to do it, and, not only that, be able to get away with it.

Not only does he relate to the drunk in the street or the Prime Minister of Australia, he actually gives part of himself to them. He has to be the most generous person I know, whether with his time, himself or his money. Apart from his charity work, he'll give as much time as is physically possible to promising cricketers. He'll help a mate out who's stuck for cash, not mind if I spend a fortune at the shops, donate memorabilia for fund raising, do a story for the media at last-minute notice ... it is almost impossible for him to say "no" (he doesn't like doing it, and most of the time it's my job).

He does this because he wants or needs to be loved by everyone, bar none. He is a crowd pleaser. All of this, of course, has its drawbacks, and it tends to be me or family who feel it most because there is a limit to how much one person can give. And then there is the question of being taken advantage of or ripped off. He has had his fair share. For Michael, everyone's a good bloke. He is very unaware of faults in people's nature, rarely talks about anyone, and can easily forgive and forget. This is where we stand opposed, or, better put, maybe complement each other. He is the "talker" (not a very good listener), whereas I stand back, observe and make up my mind. You could say I don't suffer fools easily. As far as business, intuition and planning, these decisions come ultimately from me. (But don't get me wrong — as far as world-wide interest, knowledge and a retentive memory, he's up there with the best of them. He is always keen to learn more, he doesn't want to miss out on anything).

Not only is Michael good with adults, the kids love him. After all, he is still one big kid at heart. Testimony to this is the Mike Whitney Cricket School, now in its sixth year, and still expanding. I watch the kids and they are mesmerised by him. I remember a situation that developed while we were travelling in Africa, on the island of Zanzibar. We decided to have a relaxing break and rent an old house (which was evidence of the British Raj back in its hey day). The building was on the more remote side of the island, by the beach in a little fishing village called "Chwaka". As soon as we arrived we were swamped by kids, obviously not used to seeing very many "white" tourists. From that moment on, he set up a rapport with the people. When we walked through the town the kids all followed behind him. We'd stop and have a drink at the local cafe (if that's what you'd call it) and the kids would wait outside for him. Language was no barrier — he'd play games with them, to the point of doing fancy tricks with a soccer ball. So they called him "Maradona". He was like the "Pied Piper", and loved every minute of it.

It would be remiss of me not to add my views of cricket from a woman's point of view. I suppose the most common question put to me is: "How do you enjoy being a cricketing widow?"

It's my life! It's only up to me to make the most of it and yes, by the end of each season, I've had it. It's difficult to adjust to a partner who is only there part-time. After a seven-month season with "the boys", it's back to "breaking in" time again. Wives have to be flexible and very understanding. And to live with someone in the public eye puts an even greater strain on a relationship, where I believe equality is so important.

I am unimpressed by the governing bodies of cricket. It is a "man's domain" and emotional ethics are out the window. Little consideration or validation is made for the wives or the family unit. I believe the cricket authorities have a lot to answer for. Once again, the old adage "to win at all costs" reigns, and this in a game they call a "gentleman's sport". In the end who really wins?

But cricket has given a lot to us. It's our livelihood. It's given us the opportunity to meet people, and see and do things that most people can only dream of. It's tough, but I've worked my life accordingly and built up a good support system of family and friends around me. I fell in love with the man and part of the package was cricket. Far be it for me to discard or surrender to it.

You know what they say: "If you can't beat 'em, join 'em."

Preface

by Phil Tresidder

Michael Whitney might have been a crash-tackling rugby league footballer. Or perhaps an iron man in the foaming surf. Maybe a mountain climber — after all, he scaled Mount Kilimanjaro.

But he chose cricket as his sporting destiny, and became one of the game's finest competitors and ambassadors. Nobody has played for his club, state or country with greater pride and resolve. He fought off a string of injury mishaps to stay in the representative arena and won the admiration of Australian cricket crowds from Perth to Brisbane. On one memorable day in Perth he destroyed the Indian team; on another he decimated the world champion West Indian batsmen.

Michael Roy Whitney is unique among the personalities of Australian cricket. Cricketers come and go on the centre stage, but few have the charisma to make them crowd favourites. Mike Whitney always had the crowd on his side. They responded to his raw courage and unfailing good humour, and appreciated his character. Nobody has ever accused him of ignoring a youngster with an autograph book, and in Sydney he established his own indoor coaching school where he has provided professional training and encouragement to hordes of young hopefuls.

The Mike Whitney story is one of dedication and accomplishment. When he takes his leave, the Australian cricket scene will be much the poorer for his departure. As a sporting character they don't come any bigger or better. The story that follows will provide infinite pleasure for the cricket buff and inspiration for the young brigade.

Mike Whitney is a champion cricketer with a heart as big as his smile ...

A Christmas Star

Santa Claus arrived late at the Whitney family household on Christmas morning 1987. It was all of 10 o'clock when the phone rang at my mother's place in working-class Matraville, a coastal suburb south of Sydney's city centre. "It's for you Michael," my mum called. Waiting for me on the other end of the line was Santa in the unlikely shape of Australian cricket coach Bob Simpson. The conversation that followed went something like this:

"It's Bob Simpson ... how're you going, Whit?"

"G'day Bob. Good thanks."

"Merry Christmas."

"Same to you Bob." I had serious doubts that the coach had rung just to wish me Merry Christmas. He continued:

"Bruce Reid and Merv Hughes are really struggling. We want to know if you can make yourself available to play in the Test?"

He was referring to the third and final Test of the three-match Australia-New Zealand series, that was scheduled to begin in Melbourne the following day, Boxing Day.

"When does the plane leave?" I said.

"Well," said Bob, "as a matter of fact, there's a ticket waiting for you at the airport ... I thought you might want to come down. The flight leaves at 3.30."

Surely no fast bowler has ever had a better Christmas present.

The house was in uproar before I even got off the phone. My mother tore into the bedroom that used to be mine, and emerged with a blazer which I hadn't worn since the under-25 Australian team's tour of Zimbabwe, back in 1983. Then I did some rushing of my own — back home to Clovelly (about 10 minutes drive) to round up my kit, and some clothes. There was just time for some very traditional Chrissie lunch — turkey, ham, potatoes, Christmas pud, bon-bons.

At 4.30pm I hit the tarmac at Melbourne's Tullamarine airport. An hour later I was in the vast cavern of an empty Melbourne Cricket Ground, where the sound of leather ball on willow resounded as the Australian team practised. After more than six years away from Test cricket, I was back with the Australian team, with men such as Border, McDermott, Boon and Marsh, Dean Jones, Steve Waugh and so on. Also there was the Victorian fast-medium bowler, Tony Dodemaide, who had turned up as a practice bowler to lend a hand. I always liked Tony; he was no Ian Botham, but he was gutsy, a fighter, and a good bloke.

I had no idea at that stage whether I was actually in the XI. As Bob Simpson had explained over the phone, two of the side's three pacemen, Bruce Reid and Merv Hughes, were under an injury cloud. After practice, we gathered at the Hilton Hotel, where I found out I was rooming with leg-spinning all-rounder Peter Sleep.

"You're going to play, mate," he said to me.

"How do you know that?" I asked.

"I don't," replied the man they called "Sounda". "I've just got a gut feeling."

When I got to the ground next morning the big three — Simmo, chief selector Laurie Sawle and captain Allan Border — were already there in the nets. The message I received was direct:

"Reid's out, Merv's struggling, you're in."

I was that pumped up. I was bowling in the nets and let the next ball really fly in a joyous celebration. I was ready.

The big three then approached Tony Dodemaide. Five minutes later he wandered back towards me, his eyes wide open.

"What's up with you?" I said.

"They've picked me in the team," he said.

And that was that. Merv had been ruled out, off-spinner Tim May omitted and Tony was in as the third seamer.

Australia went in one-up in the series after winning the first Test in Brisbane and drawing the second in Adelaide. For much of this third game things ran beautifully for the home side. We bowled first, and I finished with 4-92, which was very pleasing. We kept them down to 317 and then scored 357 with my roomie, Peter Sleep, getting 90, and Tony Dodemaide 50.

In the second innings Tony took 6-58, to establish himself as the first player since Albert Trott way back in 1894-95 to score a half-century and take five wickets in an innings on Test debut.

The Kiwis scored 286 in their second dig, and we needed 247 to win — a seemingly modest target. When we reached tea on the last day needing 71 to win off a minimum 28 overs, with six wickets in hand, it looked comfortable. So comfortable in fact that my mother and sister Christine decided to head back to Sydney. They thought they'd get going early to avoid all the hassling around after the game that would follow the "formality" of victory.

In hindsight the early departure stands close alongside that of the cluster of media men who chose to leave the 'Gabba early on the last day of the most famous Test match of all — the tied Test between Australia and the West Indies in 1960. When Joe Solomon threw down the stumps to bring off that sensational tie, the media boys were at 30,000 feet, en route to Sydney. So it was with my mum and Christine as I produced my finest ever performance with the bat.

As the number-11 batsman, I was pretty relaxed as the last session of play began on that fateful late December day in 1987. Even when Peter Sleep was out, lbw to the champion Kiwi opening bowler, Richard Hadlee, to put us six down, with 38 get, the butterflies were still dormant. But then, without addition to the score, our one remaining specialist batsman, Mike Veletta, went to sweep their off-spinner, John Bracewell, but mistimed and was out caught by Dipak Patel.

Things had changed.

In the dressing room, I had been busy packing my gear. That day the selectors had named the side to go to Perth for the upcoming one-day internationals, and I was in. I was still fiddling with my kit when Hadlee knocked over our keeper, Greg Dyer, caught behind, to make the score 8-216. Instead of packing my things away, I was taking my pads out of my kitbag, and strapping them on.

Craig McDermott walked out to the middle to join Tony Dodemaide. With seven overs to go, Hadlee took the new ball. Two overs and one ball later, Dodemaide was lbw, to the dismay of the ever-quietening crowd. Thoughts of a win were out the window now. With this wicket the New Zealand ace had equalled Ian Botham's then world record of 373 Test wickets, and taken 10 wickets in a match for a world record eighth time. There was still one wicket left, and Richard Hadlee was fired up and raging.

All along I had been thinking that I wouldn't be needed — that we'd coast home to victory. Now I was on my way out to the middle! It seemed somehow unreal; the collapse had been so swift.

"Billy" McDermott was not bad with the bat, but my record was not real good. I figured, considering the balance of things, that Hadlee was looking okay. There were four overs and five balls to go.

Before it began I had this mid-wicket conference with McDermott:

"Just take 'em on the body," he said, pumped up, eyes blazing. "Get forward, get forward ... Get forward!"

I started to think: I'm more scared of him than I am of Hadlee!

I feigned calmness. "I'm cool," I said to Craig. "You just worry about what you've got to do."

As I took block, Martin Crowe was singing in slips: "How do you feel ...

when Richard runs in, and you're the last?"

The Tooheys ad. In 1981, I'd been part of a Tooheys beer promotion that had me scoring the winning runs off the last ball of a match against the West Indies.

"You think you're really funny, Crowey," I said.

They were all having a giggle.

The first ball from Hadlee jagged back and hit me on the inside of the thigh. There was a huge appeal. Not out. It was too high. "Don't rub it," I said to myself. "Tough it out, don't show 'em it hurt."

We survived that over, and the next from their young paceman, Danny Morrison, who was charging in. Three to go, and Hadlee to bowl two of them.

The first ball of Hadlee's second-last over was a wayward delivery down the legside. In the manner of a genuine batsman I flicked it down to fine leg, who was posted very wide and who happened to be Ewen Chatfield — not the fastest mover on a cricket field. It was going to be an easy three. My total of Test runs at that point was four, in two Tests. A three would have been something special.

I bolted the first, turned for the second, and there was McDermott standing with palm extended like a traffic cop.

"No!" he boomed.

I wasn't going to argue.

Billy negotiated the over and I was left to face Morrison. I went forward to the first ball and it hit me halfway up the pad, fairly adjacent. The shout could have been heard in Auckland. But umpire Dick French from NSW took a real long look ... and turned it down. Good on you, Dicky boy, I thought to myself. The second ball drifted in on me, and I forced it out through mid-wicket. Easy three here. Once again McDermott planted himself after the first.

"No!"

The third ball hit McDermott halfway up the pad, fairly adjacent. I looked at umpire French out of the corner of my eye. He had a good long squiz, then turned it down. Billy survived the over, pinned down by Morrison's accuracy ... and a bouncer last ball.

One over to go. There was plenty hanging on it. Hadlee chasing the world record, AB chasing his first series win as skipper, all we Aussies hunting the Trans-Tasman Trophy held by the Kiwis since 1985-86.

It was Hadlee's 31st over of the innings, and I was thinking, he has to be tired. Billy counselled me in mid-pitch, eyes still blazing. "Get forward! Get forward!" I was *definitely* more scared of him now than of Hadlee.

On the first ball of the over I could see the seam, and it was swinging away. I shouldered my bat and it zipped past my chest, thwacked into keeper Ian Smith's gloves and knocked him back a few paces. That one shook me up a bit — it really flew. I blocked the next, then left the third. The fourth was a yorker which I managed to dig out without much style or grace.

Before the fifth ball the Kiwi captain, Jeff Crowe, decided to bring the field in. A bit late, mate, I thought. You should have done that four-and-a-half overs ago. For some reason Crowe had taken a fairly conservative approach. The bloke had had a nightmare tour actually — just couldn't get among the runs.

The fifth ball went searing past outside off stump, left well alone by a relieved Whitney. It was down to one. The crowd was in a frenzy.

I was strolling out and patting down the pitch after each ball, just like a real batsman. While I was doing it, I was thinking to myself: "Why do batsmen do this?" I was trying to make it look like I knew what I was doing.

Richard Hadlee rested at the top of his mark for a long time before delivering the final ball. Predictions jostled for attention in my mind. The first thought was that Hadlee would try and bounce me; the second that he'd have to go for the stumps. In fact, the great fast bowler sent down perhaps his most innocuous ball of the day, an off-cutter which didn't seam, and which I got safely behind. Hadlee picked it up and shied a shot at the stumps, but I had jumped safely back inside the crease.

Pandemonium reigned. The crowd had been banging on the tin signs around the ground; now they erupted in a sea of colour, and a thunderous roar.

I ran up the pitch and hugged McDermott. Then I shook Hadlee's hand.

"Well done," he said, in the midst of his disappointment.

He threw an arm around my shoulders and we walked off the field.

To share such a moment with one of the greatest of bowlers remains a special memory for me. I had, and have, enormous respect for Richard Hadlee. He was the quintessential pro. Everything he did was done with the idea of improving his bowling. He was the first guy to throw out the popular theory that a fast bowler had to have a mammoth run-up. The West Indians had set that trend. Hadlee changed the whole thing with his short run — focussing on controlling his rhythm and perfecting his action.

Billy and I ran off the field and up the path to the dressing rooms together. There, outside the rooms, was Debbie Payne, then my girlfriend, now my wife, and I gave her a hug. I told her I'd been scared, and I had been. Not of the bowling, but of the weight of responsibility of trying to save the game, and win back the Trans-Tasman Cup. Allan Border was waiting at the door to congratulate us. David Boon rushed up at the exact moment that I raised my clenched right fist in a moment of exultation. It caught him flush on the chin.

Back on the field, at the presentation ceremony, Ian Smith came up to me and gave me the match ball. "This is for you — you've earned it," he said.

The ball with which Richard Hadlee broke one world record and equalled another, and against which Michael Whitney of NSW and Craig McDermott of Queensland managed to save a Test match will remain forever among my treasured cricket souvenirs.

In some ways the dramatic events at the Melbourne Cricket Ground over those summer days in 1987 encapsulated the cricket career of Michael Roy Whitney. I'm not talking about saving Test matches. I'm talking more of the *unexpected* moments that have punctuated my life in cricket. This time it was a Christmas Day phone call, an 11th-hour summons to join the Australian team and then, amazingly, a chance to save a Test. A chance, I'm happy to say that was taken, and is now filed away for the sweet sharing of memories with other Whitney generations.

In 1981, it had been a phone call too, an out-of-the-blue invitation to join an Australian Ashes touring team. I still pinch myself over that one. I was just a knockabout kid, adding to my education in the great university of cricket with a spell in England's Lancashire leagues. One day a nondescript league player ... the next a Test cricketer!

Again, the unexpected, so much more fruitful for me than things actually *anticipated* in my career. In 1989 it seemed the entire cricket world expected me to go to England as a member of Allan Border's Ashes team. I expected that too. But the selectors thought otherwise, and I stayed at home. The story was repeated to some extent in '93 as well.

In my life I have always been happy to take chances, to go with the flow. The opening of my mind through travel, and communication with people from all over the world, has been a joy. My philosophy has always been to have my mind open to the possibility of good things happening, and then to seize the moment when they do.

The lovely game of cricket has been the continuing thread in the life and times of Mike Whitney. A game which I first played on a paddock in Matraville has taken me across the world, enriched my life and provided fun and friendship ... but sometimes pain and drama. The ancient game is the very heartbeat of my story.

Let me tell you about it ...

The Young Whit

Sport has always been in my blood. As a kid I knew it. In these growing years all I ever wanted to do was play footy, run and jump in "Little Athletics", ride my board on the big waves at Maroubra ... and bowl fast. School was a bit of a drag, but I weathered the storm and enjoyed it.

As a teenager, I ran a bit wild. These were the '70s, the tailend of an era of peace, love, hippies, and flower people. As young as I was, I was consumed by all that. I had pictures of flowers on my bedroom walls. Peace, love and hope they were for me.

Surfing was my great escape, and I started going up and down the coast with my mates. Even today, I still love it. It gave me the opportunity to separate myself from land, to get close to nature, to just get away. I've always loved nature and things that are free. I don't like going to zoos, and seeing animals caged up, which is why I enjoyed Africa, and the great game parks where the animals roam wild, as much as I did.

I love the power of nature, and have done so for as long as I can remember, from my very early days growing up in Paterson Street, Matraville, a working-class suburb in Sydney's eastern suburbs. My mother came from Paddington, near the city centre, while my father was from Eastlakes, right near the Rosebery racecourse that no longer exists. My parents met at a dance hall. My father was a sailor, and after they married they lived in my grandmother's home in "Paddo" for a time.

My aunt, mum's sister June, also lived there with her son. We affectionately call her "Dear" to this day, because when we were kids, my sister, Christine, and I would run to meet her, and she would say to each of us: "Hello Dear." And we'd innocently reply: "Hello Dear." I remain very close to my aunt. Until she moved to Gosford a few years back she used to come out to the Sydney Cricket Ground every day that I was playing, and sit in the same seat, next to my mother in the Ladies' Stand.

I can remember my parents talking of the shock of moving to their own residence in Matraville, a few kilometres south of Paddo. I was born on February 24, 1959, just a few months after my parents had moved into their new home. I can understand what sort of an impact the transition would have had on them. At that time Matraville must have seemed like the end of the line. Indeed, it was. The tram only ran as far as the suburb of Maroubra, which meant they had to walk the remaining two and a half kilometres home.

We had an ice chest on hire purchase and no carpet. All the houses in the street were the same. Today you can go down Paterson Street and the houses are all brick veneer with extensions. They were mostly young families, which meant that, as I got older, there were plenty of participants in the games of footy we played in the street. I quickly became part of a tightly-knit group, and can still remember the shock and horror we felt when one of the group, a boy next door, died in a swimming accident.

My father had a job with the Boral company, driving a bitumen truck, and he took a second job at night. He wouldn't let my mother work, which meant that I saw very little of him. Before he died, when I was aged 16, he had scarcely seen me play more than a handful games of cricket. But my mother later told me how keen he was for me to play football. He reckoned football would make a man of me. At five years of age, I played footy for the Matraville Tigers, but then my father met Gorden "Gobes" Ella, father of the ultimately famous Ella brothers, so I joined them at La Perouse. Most of the kids in the team were Aboriginal; I was one of the few "white" boys in the club.

At school I discovered I was a pretty fast runner. An athletic field had been built in the nearby suburb of Pagewood, so my mother took me down to enrol in the Little Athletics, a concept which had begun in Sydney and involved organised athletic events for young kids. I was a bit of a hit, winning everything I could. The Little Athletics quickly spread to Victoria and West Aussie, and at age 11, I earned a trip to Melbourne. Flying down to the Victorian capital, my first trip in an aeroplane, was an outrageous experience and, once there, I was billeted with a Melbourne family. A year later I competed again, and today I can still recall a kid from Western Australia who turned up with big wraps on him. His name was Gary Honey and he won the long jump, but I beat him in the triple jump. Gary went on to win a silver medal in the long jump, beaten only by the awesome Carl Lewis, at the 1984 Los Angeles Olympic Games.

At that stage in my life, my ambition was to go to the Olympics and stand up on the winner's dais. I joined the Botany Harriers athletics group as a sub-junior, but I wasn't very big and the older boys I met seemed like monsters. They were half a metre taller and I'd line up with them in sprint races and come in last. I couldn't hack that, so I chucked in athletics.

I played junior league football until I was 19, but, for most that time, I thought of myself as a bit soft. If I got belted I used to cry. Then I joined

Mascot Juniors club and met these guys who were really tough. If you didn't cut it with them, you got the arse, so I toughened up real quick.

My father worked his butt off for the family, often through weekends to look after us all, so he saw little of my sport and had no real influence on my sporting progress. But, when I played for La Perouse, he offered me 20 cents for every try I scored, which was big money then. One year I broke the club record with 34 tries and it cost him a motza. As I said, I was 16 when he died, through cancer of the liver. We knew it was coming but it was still a terrible shock.

It was not long after this time that I started to run a bit wild. After the loss of my father, my mother had become very protective of me, which led to conflict. If she ordered me home by 9pm, I'd walk out of the joint a little rebellious and stay out drinking a bit and doing things I shouldn't have. I know she didn't enjoy those years, but if I got anything out of them it was that they toughened me up.

I slowed down a lot as I got bigger, so in the footy I moved from the backline to the second row. I enjoyed the move, because it meant I was really in the thick of it. When we used to run out on the field, for the Mascot C-grade, you could guarantee from the first scrum there would be a biff. Always a stink on, and then, after the game, we'd go down to the hotel for a grog session. That was the way we played rugby league. I'm sure it influenced my make up as a cricketer, helping to forge a keen competitive spirit.

I was never sent off the football field by the referee, and I never missed practice. I remember playing D-grade for La Perouse and sitting on the sideline because the coach, Ken Williams, wouldn't give me a run. If he ever did it was with only five minutes to go. I pleaded with him to give me a game and he said: "Okay, you can play next week."

But next week came and I was on the bench again. Five minutes to go and he said: "You're on."

"No I'm not," I replied.

"But I've just pulled a bloke off for you!" he exclaimed.

I started taking my boots and socks off, and my jumper and then I said: "Mr Williams, you can stick these up your arse."

I never played for La Perouse again.

I went and played with a gun side at Kensington. I only went there to win a competition but we got beaten in the major semi-final. A guy called Rodney Churchill was in the team and he used to get his father, Clive Churchill (perhaps the greatest rugby league footballer of all time), to come down occasionally to our training. He'd take us for a run, teach us some ball skills and, although he'd been retired from the big-time for many years, could still show us those kicking skills that made him famous. It was fantastic.

Football was my number-one team sport for much of my teens, but even so, by the time I was 16 I had managed to work my way up to the Botany United B-grade cricket team. All my weekend cricket to this point had been with Botany United, where a big, jovial, hard-working bloke named Alan Cook was club captain of all the junior teams. Alan had a considerable influence on my early career. He was one of those guys that every sporting club has to have — the bloke who would drive around on a Saturday morning, pick up all the kids in his car, and take them to the game. Then he'd have to organise everything down at the match, make sure the kit and the balls was there, umpire if he had to, and generally work like steam.

The club barbecues used to be held at Alan's place at Botany, and there'd always be a keg on. Alan would sneak a middy around the back of the shed to my best mate, Wayne Martin, and me — and it was probably there that I first tasted beer. There was never any drama with Cooky — even on the day "Mardo" and I discovered his pipe in the car, and made ourselves as sick as dogs by lighting up.

I was shaping up okay with the bat and the ball. I remember playing a team from Marcellin College, Randwick, who had a former captain from the Randwick grade club, John Brennan, looking after a team of 16-year-olds. He used to score a truckload of runs. This particular game was being played at Pioneers Park, at Matraville, on a concrete pitch covered by mats. I was bowling to John Brennan. I had discovered the previous season I could bowl a bouncer if I flung the ball onto the concrete in the gap between the two matting strips. If I could hit that it would take off, and I soon had John ducking a few sharp flyers. Early the next week, I received a call from the Randwick grade club secretary, Lyall Gardner, who explained that one of his members had spoken about me, and said I was quite sharp. Lyall asked if I would come down and try out with Randwick. I said "Nope", and hung up the phone.

At the time I was into surfing and just hanging around the beach. But Lyall wouldn't let go, and hounded me to make myself available. Finally, one Saturday morning, he rang me with a plea. A player had pulled out of Randwick fourths, and they needed a bowler. Mum told me I should play, so I said yes.

"Mate," I said to Lyall, "I've got no spikes, no long white trousers. I've only ever played in shorts and rubbers,"

Fortunately, Wayne Martin, loaned me some whites. He was the only bloke I knew who actually *owned* a pair of long cricket trousers. Mardo and I go all the way back to our first day at kindergarten. We're like brothers after a friendship that has never wavered in 30 years.

When I arrived at the ground, the opening bowler, John Warwick, opened his kit bag and six pairs of old boots fell out. One pair fitted.

"How many pairs of socks have you got?" he asked.

"One" I said.

"Always wear two pairs," he told me, "it will stop blisters."

From that day, I've always worn two pairs of socks when I'm bowling. We bowled, I took four for 16 ... and was really blown out. That was basically the start of my cricket career.

But I wasn't going to forsake the surf. It remained part of my life. I was a goofy-footer board rider, which means your right foot is forward on the board, and, when you are going to the left side of a wave, your body is facing the wave. If you are going to the right, your back is facing the wave. I've always been left-handed in everything I do single-handed. But two-handed, like golf, batting or baseball, I'm right-handed.

A bit weird, I suppose, which recalls a funny story. When I was a kid at kindergarten, being left-handed was a definite no-no. I had an old lady teacher, who decided I was going to be right-handed after all, and took to me when I struggled with the conversion. I arrived home with welts across the backs of my legs. My mother said: "What's these?" I didn't want to tell her but she got it out of me. The next day, my mother marched to the school and told the teacher if she touched her son again she (my mother) was going to belt her (the teacher). That solved the problem ... and later on the teacher gave my mum a present at Christmas.

I guess my mother and I are fairly stubborn characters. As I grew older, I became more and more rebellious. She would whack me, and I would say: "Mum, you're wasting your time. I'm bigger and it doesn't hurt any more."

I remember the days she chased me around the backyard, I used to feint to go one way, then sidestep and bolt up the side passage. But for years I couldn't get away from her. Then one day I did! I was stoked.

My hair fell down over my shoulders and I wore a ring in my ear. The surf scene was right up my alley. We didn't want to work at school, but would get out early in the morning, get down to Maroubra Beach and just cool out. And there were always girls hanging around. We would drink at the Maroubra Bay Hotel, where the scene then was alcohol, some drugs, and wet T-shirts.

Sharks? There were plenty, all the way up the coast! I remember one day, when we were surfing at Greenmount Point, on the Queensland coast. I was in the water with a mate, and a third bloke was out with us on a surf-ski. Suddenly, a big fin came out of the water, no more than 10 metres away. We saw it and froze, but the bloke on the ski panicked and paddled full pelt for the rocks. He crashed his ski and scampered to safety. Out came the fin again, and it was a dolphin! This fellow had smashed his ski to pieces. It was a classic!

In the surf there is an unknown world beneath you. We saw sharks but

I've never been scared of things like that. It would be horrific to be taken by one but if it happens, it happens. If you're meant to be there on the day and a three-metre white pointer is swimming up the coast and it takes you, then one, you're unlucky, and two, it's part of your destiny. I'm a great believer in fate.

The summer after my initiation with Randwick I was back, in fourth grade, and we won the competition. The fourth grade final that season, 1977-78, was scheduled for Kensington Oval, but, on the Sunday before, I played a rugby league trial and damaged my knee when I stepped onto a sprinkler hole that had been left uncovered. I turned up the next Saturday for the cricket final carrying a torn knee cartilage and limping badly. The captain, Paul Hill, was dismayed. "What have you done?" he asked, and I told him. I asked Paul to keep it a secret. Fate? It rained and we were the premiers without having to bowl a ball!

After that year in the fourths with Randwick, I went off to England, on a social cricket tour with the Randwick Wanderers. The year was 1978. I went because my knee was playing up and I couldn't play football. If I hadn't hurt my knee I would have missed that trip ... and an outrageous opportunity to play for the Surrey Second Eleven. That changed my whole life. Tom Hansell, an Englishman who had played a season with Randwick, met us and told me he needed a player for a match between the county staff and Surrey. Would I play? I took four for 40 and knocked over Alan Butcher and Monte Lynch, two guns striving to play for England. Next came an invite to play a three-day game for the Surrey Second Eleven against the Combined Universities. I got a few wickets and was on my way, together with tour-mates David Tink and Gary Richardson, to play against Sussex.

The Sussex team we faced had an opening bowler, 193cm tall, with long blond hair and moustache. He was South African, making his debut and could bowl sharp. He was huge! Fred Titmus, the crafty former England off-spinner, was our captain. We batted first, and when my turn came along, I was able to scramble a few runs before they called up this big fellow, whose name was Garth Le Roux. Straightaway, he bowled a ball that kicked up and I returned a simple catch to him. I swore all the way to the pavilion, where Titmus, smoking a cigar, looked at me and calmly said: "Michael, I don't think I've ever heard anybody manage so many f-----s from the wicket to the dressing room."

After that debut season in English cricket, Le Roux came to Australia and starred in the second year of World Series Cricket. I returned to the Randwick lower grades, to continue my cricket education. My first game back was in third grade, and I managed to score 40, against Gordon at Killara Oval. In that dig I hit a couple of big sixes, and the following week I was promoted to seconds, where I stayed for the remainder of the season.

Halfway through the following season, 1979-80, I received the call to first grade. I remember much of that debut game with great clarity. It was against Balmain, at Coogee Oval, and one remarkable thing about the match was that it featured *four* left-arm opening bowlers. I opened for Randwick with the late Tim Towers, son of a famous father, the rugby union legend, Cyril Towers. Balmain's attack was led by Chris Fitzgerald and a young bloke named Mark Baldwin who, like me, was making his first-grade debut. Tim Towers, who died tragically of cancer at the time I was on tour with the Australians in the West Indies in 1991, was another who had a profound influence on my early career — a terrific bloke who took me under his wing, and talked to me about what it was to be a first-grade bowler. Tim was Nature's Gentleman.

The funny thing about my first wicket in first grade that day is that, despite all the other little things I can recall about the game, I can't remember who I got out and I can't remember how I got him out. However, I can still picture the dismissed batsman in my mind, walking off the ground, with all my team-mates gathered around me. I guess the reason for the gap in my memory over this significant career moment lies in the number of wickets I have taken at Coogee Oval. At last count, my wicket-tally for Randwick was up over 400 — and very many of those have been at Coogee by the sea

I finished that season, in which Randwick won the first grade premiership, with 38 top-grade wickets at 12.84, a good enough return to put me second on the competition averages. By season's end, after I had taken 5-20 against Bankstown in the final round and 4-28 in the final against Penrith, some critics were writing of me as a potential Sheffield Shield cricketer. I liked that idea, and worked harder at my game during the months before the 1980-81 season than I had ever done in the past.

A place for Mike Whitney, the larrikin kid from Matraville, in the sober atmosphere of first-class cricket was beckoning.

Learning The Game

On the back page of the Wednesday, October 8, 1980, edition of the Sydney *Daily Telegraph*, was a story, written by one of their cricket writers, John Taylor, which told of the selection of the NSW side for the first Shield game of the 1980-81 season.

"SURFIE IN STATE SIDE" screamed the headline, and Taylor's story below told of my elevation to the heady heights of Sheffield Shield cricket.

Randwick's 21-year-old left-arm opening bowler, Michael Whitney, who spends most of his spare time surfboard riding at Maroubra, was chosen last night in the NSW cricket team.

Whitney is the only newcomer in the State side for the season's opening Sheffield Shield match, against Queensland in Brisbane, starting on October 17.

While Whitney didn't expect to break into the Shield side yet, State coach Peter Philpott agreed with the selectors that he is ready for the big-time.

"He'll bowl better on first-class wickets," Philpott said.

"What's more, he will put pressure on Len Pascoe, Geoff Lawson and Graeme Beard," Philpott added ...

In an interview with Brian Mossop, of the *Sydney Morning Herald*, I gave my reaction to the news.

"This time last year I was playing second grade," I told Mossop. "I've never even played State Colts. This is crazy. I'm more surprised than anything, but I'm very pleased."

Mossop described me as "raw", but suggested I had "a mature approach to bowling and a willingness to learn that is bound to receive encouragement from the more experienced Pascoe". Also included in the *Herald* article was this quote, which came after Mossop had asked me about my batting.

"I hate those quick bowlers!"

I still had some unpleasant memories of facing Geoff Lawson, at full steam, in a Poidevin-Gray (under-21) match two seasons before.

LEARNING THE GAME

The first thing I had to do was seek time off from my employer at the time, Qantas, where I was working as an apprentice ground engineer. Then I was on my way.

They picked three pacemen for that first game — Pascoe, Lawson and me — and the team also included Beard, who doubled as a very economical medium-pacer and an off-spinner. I had been included in the training squad that had worked in the pre-season, then done well in some trial games, which earned me the spot in the top side. I remember knocking Dougie Walters over in a trial at the Uni of NSW — caught behind. He was my hero, and to get his wicket was very special for me.

I was 21 years of age, facing a Queensland team which included the likes of Greg Chappell, Allan Border, Martin Kent, Trevor Hohns, Jeff Thomson and Carl Rackemann. In our team were some of NSW's finest — men such as Doug Walters, Rick McCosker, Peter Toohey, Lawson, Pascoe and so on. We bowled first, and when my turn came I got my Sheffield Shield career away to a dream start ... after a very shaky opening.

Greg Chappell gave me a real caning early, after Lenny Pascoe dismissed Martin Kent with a beauty — a ball that pitched, and left him sharply. Chappell joined Kepler Wessels at the wicket, and proceeded to take me apart as clinically as a surgeon performing a delicate operation. I bowled eight overs in my first spell, and conceded 40 runs. Out of that entire spell I reckon Wessels faced only three or four balls. For the rest of it Chappell just milked me — the new kid.

It wasn't until years later that I understood what he had done. I had little control — just tried to bowl super-quick. Chappell would wait, and simply hit the bad balls for four. I made up some sort of ground on him later when I caught him at mid-on, when he was 94. Greg tried to loft his brother Trevor, and it was a real buzz to take the catch, my first in Shield cricket. On the bowling front, things improved for me as the innings wore on.

My first Shield wicket was a bloke named Wayne Broad. I bowled him with a full toss which sneaked through and removed his leg stump. Next man in was their wicketkeeper-batsman, the former New South Welshman, Ray Phillips. First ball I bounced him; Phillips fended at it but only gloved it through to our keeper, Steve Rixon. This was outrageous — I was on a hat-trick! Geoff Dymock was next man in and I fancied myself as a real chance. But Dymock nonchalantly blocked whatever it was that I served up to him, which was a real bummer. The Queenslanders were all out before stumps on that first day, and my figures read 2-52, off 15 overs, after a tough but highly-pleasing first outing in first-class cricket.

That night, however, I ended up in a spot of bother ...

As the young punk in the team, I was rooming with our skipper, Rick McCosker. I suppose it was worked out that way so he could keep an eye on me. Before the game, Rick had given me some advice: "You do whatever you want to do," he told me. "But if you get on the grog and can't perform next day, then you're only cutting your own throat And if you come in late, don't wake me up."

Then the skipper added a rider: "And be very wary of Doug."

In a bar at the Travelodge near Storey Bridge that evening, the members of the NSW team gradually drifted away until there was only Dougie and myself left. That suited me fine. When the bar closed, Doug suggested that we might go downtown — and I jumped at the chance.

We arrived at a nightclub called the "Underground", a legend in Brisbane, where there was a lengthy queue of people, waiting to get in. Dougie took a suck on his Rothmans cigarette, looked over the mob, and caught the attention of the bouncer on the door. Suddenly the crowd parted in the way it must have been done when Moses did his bit with the waters — and we were in. This is fantastic, I thought. Doug knew the manager of the place — who bought us a drink. Doug also knew the assistant manager — who bought us a *couple* of drinks. The bouncer was having 10 minutes off and he came over and shouted some drinks. After that we had a few shouts ourselves.

By the time we called stumps and headed back to the hotel I was absolutely legless. When the cab dropped us back home, Dougie jumped out and strolled inside, leaving me to pay the freight.

Even in my muddled state, I was able to remember Rick's instruction not to wake him. As I stood outside the door of the room fumbling for the key I at least did it quietly. I finally negotiated the door, but promptly fell over the mat inside. A wobbly tiptoe across the room and I was in bed — fully clothed.

Rick was up early as usual, having his traditional tea and toast. I woke hazily, with a brewery coming out of my mouth. Rick looked down at me without pity.

"You went out with Doug, didn't you?" was all he said.

I was in a semi-crashed-out state at the ground, and every now and then the skipper would walk past me and poke me on the shoulder to wake me. That night, I took things quietly. Lesson One in the great Education of Sheffield Shield cricket had been well learned.

In the second Sheffield Shield match of my career, during the same season, 1980-81, a confrontation between my team-mate, Len Pascoe, and the Victorian captain, Richie Robinson, made me wonder whether I had strayed into Federal Parliament at Question Time, rather than a game of cricket. In the match, played at the SCG, Len bowled an over that lasted at least 10 minutes, and throughout it all, he and Robinson sledged each other furiously.

It all started when Len bowled Richie a bouncer first ball, and followed that up with a gobful. Richie retorted that the NSW fast bowler was too old, and *definitely* over the hill. Lenny was steaming as he went back for the next one. He lengthened his run by 10 metres or so, and let fly another bouncer which sailed over Robinson's head.

"Bookshelf," Len screamed at the Victorian, "I'm going to kill you — I'm going to stick one up your nose."

Richie is known as "Bookshelf", after the publishing company, Angus and *Robertson*.

The sledging and anger intensified throughout the over. At one point umpire Rocky Harris called our skipper, Rick McCosker, over and instructed him to get Lenny to settle down.

I was just a kid fielding out at mid-wicket and couldn't believe what was going on. After the match, Lenny put an arm around me and said: "Listen son, don't take what happened out there to heart. It's just cricket — things like that happen out on the field."

Len Pascoe was an amazing bowler — a tearaway as a young bloke who improved with age, despite the handicap of failing knees which took a toll on his fitness. He taught me very early that if you're a quick bowler, then you have to be prepared to run in all day. I remember him saying to me in a match one day, with the clock registering 5.40pm, that if your skipper wants you to bowl the last hour of a day's play, then you have to be ready to do it.

I ended up with four first-class appearances that season, three Shield games, and a match against the touring New Zealanders. I didn't set the world on fire, but it seems I impressed a few people. In his book *Phoenix from the Ashes*, written after the 1981 Ashes series in England, England's captain Mike Brearley explained how, when he made enquiries in early 1981 as to a possible overseas import to open the bowling for his county, Middlesex, both the South Australian captain, John Inverarity, and the Queensland captain, Greg Chappell, had described me as the best long-term fast bowling prospect in Australia.

The kind words of praise from Inverarity and Chappell didn't result in an offer, as Middlesex wanted a proven performer. In fact they eventually signed the great Jeff Thomson, who had strangely missed selection in the Australian touring side. But, even without an offer from the men of Middlesex, I was heading for Britain, to a little village in the north of England, to play in one of the famous Lancashire leagues.

The experience gained in England, I hoped, would help my bowling, and boost my chances of playing Test cricket ... somewhere down the track.

The Twists of Fate

When I flew out of Sydney's Kingsford Smith Airport one day in April, 1981, I had no clue of the momentous events that awaited me 20,000 kilometres away. I was off to play with a club called Fleetwood, from a village of the same name, in the Northern League in Lancashire, England. I didn't know a thing about the place, but two Randwick players, Mal Brown and Eric Higgins, had been there the year before and enjoyed the experience. Brown had written me a letter announcing that the club wanted a quick bowler for the 1981 season ... and I was on my way.

There is something that sticks in my mind very strongly about the lining up of that deal. Sportswriter and sportsman Phil Tresidder, my mentor and friend from Randwick, insisted that I had a clause added in the contract insisting that if, by chance, I was needed by the Australian team (who were touring England that year), then Fleetwood would be obliged to release me. I remember saying to Phil: "Don't be silly, I'm not going to get picked."

After a brief sojourn in Earl's Court in London, where there were wall-to-wall Aussies, I took a train north, to Blackpool, and then on to Fleetwood. The chairman of the club, Frank Knapman, who I count still as a great friend, picked me up at the station and promptly took me to the pub to introduce me around.

From there it was on to my lodging place for the summer, the home of an elderly couple, Edith and Eddie Funk. I was 22 years old and looking for a good time. The thought struck me immediately that living with an elderly couple could be something of a problem.

On the first night in Fleetwood I went out for drinks, and arrived home around midnight. Eddie was waiting for me, with a pot of tea and a plate of sandwiches. On the second night it was 1am before I made it home, and Eddie was there again with the tea and snacks. On the third night I rolled in at 2.30am and Eddie was there asleep, with the sandwiches on his lap.

Next morning I had a heart-to-heart with kindly old Eddie. "Look," I said. "There are probably going to be nights on which I don't get home at all!".

"Ooh," said Eddie. "Is that right?"

From that moment on the Funks knew they had a larrikin on their hands.

They were kind and wonderful people. When I left them six months or so later I remember Edith, who was over 60, commenting dryly that she felt like she had now completed finishing school. They gave me a key to their house, and treated me as a son. We still keep in touch and I still have that key.

My fee at Fleetwood was 1500 pounds all-up — around 65 pounds a week, which was no fortune. My first appearance was against a club called St Anne's, whose professional that season was the magnificent West Indian batsman, Rohan Kanhai. The local press did a great job in building up the confrontation between Kanhai, the proven international star, and the young bloke from Australia who had played only half a dozen or so state games, but who had a reputation as being a bit of a wild man.

It was bloody freezing that first day. I remember putting on a singlet, tee-shirt, two shirts, two short-sleeved jumpers and a long-sleeved jumper — and still feeling chilled when I went out onto the field. The wind was bitter, and strong enough to blow the bails off.

Despite the weather, I had the great thrill of getting rid of Kanhai early. He went for a drive, and the ball held up on the pudding wicket and he spooned it into the covers. It was a fabulous scalp to get; Kanhai would score a lot of runs as that season progressed.

The fifth game of the Australian campaign in England was scheduled to be played in the last couple of days of May at Bristol, against Gloucestershire, who that year had three outstanding internationals in their ranks — Mike Procter of South Africa, and the Pakistanis, Zaheer Abbas and Sadiq Mohammad. At the time of that match Procter was out of action with a knee injury, and Gloucestershire cast around to find if there was an up-and-coming import worth a game for the county.

The New South Welshmen in the touring team — Steve Rixon, Graeme Beard, Trevor Chappell, Geoff Lawson, John Dyson and Dirk Wellham — put in a plug for me, and I received a call asking if I would be interested in coming down and having a trial with Gloucester.

There was a touch of irony in that call. At the end of the 1980-81 home season, Esso scholarships, for four promising young Australian players to go to England, had been handed out. Queensland's Carl Rackemann, South Australia's Wayne Phillips and Stuart Saunders of Tasmania had taken them up, but Dirk Wellham, who had been given one as well, had been obliged to forgo the offer when he was chosen for the Ashes tour. His scholarship was then offered to me, but Fleetwood declined to release me from the contract I had with them. So the remaining scholarship was given to another young NSW batsman, Greg Geise, who went to ... Gloucester.

When the invitation to trial came, I packed my gear, accepted a lift to Blackpool station and then took the train to Bristol. I was like a kid from *Boys' Own Annual* as I stood on that old station with my port, the station master's whistle trilling in the background.

I stayed with Greg Geise and his wife Kim, and next day headed down to a centre-wicket practice. I remember batting that day, and facing a big young bloke named David Lawrence, an English-born bowler of West Indian descent, who took a run of about 80 metres and bowled like the wind. He really stuck it up me. My diary entry that day reads: "17 years old, 6ft 3ins tall and crazy like me". Lawrence knew I was there to take someone's spot — and he wasn't having any of it. He was a boisterous sort of a bloke, with enormous potential, and he went on to play Test cricket. He came out to Sydney one season and played for the Manly club, but hurt his back and had a pretty poor year.

When it was my turn to bowl I had a bit of luck straight away. A bloke named Barry Dudleston came in and I bowled him with an inswinger, first ball. I remember looking over at the pavilion as I was walking back and seeing Tony Brown, the Gloucestershire secretary, brandishing some papers and signalling me to come over to his office. It seemed that Dudleston was something of a legend in that part of the world — captain of the Second XI and a batsman who had scored more than 14,000 runs for Leicestershire and Gloucestershire. To clean him up first ball was a tactically sound thing to do!

Brown subsequently spelt out the terms of a contract they were offering me: a car, 1000 pounds to sign, 1500 pounds for my return air fare, 85 pounds for every three-day game, 70 pounds for one-day games. My head was spinning with all the figures; after all, I was on 65 quid a week at Fleetwood. I rang the chairman of Fleetwood, and he suggested I bring the contract back with me. I did that, and, on the agreement of the club, I signed a contract with the county. I didn't get to play in the match against the Aussies, but I did have the opportunity to play a few games for them. It was a real buzz. They gave me a brand new Fiat Miafiori for my exclusive use during that time.

The first game I played for the county was against the touring Sri Lankans in mid-June. The thing I remember most about that match is that every Sri Lankan batsman wore a helmet and had a Stuart Surridge jumbo bat. They were all about 167cms (5ft 6ins) tall, and all batted the same way. I had the sense that for every wicket we took we might have had the same bloke walking up the pavilion stairs — then coming straight back out again. If you pitched it up they'd whack you, and if you dropped short they'd try to pull you. I took 4-86 in their second innings, but the game was a high-scoring draw.

I spent a lot of time driving between Fleetwood and Gloucester that English summer. Wednesday, Thursday and Friday, I'd be playing for Gloucestershire; on Saturday I would represent Fleetwood in the League; and then occasionally on Sunday I would play for Gloucester in a 40-over John Player League match. This schedule sometimes involved a lot of time behind the steering wheel, and could be very tiring — but I was getting good money and playing a lot of cricket. My first experience in the world of professional cricket certainly hardened me up.

On August 9, I took 2-9 from my allocated eight overs in a John Player League match against Surrey at Cheltenham. The game was televised on the BBC, and among the watchers was the Australian camp. When I finally made it back home to Fleetwood, fairly well pleased with myself, I returned a phone call from Tony Brown. The news was almost unbelievable. Fred Bennett, the Australian team manager, had rung and asked the club to give me a release so I could play in the fifth Test of the Ashes series, at Old Trafford in Manchester.

"Bullshit, Tony!" was my response.

"It's true, it's true," he insisted. "But, if you don't hear from him by Tuesday night, we want you down here in Cheltenham to play in a three-day match against Hampshire starting on Wednesday."

I sat by the telephone for three days, but there was no contact from Fred Bennett. I thought to myself, this Pommy bastard has had a lend of me, but didn't say much about it to anyone. I had read in the press that two of the Aussies quick bowlers, Geoff Lawson and Rodney Hogg, were injured, but I knew nothing more — apart from Brown's intriguing phone call.

So, I went to Cheltenham, and as I arrived at the ground the Hampshire bus was pulling up. First off was a young West Indian, Malcolm Marshall, who was developing quite a reputation that year as a fast bowler.

We ended up batting, and Marshall, who was only a youngster then, bowled *real* quick. At a certain point, when we were struggling at three down, the whole team was padded up! It was at this point that they brought a telephone to me in the pavilion, on a long extension cord.

"Phone for you, Mr Whitney. It's Fred Bennett."

"Fred Bennett here, Michael," said the voice. "We have organised a release for you from both Fleetwood and Gloucester, and we need you. The Test starts tomorrow. We want you here as soon as possible, so I want you to jump in your car, and drive up here now. We'll see you at the Grand Hotel."

The memories of what followed immediately are blurred. I simply couldn't believe it. I recall Zaheer Abbas warmly wishing me good luck. What a fine player he was. During that season I had seen him score a century and a double century in the same county match. A majestic, wristy player who was a delight to watch.

I left the game as soon as I could, gathered my things, and drove up the motorway to Manchester. At the hotel I met the Australian manager for the only the second time, and addressed him as "Mr Bennett".

"Call me Fred," he said.

Australian captain Kim Hughes was there with him, and I addressed him as "Mr Hughes".

"Call me Kim," he said.

"Call me Whit," I answered, and we had a bit of a laugh.

"Now then," said Hughes. "This is what we plan to do. You'll be bowling first change tomorrow after Dennis Lillee and Terry Alderman."

Just like that.

I was still doing my impression of a stunned mullet. I was over here to play some League cricket, and suddenly I was in the Australian Test team, playing alongside some of the finest players in the game.

Fred Bennett handed me the key to my room. As I was putting it in the lock, the door opened, and Ray Bright, the left-arm spin bowler from Victoria, walked out. He introduced himself and said he was shifting to another room.

"You're in here," he said.

I had no idea who I was rooming with. I carted my kit in and plonked it in the corner. On the other side of the room stood a large port, with a name embossed in gold on it.

"D.K. Lillee" the inscription read.

If everything else that had happened wasn't enough, this really blew me away. They had roomed me with a legend. I was not only playing in the same team as him ... I was staying with him!

Doug Walters was my all-time hero when I was growing up, but Lillee, Marsh and the Chappells were only a leg glance behind. Now I was rooming with the great fast bowler ...

Half an hour later Lillee entered the room and I can recall sort of half standing to attention when he came in. I remember him saying: "Relax, Michael". Then, we talked. He didn't try to tell me how or what I should bowl.

"You're playing for Australia now, and you might want to think of all the people who are supporting you back home," he said. "It's a big chance, and you should try and make the most of it. If you give 100 per cent that's all you can do. We're not expecting you to go out there and take eight or 10 wickets. If you go out there and do the very best you can, you will have done your job."

Geoff Lawson that night invited me out to dinner. My great friend and fast-bowling colleague was not renowned as any sort of gourmet (at that stage of his life, anyway), so dinner was a trip to the nearest Wimpy fast-food bar. Between us, as we talked cricket, we scoffed half a dozen burgers. An old drunk came into the restaurant, slumped at the next cubicle to ours, and pulled out a bottle. This was my celebration dinner. I was in the Australian team, a champagne and caviar experience in my life, and I was eating burgers, and keeping an eye on the drunk next door.

That night I called my mother, and she cried on the phone. Or was it me? Next morning the telegrams started to arrive — there must have been over 100 of them by the time we left for Old Trafford. I knew that at the ground there was going to be a large group of people from Fleetwood who were coming along to give me a cheer. I was warmed by all the support.

By that first morning of the Test, D.K. Lillee and M.R. Whitney were on pally first-name terms. You know — Den and Whit. We headed down to breakfast together at about 8.30 in the morning, and there wasn't another cricketer to be seen. "Are we a little bit early?" I asked the great man.

"No, we're a little bit late," he replied.

In all the hysteria and excitement of the previous day I hadn't cottoned onto the fact that the team bus was to leave at 8.15am. Fred Bennett had certainly mentioned that at the team meeting but the message hadn't quite reached me up on Cloud Nine. I really freaked out when I realised that morning that the bus had gone ... without me!

"It's cool, mate," said Dennis Lillee. "You're with me. I've organised a lift to the ground — so don't worry about it."

He went back to the cornflakes.

So we had our breakfast and met up with the lift that Dennis had arranged. On the way to the ground Dennis chatted casually with the bloke who was driving us. You couldn't imagine anyone more relaxed or unworried.

Meanwhile, I was *churning*. It was my first day of Test cricket, and I'd missed the bus. All I wanted was to be with the team.

When we reached the ground I was out the door and off and running as soon as the wheels stopped turning. I hurtled through the car park at Old Trafford, and up to the members' gate.

Waiting for me there was a bloke you all know. The man in the green coat. This particular version of the species threw out and arm and blocked me. "Now, who might you be?" he asked. It is worth noting that I was not in blazer or uniform or anything like that — simply because there hadn't been time to organise any such thing. I wore jeans, a pair of street shoes and an Australian tracksuit top which John Dyson had lent me.

D.K. Lillee had gone his own way. He probably had a private entrance to the ground, and I was all alone — posted there trying to talk my way in. The bloke just wouldn't budge. I told him I was the new Australian fast bowler who had been brought into the Test to replace Rodney Hogg and Geoff Lawson, but he wasn't having any of it.

"Look lad," the green coat sneered. "I've been on this door for a long time, and I've heard plenty of excuses from people trying to get in. But yours is one of the best efforts I've ever seen, what with the kit and the tracksuit and everything."

Finally, in desperation, I said: "Mate, just do me a favour and ring the dressing room, will you?"

With some reluctance he did — and whatever was said at the other end got me through the gate.

The green coat pointed me in the right direction and I rushed up the stairs, head down, bum up — and promptly collided with a cricketer going the other day. He was sent sprawling, his bat and pads rolling down the staircase. I looked down at him to apologise, and promptly realised that I had knocked down England's opening batsman, Geoffrey Boycott. My apologies were profuse, and I introduced myself to him.

"Aye lad, aye," said Geoffrey. "You're young lad who's making debut today, aren't you?"

"Yeah, that's right, mate," I answered.

"Well, good luck," said Boycott. "But not too much ..."

He continued on his way down the stairs.

Finally, I made it to the dressing room. My first vision was of Kim Hughes, arms folded, stern of face and foot tapping.

"Um, Kim ... ah, ah," I fumbled.

"Don't worry Michael, don't say a thing," he said. "You're with Dennis, aren't you?"

Kim went out and lost the toss, and England's captain, Mike Brearley, decided to bat. It was a typical Manchester morning — jumper weather, with low clouds hanging over the ground. My main emotion was still one of disbelief as I made my way down through the stand and out onto the ground, walking alongside Hughes and Marsh, Lillee and Alderman, and all the rest.

After 15 overs the Poms had lost two wickets. Graham Gooch and Boycott were gone, and Chris Tavare and David Gower were in the middle. Kim Hughes threw me the ball, and said: "Good luck, mate ... good luck."

Over the years a lot of people have bagged Hughes. I just want to say I found him terrific during the three or four weeks I was with his team. "If there's anything I can do to help," he said to me. "Don't hesitate — even if it's three o'clock in the morning."

I had plenty of respect for him as a cricketer, too. He was a risky, extrovert player, who liked to invent shots, but an excellent bat. When I bowled to him in Shield cricket I always thought I was a good chance of knocking him over, because he liked to play the spectacular, but risky, down-on-one-knee cover drive. But, while you might get him now and again, he was the sort of batsman who could take an attack apart.

He threw me the ball on this gloomy Manchester morning, and I marked my run. To say I was nervous would be a big understatement. I bowled from the scoreboard end, to Tavare, and the first one reared slightly, and he nudged it away to square-leg. It was a fair start, a reasonable ball. Then, as I walked back to my mark, it started to rain ... and next thing we were off the ground. We didn't come back for 87 minutes. When I finally completed that over, it must have been the longest debut over in the history of Test cricket. It took an hour-and-a-half from first ball to last.

The fourth ball of that first over was to David Gower, who, in typical cavalier style, slashed hard at it. The ball flew at head height to first slip Graeme Wood, but went straight through his hands and smashed him in the mouth. He dropped to the turf, and they carried him off. I couldn't believe it.

In my second over, Gower slashed again at one just outside off, and this time Graham Yallop, in the gully, took the catch. I was ecstatic — I had my first wicket in Test cricket after bowling less than two overs. Later on, I had their number three, Chris Tavare, caught by Terry Alderman at first slip for 69, after he'd batted for 285 minutes. At stumps, the Poms were 9-175, and I had 2-31.

At the end of my first day as a Test cricketer, I walked off with my head held high. I remember that, when I got back to the dressing room, I opened my locker, took off all my clothes, except for the baggy green cap, and just stood there and stared at the mirror on the back of the locker door.

Yeah, I thought, this is right up your alley, son. Two wickets in an Ashes Test at Old Trafford ... Bowling for Australia with Dennis Lillee and Terry Alderman ... The Poms on the ropes.

This is just insane!

In the euphoria of the moment I grabbed my towel, and walked across the hallway into the shower. There were some of the guys in the shower, and I bowled down the other end where the showers were empty, turned on the tap and let the water run over me. I was still thinking how great it all was — that I was actually playing in a Test match for my country.

I spun around after a while — and there in the showers with me were most of the English cricket team — all of them smiling and laughing.

I had walked into the wrong shower!

Grabbing towel and shampoo I beat an embarrassed retreat. I recall Ian Botham making some comment as I went, about convicts — something along the lines of: "You'd better get out of here or we'll put you in irons."

It had been quite a first day in Test cricket — arriving late, picking up a couple of wickets ... and joining the opposition in the shower.

We ended up knocking them over for 231, but it could have been even better, as the local Lancashire fast-medium bowler, Paul Allott, playing, like me, in his first Test, belted an unbeaten 52 from the number-10 spot, as they added a frustrating 56 on the second morning. I finished with 2-50, from 17 overs, which was a gratifying start.

In the second innings it was a different story. Ian Botham took charge, and I had the unhappy experience of dropping him, a difficult chance admittedly, when he was 32. The cricketing bible, *Wisden*, later called it "nearer quarter than half a chance". Terry Alderman had taken the new ball, and Botham opened up on him. He tried a big straight drive, which he miscued slightly. I was at mid-off and the ball flew miles in the air over my head and towards the fence. I chased it madly and managed no more than a fingertip on it about 10 metres inside the fence. I dropped it. I remember some bloke in the crowd calling out to me: "Why don't you bugger off back to Fleetwood?" I told him to shut his Pommy mouth.

Botham went on to get 118 and said later it was his greatest innings. It sure changed the whole game. He hit six sixes, including three in two Lillee overs, and a remarkable pull over wide long-on off Alderman. His second 50 took just 26 balls and 28 minutes. England, after being 5-104 (a lead of 205), were all out for 404, leaving us the unlikely target of 506 to win the Test.

I had got a globe, batting number 10, in the first innings and in the second was relegated down the order. We still needed a truckload of runs and had to bat a session and a half to save the match when I came in. Allan Border was there on 100-and-something and I managed to hang on with him for 40 minutes. I took a few on the body and really tried to guts it out.

The Poms took the new ball and I could see bustling Bob Willis disappearing into the distance on that enormous run of his. I was pretty nervous. A couple whizzed past my chest, and then he bowled an inswinger that I went forward to. It hit me on the pad and lobbed to Mike Gatting at short leg. Gatting appealed and this bloody umpire gave me out. I stood my ground, but they were already running off.

"I never hit that," I yelled to AB.

"We've got to go, Whit," he called back.

I thought, bugger that, I'm standing my ground. Then I looked around. A sea of Poms had jumped the fence and were heading for the middle. Discretion being the better part of valour, I bolted, weaving my way through the mob with my bat and helmet held high in the air.

After the Test, I stayed on with the team, and played matches against Leicestershire and Sussex. In the Sussex game I opened the bowling with Rodney Hogg, who had come good. The chance was that whoever bowled best in that game out of the pair of us would play in the Sixth Test.

THE TWISTS OF FATE

I was real keen, and in the first innings I bowled well, and took 5-60. Hoggy bowled a mountain of no-balls, a couple of wides, and just didn't find his line. We built up a reasonable first-innings lead, with Kim Hughes scoring 52. Late in our innings, Hoggy nicked one, and Ian Greig (Tony's brother), who was fielding at slip, snared it on what seemed to be the half volley. He promptly claimed the catch, and the umpire stuck up his finger. Later on I said to Hoggy that I thought the ball had bounced.

"So did I," he murmured.

Hogg had these crystal blue eyes, and he wasn't a bloke who said much. But it was apparent that he wasn't happy.

In the second dig he bowled all over the shop again ... until Ian Greig came in. At that point he went up about 10 cogs in speed and direction. The first four balls of his first over to Greig were like lightning — just unplayable. Greig, incidentally, had made the mistake of wearing a cap, rather than a helmet. With the fifth ball of the over, Hogg struck him a painful blow on the inside thigh, and down went Greig. After a delay, he took the sixth ball right between the eyes and crashed to the ground.

I can still picture Hogg standing over him saying: "Cheats never prosper."

Despite the seriousness of the moment, it was hard to hold back the smiles. They carted Greig off and took him to hospital for brain scans. Fortunately he was okay.

I was selected to play the Sixth Test at The Oval, and had the pleasure of staying at the Waldorf Hotel in London. The match ended up a draw, and the image that sticks in my mind is of Dirk Wellham being dropped at mid-off by Geoff Boycott when he was 99. Dirk went on to get a century on debut. We all laughed at Boycott's misfortune. He of all people, the serious, stern, meticulous professional.

Australia lost that Ashes series, but young Michael Whitney of Sydney's Eastern Suburbs was thrilled to have had the chance to be part of it. The rest of the team went home — and I went back to the fishing village of Fleetwood. Complete strangers, in Fleetwood and beyond, would stop me in the street and ask me how I was going. The twists and turns of sporting fate had suddenly turned me into a celebrity.

How Do You Feel?

Because Dirk Wellham had scored a century against England on debut and because I had been plucked out of obscurity to play Test cricket, the pair of us were big news when we came back for the start of the 1981-82 Australian season. Around this time, the brewing company, Tooheys, decided to make a television advertisement based on cricket for their "Feel like a Tooheys" campaign, and one day I received a call from the Mojo advertising agency, who were looking after the deal.

After a bit of to-ing and fro-ing, my manager of the time, Austin Robertson, negotiated a contract. It wasn't worth a lot of money — a couple of thousand dollars, I think — but it was nice to be involved. The NSW keeper, Steve Rixon, was booked up as well, and in the end they decided not to use Dirk.

They gave me the script to check over, and one sentence that sticks in my mind read: "Mike Whitney to drive Joel Garner through the covers for three."

Hmmmm. Now, here we were talking about a bloke who had perhaps never bowled a drivable half-volley in his life. With Joel it was either the searing bumper under the throat, or the yorker that hit you on the foot and crushed your toes. There were no in-betweens.

"Don't worry about it ... we'll do it all with mirrors," they said. That's all very well for you, I thought. I remember asking the director if he knew anything about cricket. He said no.

The West Indies were in Australia that year and it was decided that Adelaide was where the ad would be made. The Windies were down there ready to take on South Australia in the first match of their tour. Steve and I stayed on there after a NSW-SA Shield game that had just been completed. We met up with the Tooheys crowd and the Windies — and headed out one morning to Football Park, on the outskirts of the city, where the advertisement was to be shot.

In the middle of the oval were 22 yards of mowed kikuyu grass. No square, no wicket — just a mowed patch. I thought: "Am I going to face the Big Bird on this?"

Apparently I was. The story of the ad was that I was to be last man in, with a chance of winning the "match". But before I went "in" they had to get the second-last bloke out and for this they conscripted a fellow named Ian McLean, an opening bat with South Australia at the time. McLean faced Garner for a while, trying to do what he was supposed to do. He got hit a few times and it had become something of a nightmare by the time he finally got one up around the throat and nicked it safely to Gordon Greenidge at slip.

I remember him peeling off his helmet as he ran off the ground and calling: "You can mail me the cheque!"

Now it was my turn. I asked about the helmet but they told me: "Nah, you're the star, you don't need a helmet."

The day at Adelaide was the first of two shoots — with plans in place for the ad to be completed at the Sydney Cricket Ground. The Adelaide ground had a tubular steel fence against which they placed 40 or 50 metres of white picket fence to simulate the SCG.

The task was for me to cover drive Joel into the section of white picket fence. Boy, I tried — and the big bloke was really doing his best to look after me. But after an hour or so it hadn't happened and Joel was super-tired.

"Whitney, man," he said. "My arm, it hangin' down."

Then the creative people came up with a new idea. Joel would come in to bowl, then they would switch the camera to me. I would play the "shot", but to get the ball to where it was supposed to be, Joel would actually *throw* it out, from behind me, towards the section of picket fence at deep cover. And that was how we finally worked it out — although, of course, I boasted to friends for weeks afterwards how I'd slogged the Big Bird all around the paddock.

Between this shoot and the next one, in Sydney two weeks later, I made a bad blunder. At that time I wore my hair long and Afro, but soon after the filming in Adelaide I decided I needed a trim. When I arrived at the SCG for the completion of the filming the make-up lady freaked out! She did all she could to get it frizzed out again, and we finally made it through.

The "crowd" for the ad was made up of blokes from Bronte Surf Club. The club received a nice donation, a barbecue and some free grog for their troubles.

It was an advertisement that they intended to run for six months. In fact it was so popular and so effective that it finished up running on TV for five years. It gave me tremendous exposure, and it put a few bob in my kick. Everywhere I went people would say: "How do you feel?" The funny thing was that plenty of them thought I was just an actor. They had no inkling that I was really a cricketer.

Come to think of it, maybe that says something about my batting ...

A Brush With Bacchus

Firebrand Lenny Pascoe was the first-choice fast bowler for NSW at the beginning of the 1982-83 Shield season. But from early in that season Len was struggling with knee problems, and Henry Lawson and I opened the bowling most of the time. We had a tremendous season. The NSW Blues had a really good team, and went all the way to the first Sheffield Shield final — in Perth against Western Australia. This was the first year that the Shield champions weren't automatically the team that finished at the head of the competition table. For the final, the selectors left Lenny out, and he wasn't too pleased. In fact he refused to be in the NSW team photo at the end of the match.

We knew it was going to be a difficult game. After all NSW hadn't won the Shield in 17 years, and we realised just how tough WA were in Perth. But we were confident, and we were ready.

It turned out to be a fairly low-scoring match and in their first innings of 259 I took 4-67. We had grabbed some quick wickets, notably their openers, Bruce Laird and Graeme Wood, and were well on top until a mid-innings salvage operation by the two Marshes, Geoff (known as "Swampy") and Rod (known as "Bacchus", after the Victorian town of Bacchus Marsh). I recall skipper Rick McCosker coming up to me and saying: "You're going to have to bowl — and we really need a breakthrough."

In the second over of that spell I decided to bounce Rodney Marsh. I dropped one short — and he pulled me for four. He glared back up the wicket at me and the message was: "Is that the best you can do, boy?"

I bounced him again next ball, only this time about two yards quicker. I really put everything into it. The ball came onto him a bit swifter than he expected and when he went to pull it he got a top edge, and was caught at mid-on by Steve Smith.

I was really fired up, followed on down the wicket, and said to him: "F------ get going!"

Marsh got about 30 metres towards the dressing room, then swung around and came back. By this time everyone was around me, congratulating me on a wicket we had really needed to get.

"What did you say?" he snapped.

"I said f------ get going. You heard me. What do you think ... I'm scared of you?" I fired back.

He kept walking towards me and soon we were chest to chest. I remember Rick McCosker and Peter Toohey coming between us to prevent anything else happening. I was pumped up, and a bit young and silly. Eventually Marsh left, and the game continued.

After stumps that day I went into their dressing room to have a beer. While there, I approached Marsh. I held the bloke in the highest esteem. He was the Australian wicket-keeper and a fabulous cricketer with an awesome record.

I had always been told to never take off the field anything that may have happened on it. As far as I am concerned once you walk through the gates in a cricket match at the end of a day's play, it's all over.

In their dressing room that night I said to Marsh: "Look mate, I'm sorry about that. It was just one of those things that happen in a cricket match."

He retaliated by giving me the biggest blast imaginable. "You carry on as though you've played 100 Test matches," he said. "Who do you think you are? You're nothing but a young prick."

I started to shake with rage, and I can remember our manager, Noel Bergin, grabbing me by the shirt and hauling me out of the WA room, and back to our dressing room. "Now cool off," he said. Soon after I learned that I had been reported to the umpires and the (NSW) team had had to settle on a fine for me. They fined me the minimum at the time, $25, which wasn't a lot of money — but which still represented a black mark against my name under the ACB's good behaviour code.

I couldn't believe Marsh had carried on the way he did — and I lost a lot of respect for him that night. Whether he'd done it simply to put me off my game, I don't know. But I'll tell you that I got enormous satisfaction when we bowled them out three days later, and especially when I took the last catch to dismiss Wayne Clark, off Trevor Chappell's bowling to wrap it up.

I did a stupid thing after taking that final catch — I threw the ball away. The winning ball from NSW's first Shield win in 17 years and I chucked it away. Some kids are probably still belting it around a backyard somewhere. It would have been a nice souvenir to have. But I did grab a stump as a memento. When I picked up my winner's medal that night I reserved my biggest smile for Marsh. We had beaten a very good team on their home turf and we sure did celebrate that night.

Happily, I can report that Rod and I get on a lot better these days!

Australian cricketers seem to be synonymous with "sledging", the name created to describe verbal abuse on the field. You hear, for example, that

Ian Chappell invented sledging. That's hard to believe. I'm sure it was around long before Ian took over at the helm for Australia. It would be difficult to brand any one guy for introducing sledging.

You can put sledging into two categories. Firstly, light-hearted sledging which may be just enough to put a batsman off, but really little more than a giggle. And then there is when it becomes really heavy; when blokes became racist, get personal, or attack your family. This type of abuse can, at times, become a little ugly.

I have been fined for sledging, and regretted it afterwards. The game was NSW versus Tasmania, in a Sheffield Shield match at the Sydney Cricket Ground in 1985-86. The West Indian, Winston Davis, was the pro for the Apple Isle that summer, and he was bowling on a pitch which had a bit of a ridge, well short of a length. Davis was exploiting this ridge, bowling up to four balls an over short, and, in some respects, you could not blame him for it. But it meant he was bowling up to four bouncers an over, and, with respect, that's not cricket.

Steve Small, the aggressive, seasoned NSW opener, smashed a century. For the entire innings Davis slanted the ball across the left-handed Small, who continually, deliberately, and for Davis quite frustratingly, slashed the ball over the heads of the slip and gully fieldsmen.

Finally it got down to me ... last man in. Davis had bounced everyone else, so I expected to get my share. I made up my mind to pull or hook him — yeah me, pull or hook him! What a joke! The first ball he bowled was quite sharp, and short. I tried to "hook", but didn't even get close and it smacked me right in the middle in the middle of the chest.

"You black bastard," I yelled at him.

He was taken aback, and promptly called me a "white racist pig". I looked up the wicket and gave him another gobful. I told him he'd been bowling bouncers all day and didn't need to bowl them at tail-enders. Basic sledging. He pitched the next ball up, and I sliced it over the slips for a single. As I ran up the wicket, I was telling him how he was going to get his when he batted. He called me a white racist pig again.

Now, I had never called anybody a black anything before in all my life. I am not a racist. Not prejudiced against colour, creed or religion. On this day it just came out. He had a go at me, I had a go at him, and umpire Dick French ended up stepping in to cool down the situation. So then I got stuck into French, saying it was all his fault for not warning Davis for intimidatory bowling. It had been three or four bouncers every over all day.

At the end of the day's play, skipper Dirk Wellham and I were "invited" upstairs to see the match adjudicator. So we went along, as did Mark Ray (the Tasmanian captain), Winston Davis and the two umpires. I can't remember the adjudicator's name, but he was a little fat dude with a moustache. I don't know if he'd ever played cricket before, but he'd taken this job for the day. He began by reading out a formal statement, which included the details of the sledging, and then he asked me if I had anything to say.

I said firstly that I wanted to apologise. I regretted referring to the West Indian's colour, but it had just come out in the heat of the battle.

"That's cool, Whit," said Winston Davis. "I accept your apology."

I then added that he had been bowling three or four bouncers an over, and that I thought that the umpires hadn't been doing their job properly. On reflection, I guess he was only exploiting the ridge on the wicket, which he was entitled to do, but to bowl so many short deliveries I thought was wrong.

Getting a bouncer first ball had upset me. Winston then explained that he was only bowling as he normally did. Mark Ray didn't say anything too controversial, the umpires had their say, and then it came back to the match adjudicator.

He looked at Winston and said: "Well, you've never been fined before under the players' code of behaviour, so I'll let you off with a warning."

Then he turned to me: "But YOU, MIKE WHITNEY, you are fined for sledging and bringing the game into disrepute. You've had a previous run-in with Rodney Marsh, and obviously you haven't learned the lesson, so I fine you $250."

Dirk Wellham looked at this bloke, laughed, and walked out of the room. I stood up and said: "You've go to be joking, mate. This is a joke." Then I stormed out of the room. I've never seen that bloke since. Thank God for that!

Because of what I achieved in 1982-83, I won a place on the Australian under-25 team that toured Zimbabwe at the end of that season. Independence had been granted to the former Rhodesia only in 1980, and we were the first Australian team to tour there since that occasion. We were sort of testing the water. It was a fairly touchy and unstable place at that time. There was a lot of dissident action around Bulawayo and regular skirmishes between two warring tribes, the Shonas and the Matabele.

At one stage on the tour a note surfaced that suggested we were all going to be kidnapped. We didn't find out about that for a while — at about the time that we discovered we'd had security men and secret police travelling with us throughout our stay.

I remember one occasion well — a late afternoon when four of us drove out of the Harare Sports Centre in an old VW bug we had acquired. Right outside the house where ex-prime minister Ian Smith had lived, and where the new leader, Robert Mugabe, now resided, we realised we had a flat tyre.

We pulled up across the road from the house, which was surrounded by a huge security fence and patrolled by armed guards. In the car were Greg Ritchie, Wayne Phillips, Dirk Wellham and me.

While the rest of us were fiddling with the tyres, Phillips strolled across the road, and tried to strike up a conversation with one of the soldiers.

"How're you going mate?" asked Wayne in a genuine Aussie greeting.

The soldier promptly lifted his machine gun, and cocked it. We all froze. Next thing there were a dozen armed guards on hand. The thought occurred that we might be dead meat. I can tell you we were happy to make a quiet and quick exit from that spot, as had been firmly suggested by the guards. I can laugh about it now, but it wasn't too funny on the day.

Despite the slight sense of unease in a country trying to find its feet, I thoroughly enjoyed the tour. I took a lot of wickets, and enjoyed the cricket. I roomed with Rod McCurdy, who, ironically, finished up playing out his cricket career in South Africa. He was a good bowler, pretty quick, if a little erratic at times, and a very ordinary batsman. Yet one day he and I opened the batting ... as well as the bowling. A match in Bulawayo was rained out, so we organised a 15-over slap-up game. The batting was comprehensively re-arranged and McCurdy and Whitney put on 30-or-so.

We had a tremendous fielding team — in fact we didn't drop a catch until the second-last match of the tour. We had guys in the slips like Queensland's Greg Ritchie and Robbie Kerr, and Tasmania's Stuart Saunders was a gun gully field. In fact everyone in the team could catch and field.

"Fatcat" Ritchie missed the tail-end of the tour after having a cyst removed. He was something of a character. One day, walking around the ground, he met up with a local who was accompanied by a pet chimpanzee carrying its baby. Ritchie invited the bloke to the dressing room, where one of the players offered the mother chimp a beer. She skolled it down — then another and another. Des Rundle, our manager, and Stuart Saunders were in the showers and they got the shock of their lives when the chimp wandered in. I think the monkey fancied them because next thing they were trying to shinny up the walls to get away. The owner had to come in, subdue the tipsy chimp, and save the day.

Ritchie was a really good player, a batsman who should have played a lot more at the very top level than he did. But he was a carefree sort of a bloke and he let his weight get away from him. In the end his fitness, or lack of it, certainly cost him.

Wayne Phillips was a player of great gifts. In the last game of that tour, a one-dayer against Zimbabwe, he scored 135 and really took them apart. He hit some enormous sixes that day. The following season, he found himself in the Australian Test team, and scored a century in his first Test innings, opening the batting against Pakistan in Perth. Four and a half

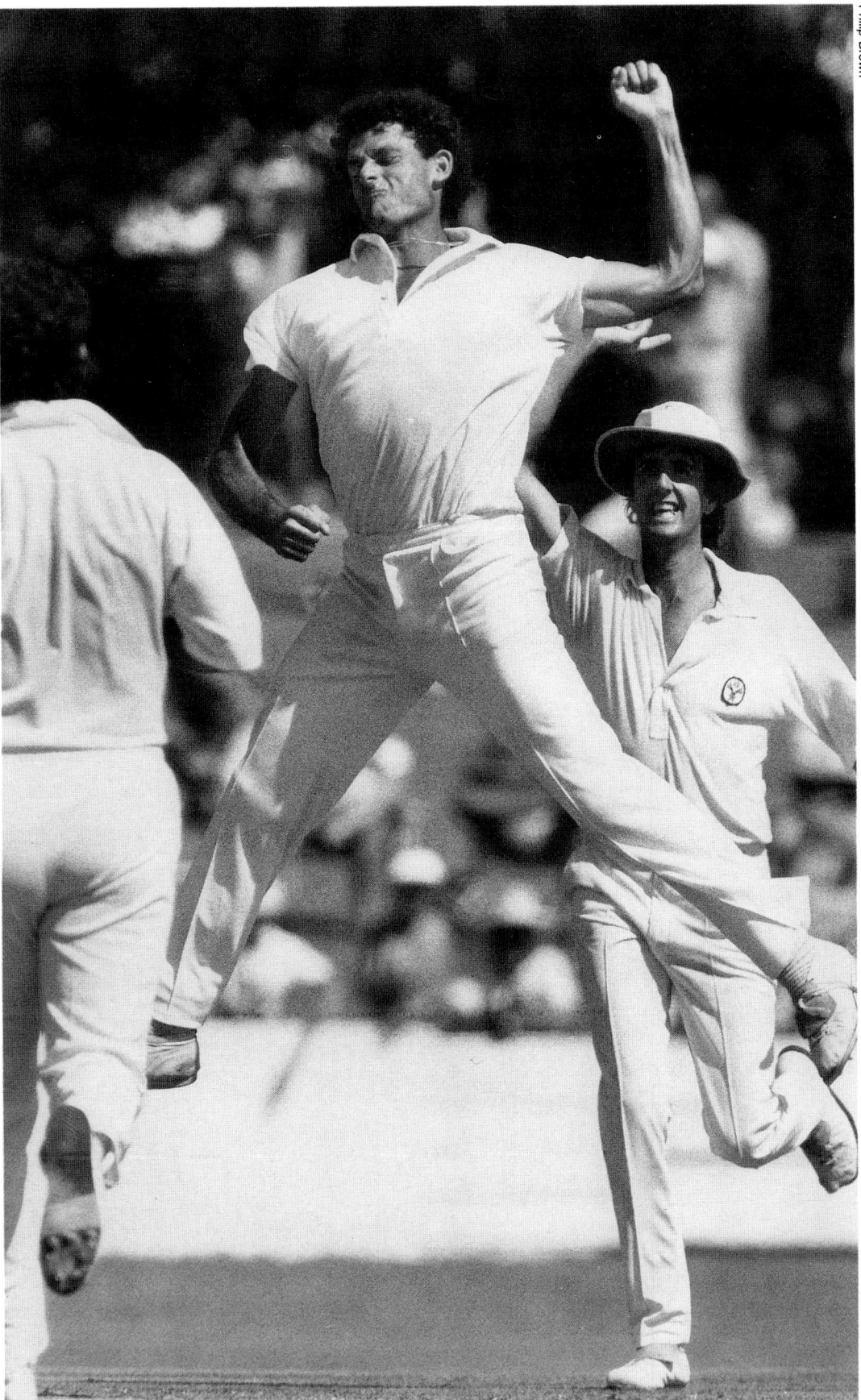

Previous page: The joy of cricket. Celebrating the wicket of Greg Ritchie, NSW against Queensland in Newcastle, November 1987. The photo won a Rothmans National Photography award for its taker, Philip Brown.

Below: One of the earliest known photos of Michael Roy Whitney, taken in the driveway of our home at Matraville.

Above right: That's me, one of the star attractions at Matraville Public School's 1965 Easter Bonnet parade.

Below: My kindergarten school photo. I'm the guy at the far right of the back row. One person in this photo I'll never forget is the teacher, if only because of the belting she gave me one day because I refused to use my right hand when writing.

Right: A very special photo, taken at an annual La Perouse United football presentation, where I won the award for scoring the most tries for the club during the season. The gentleman in the background is my father, Roy. The presenter is Eric Simms, fullback in the great South Sydney rugby league teams of the late '60s and early '70s and one of my early sporting heroes.

Below: The La Perouse United "I" Grade side of 1970, a side that included, among others, the future Australian rugby union internationals Glen Ella (back row, third from left), Lloyd Walker (fourth from left, front row) and Mark Ella (front row, second from right), and the future Australian fast bowler, Mike Whitney (to Lloyd's left).

John Elliott

Opposite page: Two photos from 1981. (Above) Bowling for NSW at the SCG, and (below) surfing the waves at Maroubra. The cricket photo, taken by John Elliott, won the NSWCA Photo of the Year.

Above: In the nets, a little wilder and less-controlled than later in my career, during my first season with NSW, 1980-81.

Left: Getting a few tips from one of the legends of NSW and Australian cricket, Alan Davidson. Right from my very earliest days, Davo has been a huge influence on my career.

Above: The end of my first Test innings, bowled by Paul Allott for a duck during the fifth Test at Old Trafford in 1981. The English fieldsmen are (left to right): Chris Tavare, Ian Botham and Geoff Boycott. I managed another nought in the second dig, despite batting for 40 minutes with Allan Border, but in the sixth Test, at The Oval, in the first innings I scored my first Test runs, an edge to the boundary. My celebrations after achieving that four were akin to how most batsmen celebrate their centuries.

Right: At the bowling crease during the Old Trafford Test. The umpire is Ken Palmer.

Below: With D.K. Lillee, during the fifth Test of 1981.

Right: Bruce Laird, the Australian and WA opener, bowled at the WACA Ground in Perth, in 1981-82. This is just about my favourite cricket photo. At the time all the critics said I couldn't bowl an inswinger, but this ball came back, took the inside edge and knocked over the leg stump. The fact the batsman was Laird, a player I had huge respect for, made the moment even sweeter.

Bottom: Run out in the 1981-82 McDonald's Cup final at the SCG by the Queensland captain, Geoff Dymock.

Patrick Eagar

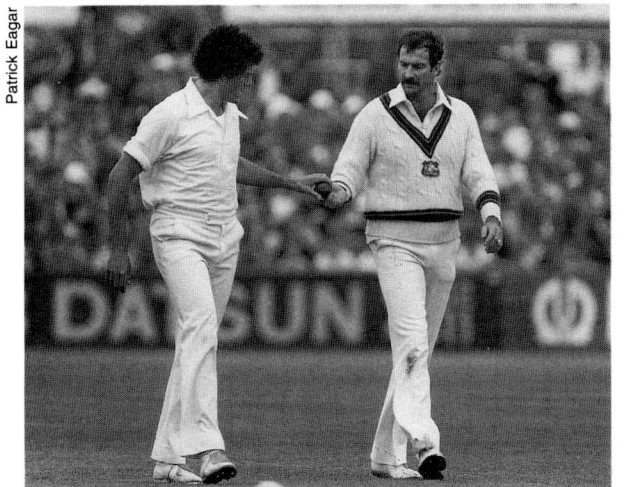

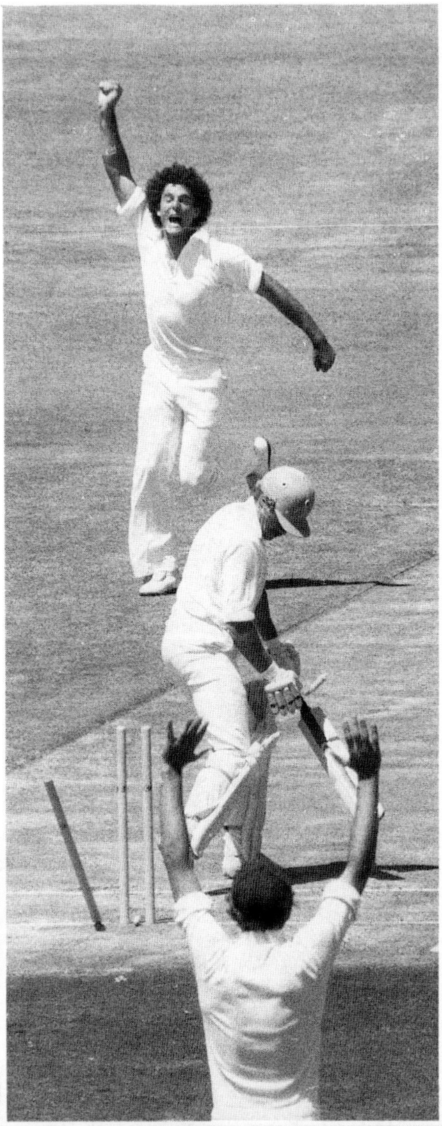

News Limited

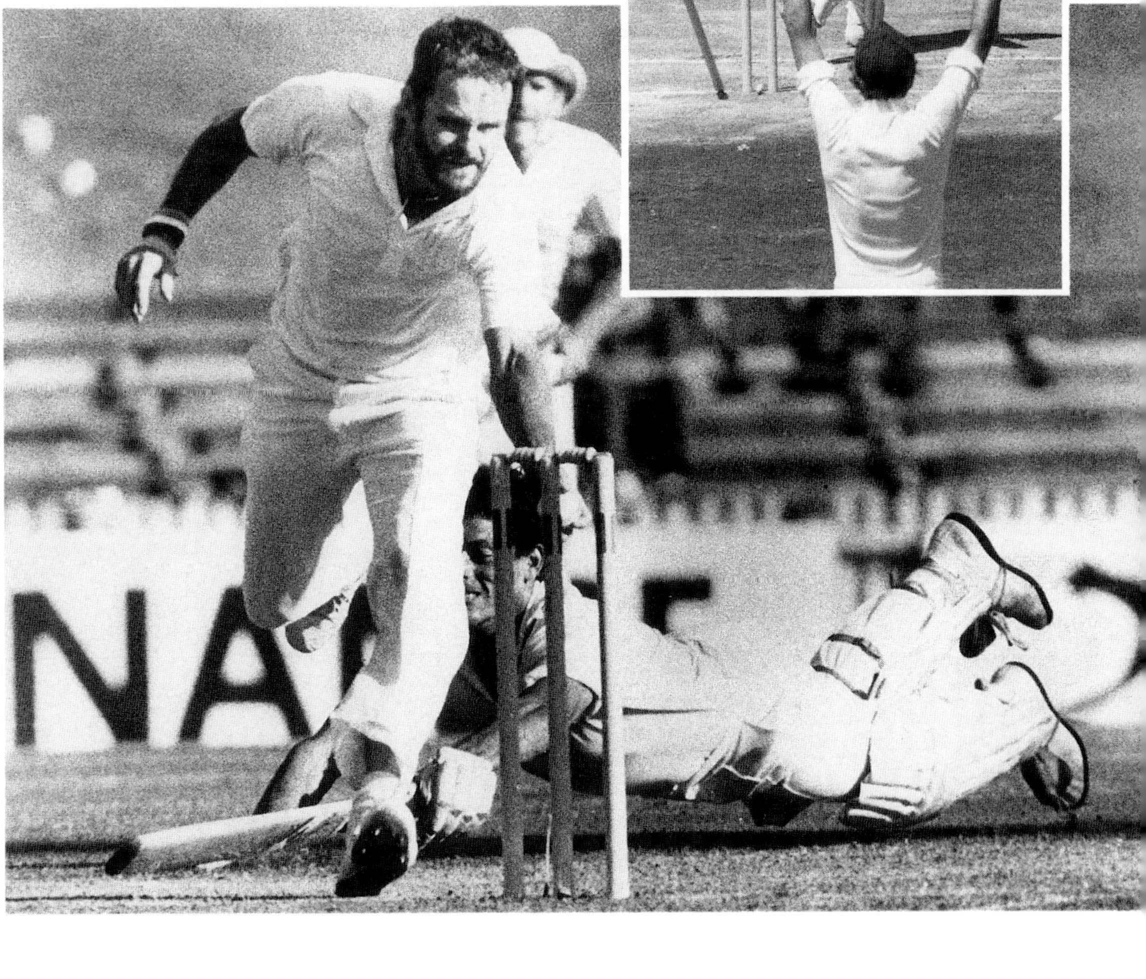

Above: My infamous confrontation with Rod Marsh in the Shield final of 1982-83.
Below: NSW, the Shield champions of 1982-83. Back row: T. Chappell, G. Lawson, D. Wellham, S. Rixon, M. Bennett; Front: P. Toohey, J. Dyson, M. Whitney, S. Smith, G. Matthews, R. McCosker.
Right: When we returned with the Shield, the first person to greet Geoff Lawson and Rick McCosker was ... my mother.

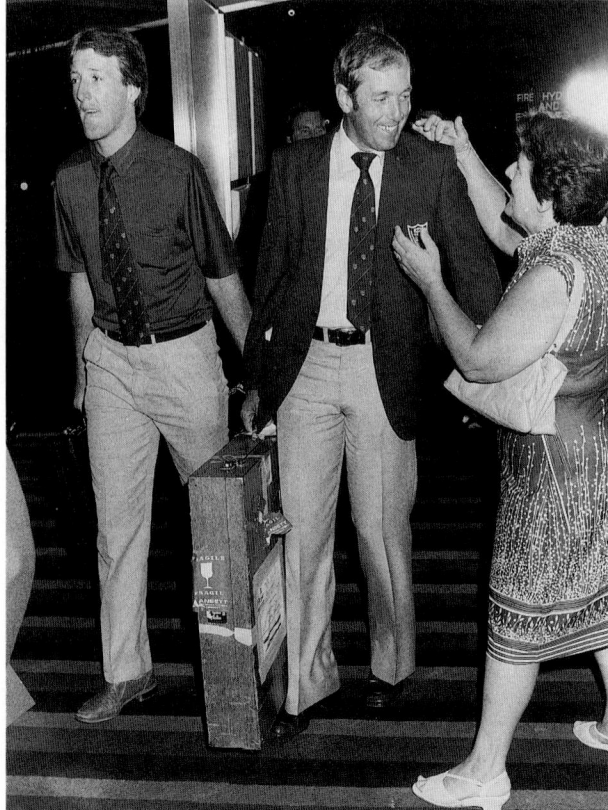

Back in the NSW XI, after more than two years out with a knee injury, January 1986.

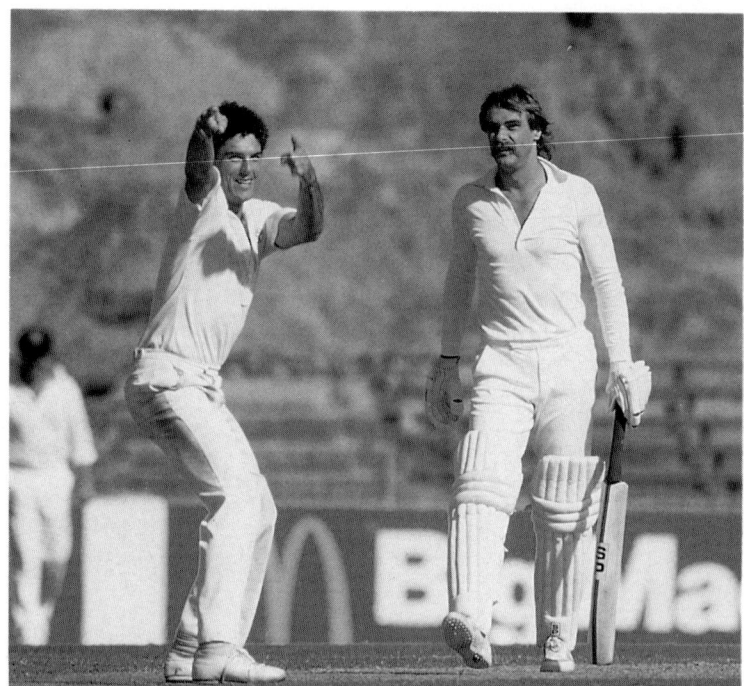

Left: Pointing Queensland tailender, Harry Frei, to the SCG pavilion after I had dismissed him late in the Queensland first innings of the 1985-86 Shield final. At the time the visitors' total was well past 400, and Harry, before he left, suggested I look at the scoreboard.

Below: Celebrations in the home dressing room after we'd hung on for a draw, to clinch the Shield in 1985-86. The NSW players and supporters are (left to right): Murray Bennett, Dave McPherson (asst coach), Mark O'Neill, Richard Done, Peter Taylor, Dirk Wellham, Mark Waugh, Rod Bower, Mike Whitney, Steve Small, Greg Dyer, Geoff Lawson, Bob Holland, Ray Tozer (selector), Mark Taylor, Bill Anderson (coach), Brian 'Strongman' Hollis (trainer).

Above: Bowling for NSW at the Harare Sports Club Ground in Zimbabwe in March, 1986. I made three tours of Zimbabwe, one with an Australian Under-25 team in 1983 and two with NSW, in 1986 and 1987.

Below: There are few, if any, people I have more respect for in the world of cricket than Geoff Lawson. He was a superb cricketer and a brilliant captain, and remains a big inspiration and close friend.

With Richard Hadlee, after the final ball of my most famous innings in Tests, third Test v NZ, 1987-88.

Above: Sharing the champagne with Mark Taylor, after the NSW team had received news of his selection in the Australian side for the fourth Test of the 1988-89 series against the West Indies. It would be Mark's debut in Test cricket. The Blues players are (left to right): Steve Waugh, Mark Taylor, Geoff Lawson, Mike Whitney, Wayne Holdsworth and Trevor Bayliss.

With my wife Debbie (above), and mother Beryl (right), the two most important people in my life.

Pictures from my most memorable bowling performance in Test cricket, the first West Indies innings of the fifth Test in Adelaide in February, 1989. Above: Gordon Greenidge, their prolific opening batsman, bowled through the gate late on the second day. Right: Celebrations after the dismissal of Richie Richardson, caught by Dean Jones at cover.

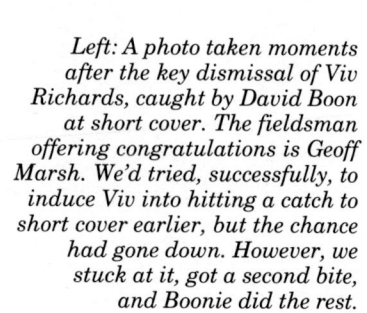

Left: A photo taken moments after the key dismissal of Viv Richards, caught by David Boon at short cover. The fieldsman offering congratulations is Geoff Marsh. We'd tried, successfully, to induce Viv into hitting a catch to short cover earlier, but the chance had gone down. However, we stuck at it, got a second bite, and Boonie did the rest.

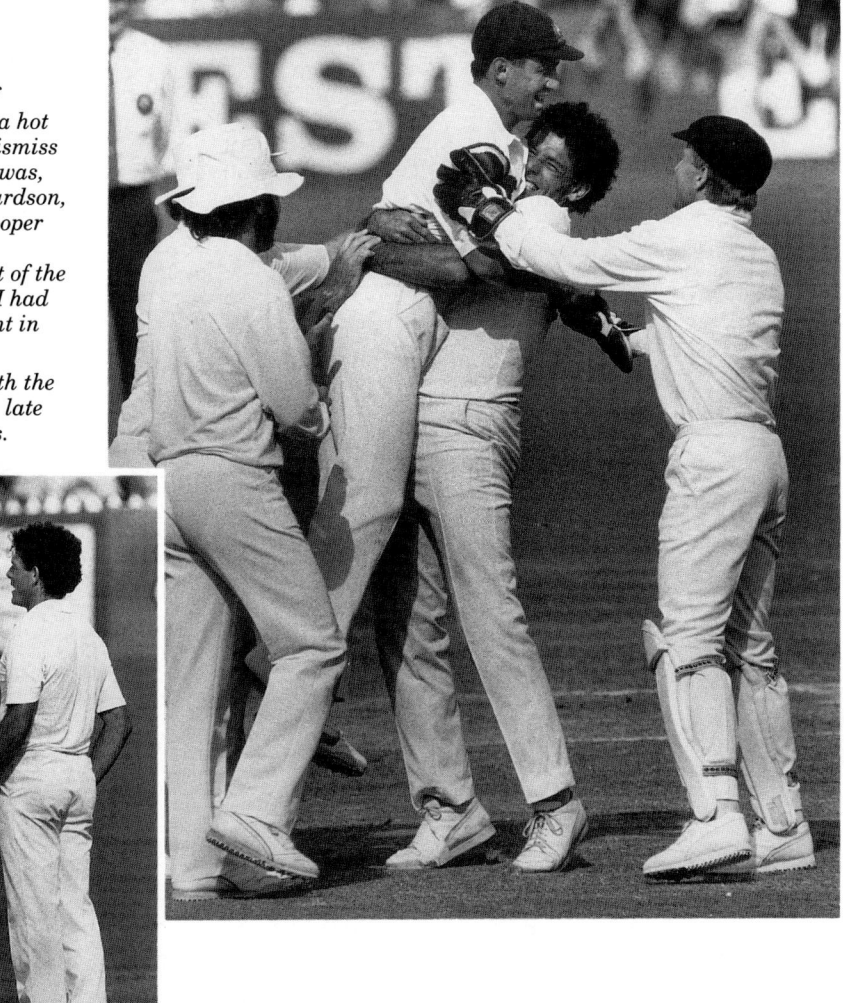

Right: A hug for Geoff Marsh after he'd held a hot catch in the gully to dismiss Malcolm Marshall. It was, after Greenidge, Richardson, Richards and Carl Hooper (caught behind by Ian Healy), my fifth wicket of the innings — something I had never done to that point in Test cricket.

Below: Face to face with the giant Curtly Ambrose, late in the Windies innings.

Right: A discussion with Jeff Dujon, who we all thought had gloved a ball through to the keeper in the final moments of the third day. The seagulls look as interested as Dujon ... and the umpire.

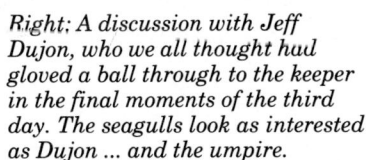

Left: Enjoying the post-performance press conference.

The two sides of professional sport. In early February, my life in cricket was a buzz, as I enjoyed my great day against the West Indies. The photo at right shows me celebrating after Carl Hooper had edged a catch behind. But that performance, and the fact I was the leading wicket-taker in the country during season 1988-89, counted for nothing when the Australian selectors chose their side to tour England in 1989. I was left behind — the most devastating blow of my cricket career. The photo below, taken by the Sydney Morning Herald's *Quentin Jones in Sydney's Centennial Park after the Ashes side was announced, offers a stark contrast to the joy of Adelaide.*

Quentin Jones

months later he would score a remarkable century in a Test in the West Indies. But later on, he did a few things the hierarchy didn't appreciate, and he got the chop. He played his last Test in 1986.

Greg Ritchie and Wayne Phillips remain two of the funniest guys I've ever met. It's a shame that in the late '80s they didn't fit the bill.

The arrival of Bob Simpson on the scene, as Australian coach in '86, meant the end for any blokes who had too much of the larrikin spirit. Bob likes everyone to toe the line, and be a unit. He doesn't like players who he thinks might disturb or influence their team-mates. Under Simpson there would be no place for a Greg Ritchie or a Wayne Phillips.

As well as McCurdy, Ritchie and Phillips, there was some other fine talent on that 1983 Zimbabwe tour:

• Stuart Saunders — a very good leg-spinner. After the tour we both went to England and played in the same league competition. Unfortunately, Stuart's English captain had no idea how to handle a leg-spin bowler and in that one English summer Stuart's talent as a leg-spinner pretty much went down the gurgler. It was a shame — he was a good prospect. Stuart and his wife Libby are two of my best friends.

• Robbie Kerr was a prolific run-scorer for Queensland, a brilliant timer of the ball who could dispatch a loose one with devastating effect without really seeming to hit it hard.

• Dean Jones was very young on that tour, but with his great thirst for runs was already showing terrific promise. On that tour he'd be sent in as a slogger in one-day games. He developed, of course, into one of the world's finest one-day players, and a first-class Test batsman, with a couple of double centuries to his credit.

• Mike Haysman emerged as an outstanding young prospect — a good hitter of the ball, with excellent technique.

• Greg Shipperd was a stodgy player, with a great defence. He never seemed like a bloke who was going to set the cricket world on fire, but he was a hard bloke to dismiss, and had a deep and genuine love of the game.

• David Boon was one of the emerging talents of the tour. His ability was obvious and he trained very hard. Here was a bloke who made it patently clear that he wanted to go on and play Test cricket.

And there were my NSW colleagues, Dirk Wellham and Murray Bennett. I'll talk about them in detail later in the book.

It was a fine team, and a tour that was a turning point for me and a lot of the other guys. We were obviously in the selectors' minds as future Test players — and many of us did go on and achieve that highpoint in a cricketer's life.

New South Wales tours to Zimbabwe that followed later were a tonne of fun. On the one in 1987 we played a match in which the scorer, a white

Zimbabwean named Wishart, reserved a corner of the scoreboard to record the number of beers he got through in the day. Leg-spinner Bob "Dutchy" Holland had the match off so we sent him around to keep the scorer company. The scoreboard carried the number "14" at the end of the day's play. The next day we sent Graham Smith along. Now, Graham is a country boy, from a tiny southern NSW township called Stockinbingal, hence his nickname "Stockers". We had asked him on the flight over whether he was the first Stockinbingal man to visit Zimbabwe.

"The first to visit Zimbabwe?" replied Stockers.

"Hell, I was the first to visit SYDNEY!"

Graham Smith managed 20 beers with Wishart that day, and strolled back to the dressing room completely unaffected.

They breed 'em tough in Stockinbingal.

The Lost Years

On a chilling day in 1984 I was told I would never play cricket again. A Sydney specialist's verdict on the knee injury I had suffered in extraordinary circumstances in Launceston in November 1983, and then aggravated by my over-keenness to get back, was more shattering than the injury itself. "I'm afraid your cricketing days are over," the doctor announced in suitably sombre tones.

I had just turned 25 and the moment of his announcement ranks among the most despairing of my life.

The story is a strange one — but, fortunately, one with a happy ending. Coming out of my successful 1982-83 season, I was full steam ahead — thoroughly enjoying my cricket for club and state. However, it all blew up on me on that fateful day in Launceston, where we were playing Tasmania in a McDonald's Cup match.

I had bowled 9.5 overs of my 10-over spell, and my figures were nice and tidy — 0 for 37. But I hadn't taken a wicket, and that narked me. The batsman on strike was a fellow named Francis Woolley and I remember saying to myself as I walked back for my last ball: "Geez, it'd be good to get this bloke."

I tried to put a bit of extra *oomph* into that final ball. It pitched just right, nipped away off the pitch and caught the edge of Woolley's bat. Next instant it was in the safe gloves of Steve "Stumper" Rixon. Mission accomplished! But back up the pitch my delighted appeal had turned into a strangled cry of pain. As my left leg hit the pitch on that final delivery stride my knee had "gone" ... just crumpled on me.

I hobbled off the field ... and out of cricket for two years.

Back in Sydney, after all the necessary investigations, I underwent an operation for removal of a cartilage and some floating bone, an operation that ended my season. But the knee seemed okay, and, as part of a personal rehabilitation process (and my continuing education in life), I went travelling — to England, South Africa, Greece and India — on an odyssey during which I must have trekked thousands of kilometres.

I went to South Africa for a particular reason. In England, while playing league cricket with the Littleborough club the previous northern summer, I had received a call from the former Australian Test batsman, Bruce Francis, sounding me out on the possibility of me joining a "rebel" Australian tour to South Africa. The deal discussed had been for a two-season contract, at $40,000 a tour — excellent money at that time (the players who eventually did choose to go, for the 1985-86 and 1986-87 seasons, in fact earned $100,000 a tour). I wanted to visit South Africa to get some personal experience of the place before I made up my mind. There was some romance, too — I wanted to see a girl I had met in Europe in 1982.

What I saw of South Africa made up my mind that I wouldn't go on any rebel tour there. I witnessed things that were shocking and disgraceful in the way whites treated blacks — a white policeman cracking a whip to chase away a small group of black men standing on a corner; those offensive "whites only" signs on the beaches in Cape Town and Durban ...

I went out of my way on that trip to meet black people and to listen as they talked about their problems. Their predicament appalled me. But I must say that, visually, I found South Africa one of the most stunning places I had ever seen, and I am delighted at the progress made towards a fairer society in the 10 years since.

Because of my knee problems any decision about me touring the country as a "rebel" cricketer was purely academic. I never had to face square-on the question — will you join us for $200,000?

Finally back home after my travelling, I was happy with the progress my knee had apparently made. I returned to formal training, and to the nets, full of enthusiasm. I played a State trial at the Newcastle University ground, and bowled 10 overs. But after it my knee really blew up, and from that point onwards it was all downhill. With the enthusiasm of youth I kept running and bike riding in the mistaken belief that the thing would get better. In fact ... it just kept getting worse.

Finally, it "went" on me again, on one of those steep Coogee hills as I pedalled home from a barbecue that Phil Tresidder had hosted for the Randwick Cricket Club at his home. I knew then I was in big trouble, and within a day or two I was back to see the specialist.

It was on a subsequent visit there, with my sister Christine along to provide some moral support, that I was told I would never play cricket again — that my knee was too badly damaged for me to contemplate carrying on. I'll never forget that moment. I walked out of the doctor's rooms with tears coursing down my cheeks. I was 25 years of age, and had been written off.

So the doctor had said. But Christine, in her way, said: "We'll see about that."

As I walked out onto the street, something snapped inside me. I swung around and strode (as defiantly as I could on my wonky knee) back into the surgery. I can still see the look on the doctor's face as I burst back into his room. He was a quiet and reserved sort of fellow, and he was definitely startled.

"I want a second opinion!" I demanded.

He sort of coughed and spluttered a bit.

"I want a second opinion," I repeated. "I've heard about this bloke Merv Cross, and I'd like to see him."

So, the orthopaedic surgeon slowly picked up his phone and rang Cross.

"Send him over," was the answer from Dr Cross.

So I headed straight across town to see Merv Cross, and within a few days was in Longueville Private Hospital, under the knife again, undergoing an operation to remove foreign bodies from the knee.

I can still remember the moment I woke from the anaesthetic after that operation. Dr Cross was there, standing at the end of the bed. In his forthright manner he leaned across and clasped my arm:

"You're going to be alright".

Just five words — and it was all I wanted to hear. If I could have leaped out of bed in celebration, I would have done so.

I knew it was going to be a hard road back, but I was prepared to pay the price. The cricket season of 1984-85 was already well underway, and as the rehabilitation process began I made a decision fairly early to write off the season in toto — and concentrate instead on building my legs and strength for a successful return in 1985-86.

I was pretty much of a lost soul during that period. I didn't want to find permanent employment because my mind was fixed on getting back to cricket — at the highest level. The last permanent position I had held was back at the end of 1982, when I had completed my apprenticeship with Qantas. With bits and pieces of work here and there — mainly coaching — I had survived. I was never on the dole, but it was a tough period. With a successful knee operation behind me, the task at hand was to get myself fit and well enough to return to cricket. The struggle was to scrape up enough money to keep that process going.

An unexpected phone call one morning helped ease the burden — and led me into one of the stranger work experiences of my life. Bob Pritchard, a bloke with an entrepreneurial bent, had started a promotions and marketing company called Powerplay International. With him at Powerplay was a lady I knew, Jill Gabrielson, who had been with PBL Marketing, the promoters of cricket in Australia, in the late '70s when they had first become involved with the game.

Jill rang me one day and offered me a job. I said to her: "What exactly does the company do?"

She explained they were closely linked to the South Melbourne (VFL) Football Club, who had just been relocated in Sydney, and renamed the Sydney Swans. Furthermore, she told me, a doctor named Geoffrey Edelsten was heavily involved in the move.

So, I went in there and took the job — car, expenses allowance ... the whole bit. At the same time they employed the venerable spin bowler, David "Cracker" Hourn, who had played for NSW during the '70s and early '80s. We were the Sales, Marketing and Promotions Department.

The experience turned out to be insane ... but some fun.

It was a decadent sort of set-up. Anything you wanted, new office furniture or whatever, you got. We had these nice offices above one of Dr Edelsten's medical centres, at Broadway, near Sydney's Central Railway Station.

As an engineer, trained at Qantas, and a broken-down cricketer, I must admit the thought occurred now and then: what the hell am I doing *here*?

Bob Pritchard gave David and me the brief on Day One. He bowled into the office and handed us the metropolitan telephone books with the words: "Well, there it is boys ... go for it."

The job was to sell the Swans to corporate Sydney. I had never had any experience in selling or phone etiquette or anything like that, and it was a struggle. In nine months with Powerplay, my only runs on the board were to sell a table of 10 to one of the many Swans functions.

It was a wild joint. There were some indications it was a potential house of cards within the first six months or so. I remember one time when they brought these people over from Perth who were negotiating to buy the company. On the day the deal fell through, Dr Edelsten came storming out of the boardroom, pulled a team photo of the Swans off the wall, and stomped it to smithereens!

Craziness was in the air much of the time. Doc Edelsten was a strange one — a little bloke who seemed to suffer substantially from the "small man" syndrome. He always wore shoes with enormous heels. We saw a fair bit of his highly-publicised young wife, Leanne. She'd park her pink Porsche out the front (the one with the "SWANS" number-plate), and come parading through the office — fur coat, wiggle and all.

There was a great air of unreality about the place, and the ultimate crash came, I'm sure, as absolutely no surprise to anyone who had brushed against the Edelsten-Swans phenomenon. I wasn't happy there, but they kept saying to me: "Mate, you're not playing cricket, but at least you've got a job."

And I'd respond: "I'm going to get back into the team, and you can bet your bottom dollar on that."

When I *did* finally get back into cricket, Bob Pritchard called me into his office and said: "You know, we just can't afford to keep you on any more now that you're going to be away playing cricket." I was happy to get out.

I worked hard during the winter of 1985 getting ready for my return to cricket. Unfortunately, I wasn't quite right when the 1985-86 grade season started, and my return was delayed until round three. And then, my comeback was the ultimate in non-events. We batted on the first Saturday, against St George, and my contribution was a stirring one not out. The next week was washed out completely — I didn't get to bowl a single over!

The next Saturday, against Waverley, I bowled 24 overs, for no wickets and 80 runs, which wasn't exactly the sort of return I was looking for. But in the next game, against Penrith, I took 2-42 from 13.3 overs, which brought a comment from the *Sun Herald's* correspondent at the game that I had shown much of my old fire.

I still had a lot of ground to make up. It was now getting close to two *years* gone from my life as a first-class cricketer. Opportunities had come and gone, and fast bowlers in their droves had leap-frogged over me.

One of them was Dave Gilbert, who had grabbed my State spot and earned himself an Ashes tour. Good luck to him. Sport, like life, is about opportunities taken (or missed).

At State practice one day, not longer after I'd made my return to grade cricket, I pulled him to one side, and did something that I had never done before, or since.

"I hope you're bowling well," I said to him.

He looked at me a bit strangely. "Why's that?"

"Because I'm going to take your f------ spot."

I can still see the look on his face. He didn't know whether I was serious, or whether I was joking.

I was serious.

It wasn't the case that "Lizard" (as we knew him) and I had ever been anything but friends. But there were only a couple of spots up for grabs. Gilbert had one, and Henry Lawson had the other. Hen was a legend, and I knew I wasn't going to get his spot ... so it had to be Gilbert.

When I did make it back, I did, in a way, replace Dave Gilbert *and* Geoff Lawson. By January, 1986, Dave was a regular in the Australian team. At the same time, Henry had broken down with a severe back injury. With the Australian team involved in the one-day international series, that left two spots open for NSW's match against Western Australia in Perth, which was scheduled to begin on January 16.

I got the call-up, along with a bloke called Phil Blizzard. When the *Sydney Morning Herald's* Greg Growden caught up with me, after the team had been announced, I was able to tell him exactly how I felt.

"To say I'm ecstatic would be the understatement of the year," I said.

"It will be so great to get into the state jumper again and run out onto the field. It is unfortunate that I get my chance because Henry is injured. But then again, Dave Gilbert got his chance when I was crook and now he's opening the bowling for Australia."

As it turned out it was an inauspicious return. We got absolutely smashed. They beat us by an innings and 46 runs after bowling us out for 83 in the first dig. I managed a first-ball duck, bowled by an inswinging yorker from their opening bowler, Chris Matthews. I then failed to get a wicket, bowling 22 overs for 84 runs as they carved out a match-winning seven for 450.

It was no triumphant return — but, boy, it was great to be back!

After the long wait, first to get over my injury and then to get back in the side, the Shield season turned out to be a successful and enjoyable one for me. Because of Henry's injury, and Gilbert's Test duties, I kept my spot in the side, and was soon back among the wickets. I finished the season with 22 at 21.95, second on the averages table for the entire competition.

The highlight was to be a real turning point in my career — my 6-65, off 34 overs, against Queensland in the first innings of the Shield final, played at the SCG. The final was drawn after a thrilling game which see-sawed one way, then the other, so, because we had finished higher on the Shield ladder, we were the champions.

The NSW opening combination in that match was an unlikely one — M.R. Whitney and M.E. Waugh. He was quite sharp in those days, was Mark "Junior" Waugh. Both teams were comparatively underpowered for the final, with leading players (Queenslanders Allan Border, Craig McDermott and Greg Ritchie; Steve Waugh, Greg Matthews and Dave Gilbert of NSW) on international duties in New Zealand, and Geoff Lawson recovering from injury. We took in an unusual bowling attack, comprising Mark and myself to open, then three spinners — Bob Holland, Murray Bennett and Peter Taylor.

The final was a great contest, full of unusual events. One of our batsmen, Rod Bower, took the first wicket. Mark and I had had no luck getting a breakthrough, and Bower had been brought on to roll his arm over for a couple of overs. He did better than that — he got rid of their opener Andrew Courtice — and finished up bowling seven overs for 1-28.

By lunch on the second day Queensland's left-handed number three, captain Kepler Wessels, was on 166 not out. I said to Greg Dyer, our keeper: "What do you reckon we can do to get rid of this bloke?"

Greg answered: "I reckon you should come around the wicket to him and push the ball across him."

Which I immediately did. Wessels went to cut the first ball I bowled to him in the opening over after lunch, which was pitched on middle and off, and leaving him. It was fractionally too full to cut and Wessels got the faintest glove — and the ball flew straight through to Dyer.

I couldn't believe it. The script had worked out perfectly.

Late in that Queensland first innings, I was bowling to Harry Frei, a left-arm seam bowler who had played VFL footy. Harry was something of a knockabout who never wore a helmet — and that's always inviting for a fast bowler. I bounced him first ball, and again on the second one, which he bunted behind square-leg and into the hands of Steve Small. It was my fifth wicket, and I was thrilled about that. I ran up to Frei and gave him not one but a two-handed signal to the dressing room.

"Piss off and have a shower," I said. At the time they were 8 for 400-and-plenty.

"Have a look at the scoreboard," replied Harry. He was a good bloke, and I had a beer with him later.

The final day was a dramatic affair, as first one side, then the other looked the victor. With 10 overs remaining, we found ourselves eight down and opted to play for the draw. Bob Holland and Murray Bennett dug in stoically. I was in the dressing room padded up, last man in.

It was Jeff Thomson's last match and he was giving it everything he had. At the other end Harry Frei was trying all the tricks of the trade, swinging the ball, bowling "Chinamen" ... doing anything he could to get a wicket. Harry would have loved to get me in there, I'm sure.

With the overs running out, the phone in the dressing room suddenly rang. It was Bob Simpson, who was then our coach, ringing in from New Zealand where he was with the Australian team. I called it ball by ball for a while, then handed the phone on to captain Dirk Wellham, who talked Bob through the final overs. Next to me, Mark O'Neill was smoking like a chimney. He had two ashtrays ... and they were both full.

The injuries that crippled my career for two full seasons and have punctuated my life in cricket are no more than part of the deal for a fast bowler. As I put down the words for this book in late 1993, I have had eight knee operations — five on my left knee, and three on the right. The left knee is my trouble spot — although people have often expressed surprise that my problems are on that side, considering that a left-armer thumps down his *right* foot at the moment of delivery. The fact is that in and immediately after the delivery stride my *left* knee is turned sharply one way, then the other. During every single ball I bowl the left knee is *twice* under serious stress. If something is going to give — then the left knee is the joint that will always be favourite.

And, even when I finally give up bowling, things don't look too flash. Dr Cross has already removed arthritic spurs from the knee, so the chances of the knee leaving me alone once my cricket days are over are pretty remote.

It's a fact of life in cricket that, if you're a fast bowler, you have to accept the realities of injuries. I don't care if you're playing for the Black Stump First XI or Australia, injuries are going to get you at some stage. For most quicks it happens in three key areas — ankles (ask current NSW speed man, Wayne Holdsworth), lower back (D.K. Lillee, Geoff Lawson), and knees (go no further than this book).

Most people, I'm sure, have no understanding at all of what a fast bowler puts his body through. The certainty of fast bowling is that if you're congenitally weak in one particular area of your body, then your craft will find you out.

But the thing about the game of cricket is that most of us are happy to pay that price. I turn 35 in February, 1994, and I can honestly say I have never for an instant lost the desire or the will to go on playing cricket — despite the pain and discomfort of the injuries I have suffered. Perhaps when my (right) knee went on me early in the 1993-94 season there were people who thought that maybe that would be the end — that at 34 I would take a graceful retirement.

Well, sorry to disappoint you — but no way. It wouldn't be me ... wouldn't be Mike Whitney ... if I didn't drag myself back to finish the season. To let it just fizzle out would be wrong. Nothing that has ever happened to me on the cricket field has ever tempted me for an instant to think about giving the game away.

However, I will admit there was one moment when my love and passion for the game wavered. That was in 1989, when, while coping with the vast disappointment of missing that season's Ashes tour, the thought of retirement did cross my mind. However, my discontent at that time was caused by something beyond my control, not by the game itself. And, even then, the thought lasted for no more than 10 seconds ...

And then was gone forever.

Bumpers, Batsmen, and One-Day Cricket

In Test cricket, intimidatory bumpers are something you just have to live with. They are part of life at the top, and batsmen accept the lethal threat for the most part without a second thought. But then, every so often, somebody gets hit and you realise, hey man, we are really playing here for keeps. As soon as there's a bit of claret in the dressing room, the whole mood changes. It's like going into battle and firing blanks and all of a sudden a live bullet is fired and somebody gets hit.

A classic example occurred when the West Indies were playing the second Test against Australia in Perth in December, 1988. I was on the other side of the continent, in Newcastle, playing for NSW in a Shield match. As Perth is three hours "behind" the Australian east coast, we were able to get back to our hotel in time to watch the last session of the Test. I was rooming with Greg Matthews and we turned the television on just as Geoff Lawson was walking in to bat. I asked Greg if he thought the Windies would "give it to him". He reckoned they would, and straight away.

We watched Henry mark out centre on the crease. I think he faced one delivery, then the next ball pitched short, directed at middle and off stumps, and climbed back at him. It just kept coming, Henry dropped his guard and turned his head away, and the ball nailed him right under the jaw. I remember looking at Greg, and he looked at me. We were both in a state of shock.

We looked back at the tele set and there was Henry lying on the pitch, not moving. For a moment we thought he was in big trouble. Then, thankfully, we saw him move his hands, while the short-leg fieldsman, Gus Logie, was trying to tug his helmet off. Henry started waving him away because he was in so much pain. Eventually they took him off to hospital where it was confirmed he had a busted jaw. It was really, really ugly.

Fortunately, the blow did not have a long-term effect on Henry's career, and he was back captaining NSW before the end of the season, and ended up going to England with the Australian team at season's end. But the sight of him stricken on the pitch certainly slowed us down for a while, even if we realised that it was, for all the pain and anguish, part of the game.

Now you have to ask if the guys who deal out the bouncers really want to hit the batsmen. The truth is they do, but below the shoulders. Nobody takes pleasure in hitting a batsman in the head. I certainly don't. If a batsman was hit on the head and wasn't wearing a protective helmet, I wouldn't like to take responsibility for that. But most quick bowlers don't mind bruising the batsman — after all, he is the enemy. First-class cricket is a tough, hard game. The batsmen certainly want to belt the ball you're bowling all over the park. The comeback you have is the psychological and physical edge that can be gained through intimidation.

I was hit on the arm in Newcastle in late 1989 by Queensland's Craig McDermott and only had myself to blame because I wasn't wearing a protective arm guard. The fact is there is protective gear available for every batsman from opener down to number 11. The dressing room is full of such equipment so if a batsman goes to the crease without it, and gets hurt, you can't blame the bowler who is trying to do the best thing he can for his side. If the bowler bounces a batsman a few times to unsettle him and shake his stroke-making confidence, then that's the way it is.

In truth, I have never met any specialist first-class batsmen who have been scared. But there are batsmen who are more susceptible to short-pitched bowling than others. Contemporaries of mine, Ian Davis and Peter Toohey from NSW, were compulsive hookers. They didn't even think about it. As soon as it registered that the ball was short they were into a hooking position. The former Australian opening bat, Andrew Hilditch, was another compulsive hooker, an unsuccessful one, and it cost him his Test spot.

Inevitably, some guys get branded as poor players of the rising delivery. Tom Moody of Western Australia, at least early in his innings, is such a player. These days, every time he comes to the crease he gets peppered with short balls. I'm sure he doesn't like being reminded of this, but that's how it is and I'll bet he's working very hard to overcome the problem. But many batsmen are fantastic players of short-pitched bowling. NSW's John Dyson was one, rock solid, and adept at weaving his way out of trouble just as Bobby Simpson did so well in his heyday. Dyson might have hooked if he had runs on the board, but it was a complete waste of time bowling short to him. He was never unnerved. Mark Taylor is similar, while Mark Waugh is a batsman who will hook courageously. He's got so much time. He'll watch the ball right onto his nose then smash it. It's incredible to watch him.

There's been a bunch of fast bowlers over the last 10 years who have been more dangerous than others and, of course, they have been mainly West Indian. But I would throw in some Australians, notably Dennis Lillee, who had an awesome bouncer and Jeff Thomson, the fastest bowler in the world when he had full steam up. Rodney Hogg was another Aussie quickie who needed prudent watching. He bowled straight and often at you, and when he bowled a bouncer he didn't waste it. Straight at your throat!

But the most dangerous bouncer bowlers in my time have been the West Indians — Joel Garner, Curtly Ambrose, Malcolm Marshall and Courtney Walsh.

When playing the West Indians, I, as a tail-ender, watched the specialist batsmen getting the bumper treatment with some trepidation. I knew my turn would come. In the Caribbean in 1991 I've never worn so much padding in my life. We were facing four fast bowlers every innings and there was simply no let-up. I tried to protect myself with an arm guard, thigh guard (inside and out), chest guard, face helmet, and pads with extra padding inside them.

I'd never worn this sort of stuff before, but we had all decided, before the tour started, that this was the way it had to be. We had been warned — you need to pad yourselves up. These guys are ugly. During the first game, at St Kitts, even the good batsmen were getting hit, and I decided ... when you get out there, think only self-preservation.

Which immediately created a problem. When I arrived at the crease, Steve Waugh was 90 not out. I wasn't fully right — I had an ear infection which had deafened me in the left ear — but I decided to try and stick it out if I possibly could while Steve reached his century. The concept of self-preservation, though, stayed firmly in my mind.

The Test fast bowler, Patrick Patterson, was bowling, and the worrying thing was that I had bounced him in the first innings. As I was walking out I was thinking that maybe that hadn't been a real smart thing to do. But Steve Waugh re-assured me.

"Don't worry mate," he said. "He's only bowling medium pace".

Well, Patrick sort of revived at the sight of me taking block. The first ball he bowled to me was short of a length outside the off-stump and, as I lifted my bat to let it go, it whistled past at 100mph and picking up speed. Their little keeper, David Williams, standing way back, reached high and dragged it out of the heavens.

I looked down the wicket and Steve Waugh had this huge smile on his dial. I walked down to him. "I thought you said he was bowling medium pace?" I said.

"That was the fastest ball he's bowled," said Steve, trying to keep the grin off his face. Re-assuring. It's been a funny thing about my batting career — every time I get to the wicket they always seem to go up a gear or two.

The next four balls hit me on the legs, and the bruises I sported over the next fortnight or so were enormous. Patterson was firing the ball straight through my pads as if they weren't there. I managed to see out the over, but, as it turned out, Steve didn't get his 100 anyway.

The punishment I took from Patterson that day reminded me of something that the great Alan Davidson once told me. He reckoned he never tried to bounce the tail-enders. Instead he tried to hit them on the legs so they couldn't bowl. It was a classic Davo statement.

Bumpers are extremely controversial, but they remain a key ace in the fast bowler's armament and I must defend his right to exploit the short-pitched ball. Even if it's Patrick Patterson doing the bowling! Since that Caribbean tour, the pace men have been hamstrung by a newly-introduced rule that restricts them to only one bouncer at each batsman per over. I don't understand why they brought in that rule. There was already in existence an intimidatory bowling law. But the umpires didn't use it, which I found mystifying. I think that if the umps had applied that law sensibly then there would have been absolutely no reason for the new legislation. I know it's tough being an umpire because there are so many rules in this game. But when you're an ump at the top level, you have to use your discretion and do what you think is the right thing. A series of bumpers to a top-order batsman is a completely different thing from a barrage at a "rabbit". Obviously if some tail-ender is getting the life bumped out of him, then the bowler must be warned and maybe eventually pulled out of the attack.

In the back of everybody's minds is the last decade of West Indian bowling, and the enormous success their formidable and often frightening four-pronged attack has reaped. I guess that is the chief reason the latest restrictive laws were introduced. But if we go back to the years when Lillee and Thomson were terrorising absolutely everybody in world cricket, we weren't complaining at all, were we? Nor were there complaints when John Snow, who had a sharp, climbing rib-tickler, was playing for England. For that matter, nobody complained back in the late '40s and early '50s when Ray Lindwall and Keith Miller were decimating the opposition. So I think it's unfair to single out the West Indies in the '80s and '90s because they've produced all these speed merchants.

If officials have brought in the new rule because of the dangers associated with batting against fast bowling then I believe they've over-reacted. With all respect, particularly to the odd batsman hurt or even killed on the field, when you play a sport, particularly at top level, you know you are a chance of being injured. If it's AFL football or the rugby codes, you can hurt your back, your neck, your legs; at skiing on water or snow, you can break an ankle; you can come off a motor bike with all sorts of fractures. No matter what sport you play you are vulnerable to some sort of injury.

One of the great ironies of the new rule, considering it was brought in a as response to the West Indian fast attack, is that it won't affect their approach too much. The rule says the ball that travels over the shoulder is a no-ball, but that's not really the dangerous delivery. The lethal ball is the one bowled into the body and this is the delivery the West Indian speedsters have perfected. They bowl just short of a length and into the body most of the time. Nobody can stop them whipping into the rib cage. Ouch!

The cricketer who is really going to be hurt by the rule is a bowler like myself. I'm classed as a fast-medium, or when I'm really wound up, medium-fast bowler and my tactics have been to get a batsman on the front foot, then exploit the bouncer as a shock delivery. I often bowl two bumpers in a row. Now, I'm not going to be able to do that. If I bowl a bumper at the beginning of an over, then, for the rest of the over, the batsman doesn't have to be on the lookout for another bumper and can get safely on the front foot.

Let me refer once again to the unhappy demise of Andrew Hilditch. His Test career came to a premature end when he got out half a dozen times to the hook shot. To me, all the bowlers were doing was to exploit a weakness in his technique at the time. It's the same as if a batsman is weak outside the off-stump and you bowl outswingers designed to snare his wicket with a nick. But as things stand now, you can bounce someone and get hit for six or perhaps get him caught down fine leg and it can be called a no-ball. This is ludicrous. As this restrictive bumper rule stands now, we are limiting the chance of seeing the most exciting shots of the game played, the flashing hooks and pulls and the dashing cuts against the steeply-rising ball.

Short-pitched bowling should be an integral part of cricket. The art of batting must remain a test of courage and back-foot technique as well as a test of the batsman's ability to play the cover drive. To take the bouncer out of the game, of even to lessen its impact, is unfair to fast bowlers, and a bonus for batsmen.

But, to be honest, we fast bowlers shouldn't be all that surprised with the introduction of a rule that will work in favour of the batsmen. Whichever way you look at it, cricket is a game loaded the batsmen's way. Speaking on behalf of the sweating, toiling trundlers, I reckon it's pretty one-way traffic. I know you're going to say I'm a bit biased, but let me put my case ...

If you play a game and each side scores in excess of, say, 300 runs, win, lose or draw, everybody will tell you what a great match it has been. But if a bowler happens to knock over a side cheaply, and keeps the opposition's score below 150 in both innings so that the game is won easily, those same people will say it has been a disappointing match.

In my view, the majority of cricket watchers see the sport as a game in which runs should be scored. Hence the view that a good "cricket wicket" is a pitch that is even and generous to the batsmen of both sides. Adelaide Oval, for instance, is regarded as being a good "deck", but 90 per cent of the time you simply have to dig batsmen out with a shovel to get rid of them.

I think the game is better served by a wicket like that at the WACA Ground in Perth, which inevitably has a bit more in it. But don't you believe that the WACA pitch is purely a bowler's dream. Sure, the bounce is good and the pace lively, but once you get set you can be very difficult to dislodge. Just recall the NSW-WA Shield match in the summer of 1990-91, when the Waugh twins of NSW, Steve and Mark, shattered a whole bunch of records with their 464-run fifth-wicket partnership. After that, the Waugh brothers would have cheerfully carted the WACA wicket around with them.

Financially, for the batsmen of the game, cricket is a gold mine. The top-profile run-scorers today are earning somewhere between $20,000 to $50,000 per year to endorse the use of a bat. I can only imagine what guys like Viv Richards, Allan Border and Ian Botham have earned by putting their names on cricket bats.

They are, of course, three of the greatest players in the game, so I won't argue they are not deserving of more payment and incentive that your average first-class cricketer. But let's compare players of similar status in the game at Test level. Let's look at Geoff Marsh and Terry Alderman for example, both Western Australians who were heavily involved in the Test scene in the last decade. Marsh has been one of the country's bravest and most prolific batsmen since he broke into the Test side in 1985-86, while Alderman was one of the best Australian bowlers of the '80s, touring England in 1981 and 1989 and taking more than 40 Test wickets in each series. But like most tail-enders, and unlike Geoff Marsh, Terry wasn't too suave with the bat. He may be lucky to get a few bob out of the company whose bowling boots he uses — maybe at best one-sixth to one-tenth of what Marsh would get for using his preferred brand of cricket bat.

Or take the marketing potential of two promising young players from my own NSW team — Michael Bevan and Wayne Holdsworth. Bevan is an exciting young stroke-maker, Holdsworth probably the fastest bowler in Australia. Bevan may pick up $10,000, maybe more, for endorsing his Kookaburra bats, which is not bad money for a young fellow who has only been in the game for a couple of years. Holdsworth doesn't get within cooee of that figure to endorse boots. Yet they're both doing great deeds in their different roles in the country's most successful Sheffield Shield team.

I realise that batsmen, and their bats, get much better exposure (from an advertising point of view) on television. But there always seem to be certain rules and regulations which hinder the bowlers from making a good quid. A few seasons ago we weren't allowed to wear coloured stripes on our boots or any advertising. That was an Australian Cricket Board rule. If a company like Reebok or Puma had boots that had coloured stripes on them, we were simply not allowed to wear them. Today, in the dress code and regulations of the Board, there is a stipulation allowing only a certain size of advertising.

Compare this with stickers plastered down the back of bats, which are spotlighted further by the "stump cam" which is now such a part of the television coverage. The bat companies are stoked. Why wouldn't they pay anything up to $50,000 in contracts with batsmen?

In the 1990s there is so much protective equipment around for the batsmen that wasn't available in the old days. During my time this has been the biggest single factor in the changing face of cricket. When I started off back in the late '70s it was extremely rare to see a batting helmet. They were just coming into vogue. Not too many batsmen wore armguards and even less wore chest pads.

One of the first batsmen I saw wearing a chest pad was Greg Shipperd of Western Australia. Opposition sides used to call him the "Walking Mattress". Well, he might have been laughed at in the early '80s, but everybody is wearing them now. Then there were inside thigh guards, thigh guards, protective padding for batsmen when they get onto the front foot, while batting gloves have advanced so much that nowadays you rarely hear of broken fingers.

And if you want proof it's a batsman's game, just have a look in the rule book. The laws of the game stipulate that if the umpire is not sure, he must give the batsman the benefit of the doubt. How about if he's unsure he gives the bowler the benefit! More times than not the batsman is out, and it's only through human error or judgment that he's given the "benefit of the doubt" when everybody else on the ground knows he should have been given out. And how many times, after the game, will the batsman confess with a grin that he nicked that ball after all?

The batsmen are being really mollycoddled. Look at the highly popular one-day games. I'm not a big fan of one-day cricket and I've never held back in admitting that. To me, the helter-skelter game is just not "real" cricket.

I'll tell you what I don't like about the one-day game. For starters, if you're a bowler, you're behind the eight ball straight away. Ninety-nine per cent of the time the pitches are made for batsmen — because one-day cricket is basically about who scores the most runs. If someone like me comes on and takes 6-30 and knocks some side over for 90, then you have a bad game, haven't you?

Then there are the fielding restrictions. If you open the bowling you must have no more than two outside the "circle" plus two in catching positions. You can't necessarily have your fieldsmen where you want them. You can't bowl wide of the leg stump or off stump. I can relate to the restriction on leg-side bowling. Bowling wide of the leg stump is crap bowling in any sort of cricket. But, wide of the off stump? I've seen blokes have a dip at one outside the off, and the ball sail straight over the top of their bat — and the umpire call "wide". If the bloke happens to connect and hammers it through the covers, what are they going to give him ... four wides? That rule really pisses me off.

And, of course, you can't bowl short ... can't bounce them. Basically, within the context of the one-day game, all you're allowed to do is to bowl within the batsman's hitting arc. And you're only allowed 10 overs. So if you happen to get hammered in the first six you either don't get another bowl, or you're playing catch-up all the time.

It hasn't happened in Australia yet, but in England there are limited-overs competitions where the length of the bowling run-ups are restricted. Now it is just ludicrous to legislate on *all* these things. You can justify leg-side restrictions because bowling down the leg-side all day would be boring and negative. But, as the rules for one-day cricket stand at the moment, basically the only place I can bowl is directly at the stumps, or just outside the off-stump, and on a good length or pitched up further into the batsmen's hitting area.

Of course, they are making all these rules for the batsman to score runs. If a team makes 150 in a one-day game that's a so-so total, but if they make 250 everybody thinks it's fantastic. That's the name of the game. It is all weighted so heavily in favour of the batsmen.

The pitches in one-day cricket are usually rock hard, devoid of grass, and offering precious little help for the bowler. The ball might swing around early but you'll never ever play on a seaming greentop. And did I mention that a batsman can bat right through the innings but a bowler is restricted in his overs, no matter how effectively and successfully he has been? Bowlers are virtually told where to bowl, but would administrators regulate how many straight drives a batsman can legally play in an innings?

The thing I *like* about the limited-overs game is that for the three-and-a-half hours or so that you're on the field it's like a continuing major adrenalin rush. There is not one moment when you can afford not to be sharp and ready. In that respect it is a very exhausting game, both mentally and physically. Play for Australia through a one-day series — and the guarantee is that you'll be absolutely stuffed at the end of it. You're either travelling, training, or playing.

Once the one-dayers are over you're straight back into Test cricket. It's at that point that people often make the comment: "Gee, they look a bit flat." Well, if the team happens to be a bit flat, it's not surprising. The workload over a complete Australian summer can be enormous.

In the season of 1991-92, one that involved a five-Test series against India, a World Series Cup that involved Australia, India and the West Indies, the World Cup, and stretched over five months, I was in every single team the Australian side fielded, either playing or as 12th man. In that five-month period I spent three-and-a-half weeks at home.

But, hang on. I'm not complaining, just explaining. On a campaign like that I had a great time, and enjoyed every moment of it — but it's really hard work. How many blokes do you know that in five months working a nine-to-five job get only three weeks or so at home?

It took me a while to appreciate the significance of one-day international cricket in terms of my cricket career. It wasn't until the West Indies tour of 1991 that I made a conscious decision to relate my performances in limited-overs matches to Test cricket. I made the one-day team over there and saw it as a prime opportunity to get into the Test side. That's the way they see the game over there — as a stepping stone — and that's the way I started to see it too. If you're playing well in the one-day side then obviously your chances of getting into the Test side are better than someone who has to leapfrog in from outside.

On that tour my whole attitude to the one-day game changed. I believe my one-day bowling found a new dimension. I homed in on what I had to do to make my bowling work effectively in the limited-overs game.

Because of my mixed feelings about one-day cricket, I've given the game a lot of thought. I believe there are potential areas for improvement in the structure of the game. For starters my preference would be for an extension to 60 overs instead of the standard 50 that prevails in Australia. I'm sure there's enough daylight for this to happen, and, with the extra 10 overs per side, the game would be more like a "real" game of cricket.

I'm sure, though, that's not going to happen — and, although it might sound strange, my second preference is for the game to be *shortened*, rather than stay at 50 overs.

Games of 50 overs follow a pretty repetitive pattern in which there is a "consolidation period" of 10 overs or so in the middle of the innings, followed by the traditional slog at the end. The way it's going, I reckon that before long the administrators will try to get rid of that 10-over-or-so period when nothing much happens. Ultimately one-day internationals will be of 40 overs, with five bowlers bowling eight overs each. I wouldn't argue with that change.

Another thing I don't like about one-day international cricket is the huge marketing emphasis placed on it in Australia — to the detriment of the traditional game. Talk to people in any Aussie street and you'd probably find they relate to Steve Waugh more as a one-day specialist than a Test cricketer, because they see so much of him in that role. The people running the game have this thing in their minds that one-day cricket almost entirely supports the rest of Australian cricket. I don't believe that is necessarily true. One day not long back I spoke to a couple of guys on the Board and asked the question: "Why don't we have a full domestic season now and then?"

The reaction was shock horror. "We'd go broke!" they exclaimed.

But would they? There are so many outstanding young Australian cricketers out there who don't get much exposure. I'm talking about young blokes like Glenn McGrath, Matthew Hayden, Ricky Ponting and Jamie Siddons. Ponting, just 18 years old, scored a century in each innings for Tasmania against Western Australia in 1992-93 — the youngest player in Sheffield Shield history to achieve that feat. Sensational!! Yet because of the over-emphasis on the one-day program, the majority of people wouldn't know as much as they should about this sort of player. They are budding champions who deserve to be seen more, and a season of purely domestic cricket would provide that opportunity.

In my view, cricket is heading the way of less Test cricket, and more one-day cricket. I regret that trend very much. I applaud the stand of the English administrators who still have enough faith to program a schedule of three one-day internationals ... and six Test matches. The Poms are inundated with one-day cricket at a domestic level, but at least they've kept the international scene purer than we have.

A Traveller's Tales

There is, of course, a good deal more to life than tearing in full pelt with a leather ball in your hand, and trying to knock down three lumps of wood 22 yards up a mown grass strip. I love cricket, but I love life more. And to me living that life to the full *must* involve travel. I think people owe it to themselves to go and see what the world is about, to experience how our fellow human beings live. I have certainly tried to do that whenever I have had the chance. Cricket has taken me to plenty of fascinating places, and I've made it my business to seek out plenty more. I'm not talking packaged tours here — I'm talking about going to out-of-the-way places, about roughing it, mixing with the locals, laughing with them, eating the food they eat. However, such a philosophy can create an occasional problem ...

In 1987, Debbie and I journeyed through the game parks of Kenya. We visited the flamingos at Lake Nakuru, toured through Amboseli and Tsavo. We experienced the majesty of the Serengeti Plains and the Masai Mara, and travelled to Nairobi and then Mombasa. From there we prepared to go up the coast, to an island called Lamu, before heading south to Zimbabwe.

In Mombasa one morning a taxi driver asked me if I wanted to change some money on the black market. Now, this was not a crash-hot idea. The Kenyan economy was in fair shape, and swapping money on the black market is not a real smart thing to do at any time. But we were low on funds and I figured any bit of spare cash we could make would be helpful.

We had about 500 or 600 US dollars to our name, and I told Debbie we would change 100 of it on the black market, before setting off for our island off the coast. She wasn't happy about it at all. They were tough on illegal money exchanges, and anyone caught was immediately sentenced to seven years' gaol. But, foolishly, I pressed on.

I sent Debbie back to the hotel where we were staying, a seedy place, and I went with the taxi driver. On a certain corner, he told me to wait while he went and organised the deal. Eventually he re-appeared and beckoned me across to where he was standing, just around the corner in a narrow lane. He gave me an envelope and told me to put the $100 into it. I was pretty wary about doing that — but he told me it was the only way that business could be done.

"Wait here," he said. "I'll go and change it for you."

Off he went down the lane, leaving me standing there. After about 10 seconds I said to myself: "This is crazy. He's probably clearing off with my money."

So I headed down the lane a little way and sighted the bloke, "on the toe", 40 or 50 metres up the lane. I took off after him, and with the added speed brought about by the necessity of getting my hundred back, rounded him up soon after he had turned out of the lane into another street.

I grabbed him by the shirt and held him against the wall. "You're trying to rip me off," I snapped. The bloke shit himself — or seemed to — and put his hand in his pocket and gave me back the envelope. I abused him some more, and told him I should punch his teeth in. I was pretty shaken up, but relieved to get the envelope back.

Anyhow, he shot through and I started to walk back to the hotel. I walked about 20 metres or so, and then tore open the envelope to get my $100 back. The envelope contained nothing but folded-up newspaper! The bastard had switched envelopes on me.

I raced back up the lane and all over the place looking for him. Funny thing, in a predicament like that all Africans look the same! Across the road was a Muslim mosque, and I figured that maybe he was hiding in there. A bloke tried to block me at the door, but I pushed him aside, and told him I was looking for a thief ... and was going in. The place was full of men praying to Allah. I checked as many faces as I could, without luck.

Suddenly the thought occurred to me that one of this crook's cronies may have followed Debbie back to the hotel, so I ended the search, and rushed back there. She was okay — just dirty on me for being gullible. I decided I would fast for the next three days in penance for my stupidity.

A couple of days later I decided I'd go back and have another look around for the thief. I pulled my hair back into a pony tail, changed my clothes and put on a pair of sunnies. I was travelling incognito to give myself a chance. I was strolling down the road where we had first met him when a bloke came out of a cafe. "Did you find the thief?" he asked. So much for the disguise. Debbie laughed her head off. It's pretty hard to travel incognito when you're a six-foot white man in the middle of Kenya. The 100 bucks was long gone.

I had occasional problems with money on my travels. I remember once being in a restaurant in the Philippines dining with a bloke from Qantas I knew. Suddenly some soldiers came in and pulled a gun on us. Then a man and a woman arrived — and the woman pointed to my friend and said she had cashed some money for him at the bank, and paid him too much. They promptly escorted him back to the bank, and I sat there under the guns of the soldiers until it was all settled.

One country that left a huge impression on me was India. It's a place where you see the absolute extremities of human existence — from devastating poverty to opulence and luxury. I walked up Janpath Road, New Delhi, one day, and there in the gutter were the bodies of two children who had obviously died overnight. Just lying there, left in the gutter. Elsewhere, I saw people who had so much.

The most striking place of all for me was Kashmir. In 1985, Tony and Mary White, Craig and Karen Charlwood, and I flew to Srinagar. We had intended to go by train, but there was great turmoil afoot. The army had gone to the Golden Temple and killed the head of the Sikh uprising. At the Australian embassy in New Delhi, we were told that to travel by road or rail was to risk death.

So we flew, and stayed at Srinagar on a houseboat on Dahl Lake. It was a beautiful tranquil place, and the setting for an extraordinary lifestyle. Tradesmen would paddle from houseboat to houseboat, selling fruit and vegetables. One day a tailor paddled up in his boat full of cloths. He could measure you on the spot and have your trousers to you within half an hour.

Our house-boat was owned by a Mohammad Gulam, a successful Indian businessman. In turn he had a man named Mansoor working for him, looking after the boat. One day I left a pair of jeans on the bed, with 50 rupees (about $5) in the pocket. When I next went to put the jeans on, the money had gone. I approached Mansoor and the look on his face immediately gave him up. He told me an elaborate story of how another house-boy from a nearby boat had come aboard when he was out, and taken the money. I wasn't concerned about the money — but the principle was important enough not to let it drop. We had looked after Mansoor pretty well during out stay, and this was a petty, but miserable act.

After breakfast next morning, served by Mansoor, I threw my plate and cutlery out into the lake. I said to him: "This will happen at every meal if the 50 rupees are not placed back in my jeans."

I told him that if necessary I would throw everything into the lake. I knew that Mansoor, in his role as house-boy, was responsible for everything on the house-boat.

That afternoon, he came back with 37 rupees, explaining that he'd found the thief, but that 13 rupees had already been spent. I let the matter drop ... and Mansoor went swimming in the lake to retrieve the plates and cutlery that had previously gone over the side.

Another amazing place is Victoria Falls, on the Zambezi River in Zimbabwe. In 1986, the NSW team travelled there while on tour. The falls are, perhaps, the most stunning natural phenomenon I have ever seen. The sheer power of it is just sensational.

I remember that when we eventually climbed back aboard the team bus after gaping at the Falls there were three players missing — Bob Holland, Greg Dyer and Rod Bower. They had taken a stroll down into the wildlife reserve which adjoins the Falls. After a while, the trio re-appeared — at speed — looking somewhat flustered.

It emerged that on their little walk they had spied though the thickets a baboon with a baby. What a lovely picture that will make, the boys thought. So over they went. Dutchy had already taken his snapshot, and Greg was getting the zoom lens adjusted when suddenly out of the undergrowth came Big Daddy Baboon.

It was suggested that no Australian cricketer has ever moved faster than the members of that intrepid trio.

On that same tour, we went to a place in Bulawayo called Chipengali — an animal hospital-farm. One of the guests was a huge lion who was obviously a bit below par. The poor animal's lack of health didn't faze Mark Waugh, who paced up and down in front of the cage, mimicking the lion. I doubt if he would have been so brave if the wire hadn't been there. Mark growled at the lion and the lion turned its back — which M. Waugh promptly claimed as a signal of his victory over the animal. Mark, however, was not too clued up about lions' anatomy. With its back turned the lion suddenly pissed all over Pretty Boy Waugh.

An M. Waugh victory?

I don't think so.

Proving The Critics Wrong

In 1987, after I had managed to keep Richard Hadlee at bay in the third Australia-New Zealand Test, we flew out to Perth for a one-day international. It was a great thrill to have been part of the side that won that series, and was particularly pleasing for AB, who to that point had never won a Test series as skipper. On the flight across the country there was a considerable celebration. In fact, we drank out the bar. "I'd like to offer you another drink, but sorry — it's all gone," said the steward.

Arriving in Perth, I showered at the hotel, then headed out into the night to continue the celebration with the boys. It turned into a very long night. The next evening the celebrations continued and I managed to finish up legless again. Back at the hotel, I went to reception to get my room key, but couldn't remember for the life of me what room I was in.

"It's 451, Mr Whitney," said the bloke manning the desk. "I remember it well because I carried you there last night."

I told the story to Allan Border the next morning, and he said to me: "You think *that's* funny!"

He explained how on the same night, after the same celebration, he'd gone back to the Sheraton where the team had stayed for the previous 10 years or so. The only problem was that this year we were staying at the Hyatt.

"Sorry Mr Border, you're not staying here anymore," said the bloke behind the counter.

The following season, 1988-89, featured a tour by the West Indies, then captained by the great Vivian Richards and at the absolute peak of their powers. Early on that tour they played a four-day match against NSW in Sydney. In the match, the Blues scored a motza of runs on a pretty flat deck. Viv and their tiny left-hander, Keith Arthurton, were bowling spin when I strolled out to the middle as number 11, and things were looking good. But as soon as I arrived Viv called for the new ball, and brought on ... Patrick Patterson.

"You've got to be joking Viv," I said.

"No man, Patrick needs a bowl," said Viv.

Peter Taylor was on 45 at the other end, and we held on for a couple of overs until he reached his 50. By this time, Patrick was running in with a great deal of fire and enthusiasm. But as soon as Taylor went to his half-century, he walked off ... just turned around and walked straight off the field. Not a word to anyone.

I think he did it to save my skin.

Viv Richards scored his 100th first-class century in that match. I remember it vividly. When Viv was on 99, Greg Matthews bowled him a bouncer, which Greg could do from time to time. I remember seeing him bowl three in a row one day to the WA number 11, Terry Alderman. The bumper took Viv somewhat by surprise and he mistimed his shot, but it rolled down to me at backward square-leg for the single he needed for the 100.

Richards was certainly one of the all-time greats, with the raw ability to tear an attack to shreds. He was starting to lose it just a bit when we toured the West Indies in 1991. It wasn't surprising; a bloke at 40 years of age is not going to be quite as agile as he was at 20. The thing I noticed about him on that tour was that every time he hooked, he hooked fine. He rarely hooked square — and that indicated to me he wasn't picking the ball up early.

Viv was a bloke of phenomenal physique, and very proud — bordering on vain. His technique was not from the copybook — he hit across the line a lot — but he had a sensational eye. You could bowl him one pitched middle and going across him, and he'd whip it square, or over the top of mid-wicket. Pitch it a bit wider and he'd smash it through the covers. He was brilliant in the field as well — a great slip field on his day, and a bloke who would *always* hit the stumps on the run. Amazing!

The West Indies galloped through the first three of five Tests in 1988-89 with faultless power, winning in Brisbane, Perth and Melbourne to kill the series stone dead. Their fearsome paceman, Curtly Ambrose, who reckoned he had never been taught to bowl, gone to a coaching clinic or read a cricket book, was the chief destroyer — busting Geoff Lawson's jaw in Perth, and taking 20 wickets in the three matches.

But fortunes swung on a slow turner in Sydney in the fourth Test. The wicket that had been the undoing of Pakistan (1983-84), the Windies (1984-85), New Zealand (1985-86) and England (1986-87) was up to its old tricks once again. Australia's unlikely hero was skipper Allan Border, whose tantalising left-arm leggies wrecked the men from the Caribbean. AB took 7-46 and 4-50, as Australia won by seven wickets.

In the wake of that win there was some speculation that I might be in the running for the fifth and final Test of the series, at the Adelaide Oval. I was in the middle of the most prolific domestic season of my life (at the time of the fifth Test I was the leading first-class wicket-taker in the country), and furthermore, more than one of the regular quicks in the Aussie team was in trouble with injury.

In the aftermath of the fourth Test win, I was having a trundle in the nets with the Australian team. I'd been asked pretty much out of the blue to go and have a bowl in the nets, and was happy to help out. After practice, coach Bob Simpson called everyone into a huddle, and made a stunning announcement. "We've got some good news for you," he said to me. "You've been picked in the 12 to go to Adelaide."

My jaw just about hit the ground. I just couldn't believe it. But what a thrill it was ... I was absolutely elated.

I must admit my feelings were slightly mixed, though. I reckoned I'd been knocking on the door of the Test team for a long time without getting in. Now the selectors had picked me for a match on what is traditionally a batsman's paradise. Were they trying to squeeze me right out?

Negative thoughts were suddenly going through my mind. Maybe I'd get belted all over the ground and then I'd be out of the selectors' hair for all time.

I was determined that wasn't going to happen.

Despite the doubts that nagged, I flew to Adelaide in great spirits, with my hopes high, only to be confronted by a newspaper article which just about knocked me for six.

Melbourne journalist Rod Nicholson was "ghosting" a column for the former Australian captain and selector, Greg Chappell. Commenting on my selection, Chappell basically "wrote" that I wasn't up to Test standard, and that he couldn't believe I had been picked to play against the Windies. The theme of the article was that there was every chance I was going to get belted all around the Adelaide Oval by Haynes, Richards, Richardson, Greenidge, Logie, Dujon and co.

Talk about a downer!

I fronted Nicholson near the Adelaide nets and said to him: "I can't believe you've written this. Every time you've ever wanted a story from me or wanted anything at all I've tried to help. I've made myself as accessible as I could possibly be ... and now you turn around and shitbag me in the press."

I made him a promise. "I'll tell you what I'm going to do, Rod. Every time I get a wicket I'm going to stick my two fingers up to you in the press box."

I then went out and took nine wickets in the match (7-89 and 2-60) and almost wore out my arm giving him the finger sign.

To Greg Chappell's credit (via his ghost Nicholson), he wrote in the paper the day after I had taken my seven-for that I had made him eat humble pie, and that it had been a great performance.

But the contents of the original article really grated on me and I never really forgave Greg for it until years later when we were co-commentators for Channel Nine at the time in 1992-93 when I was away from cricket with a broken foot. That day I had it out with Greg, telling him what I thought of what he had done. We talked for a long time and at the end of it a relationship of some substance and mutual respect had been established. Communication is a great thing.

The fifth West Indies Test of 1988-89 remains a magnificent memory for me. In their first innings I bowled perhaps as well as I ever had or have and the scalps I gathered were some beauties, including Gordon Greenidge, Richie Richardson and Viv Richards.

It was one of those golden games that can happen in a life in cricket, a innings when nothing seemed to go wrong. I persisted all the time with line and length and the ball just swung "Irish". When Imran Khan had played for NSW in 1984-85 I had talked to him at length about swinging the ball Irish, which is a bowling skill that has been turned into an art-form — by whatever means — by quick bowlers from Pakistan. A roughening of the ball on one side, and moistening on the other, can cause it to swing the "wrong" way. A ball delivered as an inswinger ends up behaving like an outswinger and vice-versa. For some reason the SCG and the Adelaide Oval rough the ball in a certain way and help in the cause of "swinging Irish".

In this match in Adelaide the ball definitely swung Irish.

I got a couple of nicks behind because of it. Greenidge was bowled. I had Richardson caught in the covers, Malcolm Marshall in the gully. Viv tried to drive a ball moving away and David Boon snapped him up at shortish cover.

It was fantastic.

In the *Sydney Morning Herald*, Peter Roebuck wrote of my bowling:

Angling the ball away from the bat and finding surprising variations of bounce, he thoroughly deserved those wickets and has booked his trip for England. It was a triumph for courage and fitness ...

On the same page, Mike Coward wrote:

Whitney bowled with great guile with the old ball to tear the heart out of the West Indies' middle order ... By dint of his remarkable achievement, Whitney has almost compelled the selectors to choose him for the tour of England this year.

My seven-wicket haul in fact took three days to complete. After we had batted for the best part of two days for 515 (Whitney, caught Dujon bowled

Patterson ... 2), I bowled Greenidge before stumps on the second afternoon. On the third day, the Windies batted throughout, to reach 8-338 at the close, and I had six wickets, for 75 (5 for 49 for the day). My seventh wicket came early the following morning.

In an interview with Mike Coward after the third day's play, I had this to say:

"I've been told my bowling is not up to Test standard or dubious and whatever. I just hope with 6-75 and two more poles left in the morning I've silenced a few people. If I never play another Test I can always say I got six-for, possibly eight-for, against the West Indies on a flat track."

And I told *The Australian's* Terry Brindle: "It's always nice to prove the critics wrong ... The criticism doesn't worry me, but I think it hurts cricket, and people, especially former players, should be more constructive."

I was truly delighted with what I had achieved in my one Test match of that glowing season. The Adelaide Oval *was* a batsman's paradise, and 1341 runs were scored in the Test for the loss of only 28 wickets. We led by 146 on the first innings, and eventually set them 371 to get on the final day. But the track had the final word, and the match was finally called off at 5.30 that afternoon when it was apparent that no result was going to come.

I remember the Test for a number of things. My own bag of wickets, of course. Dean Jones plundering his highest Test score (216), and Merv Hughes carving an unbeaten 72 to show that he wasn't just a pretty face.

And I remember poor Tim May, our off-spinner, getting hit on the foot by a yorker from Ambrose. His foot was unbelievably swollen and we stood and watched him get cortisone injections in the dressing room. Now Tim is not the bravest man in the world and the needles the doctor was using were like javelins, but we were there being as helpful as we could, geeing him up. Maysie was as white as a sheet and blokes were saying: "Jeezus, look at the size of this needle!" and "Have a look at that needle will you ... it's as big as a spear."

There is one other thing from that Test that will never leave me. On the third day of the Test I received a standing ovation as I left the ground. Afterwards there were endless press interviews. Finally, all of that was finished. By then it was quite late, and everyone had gone from the room except me. That was the way I wanted it. I was happy to be on my own to fully savour the moment.

I jumped in the shower, and yelled loud enough for all the world to hear ... just one word ...

"Yeeeeeeeeeeeees!"

"How Can They Do This To You?"

On March 17, 1989, the day they picked the Ashes team for England, I was in a car with my sister, Christine, heading out of the city, the car radio tuned to the ABC. It had been a fantastic season of cricket for me. With 49 wickets, at an average of 24.92 I had been the leading wicket-taker for NSW in first-class matches, with a best performance for the Blues of 5-66 against Pakistan. With 58 wickets at 23.62 I was also the top wicket-taker nationally for the season. I was now up to 203 first-class wickets, ranking me in the top 12 all-time wicket-takers for NSW. Within a month, I would be named the Tooheys NSW Cricketer of the Year.

I hadn't allowed my hopes to go too high — but I was buoyed by the fact a number of the critics had named me in their teams as they speculated what the selectors may or may not do.

We were on the corner of Heffron Street and Bunnerong Road, Pagewood, when the news came through. I can still hear the words intoned by ABC cricket commentator Jim Maxwell over the car radio:

"And the biggest news of all is the shock omission of NSW pace bowler Michael Whitney."

I was just numb. Next to me, Christine was muttering "Those bastards. Those bastards ... how can they do this to you, Michael?"

For one of the few times in my life I was genuinely struck dumb. I couldn't speak.

I dropped Christine at Mum's place, and headed home to Clovelly, to the unit I was living in at the time. The main emotion was one of stunned disbelief. What more could I have done to make my claim for the tour?

I thought of the two basic realities of a career in cricket, or in any sport — that there are two things you have no control over: injuries and selection. How true is that?

I wasn't alone for long. There was a knock on the door, and my mother and sister were there to try to find the words to say what we all felt. My mother was absolutely devastated. She knew how much making the tour had meant to me.

I have never been more upset in my life in cricket. Soon there was another knock on the door. This time it was Geoff Lawson, my great friend and NSW team-mate. Henry had made the team. Simultaneously the pair of us burst into tears.

"I can't believe they haven't picked you," said Henry. "You deserve to go more than I do."

That to me was a very humbling statement coming from someone who had just been chosen for his third Ashes tour.

We must have been quite a sight, the four of us sitting there in the lounge-room crying. I ushered them out after a while. I had a tough day to face, and it was best I did it on my own.

Before long, the phone was running hot. The messages stacked up on my answering machine: all the TV stations, half-a-dozen radio stations, the print guys. All of them looking for a story and, no doubt, hoping that I would come out and rip into the selectors. I just knocked the whole thing on the head and refused to say a word. I was hurting badly, but I was determined to conduct myself with dignity. There would be no public sour grapes, no matter what I was feeling.

For weeks I didn't say a word publicly about my non-selection. Finally I did an interview with Channel Nine and they asked the obvious question:

"Why do you think you weren't picked?"

I told them I honestly didn't know. And I didn't, and don't.

In the days, weeks and months that followed many theories emerged. One doing the rounds was that I couldn't get top-order batsmen out. Another was that left-armers weren't going to do the business over there against the style of the English batsmen. Any credence that second theory might have had was gunned down four years later when the selectors picked the Western Australian left-arm quick, Brendon Julian, to tour England in 1993.

Three or four days after the team had been selected, I phoned Australian coach and selector Bob Simpson at his home. After brief pleasantries had been exchanged I posed the question: "Bob, I just want to ask you why I've missed the tour. Is it something that I have done, or something about the way I go about the game?"

I'll never forget his answer.

"Michael, I can't tell you why you haven't been picked," said the Australian coach.

"To do that would be like opening a Pandora's Box."

I remember thinking: I can't believe he said that to me. I mean, this was a conversation between the pair of us in total privacy. I believed I had his total confidence. Yet he fobbed me off with his "Pandora's Box" answer.

I have never really come to terms with him saying that to me — never been able to get over the fact he felt he couldn't level with me, whatever the answer may have been.

To this day I don't know the reason I was left out. One by one in the following season I asked the other selectors, Lawrie Sawle, John Benaud and Jim Higgs, why I had missed out. Each of them, in a roundabout sort of way, insinuated that they had gone for me — but the other blokes hadn't.

By the end of it I was thinking well, if he picked me, and he picked me, and he picked me, then how come I wasn't on the tour?

In a newspaper article written in late 1993, John Benaud threw some light on the deliberations that day. By then Benaud was no longer a selector — and he wrote a piece outlining the three toughest selection decisions of his time on the panel. On top was the decision to leave me out of the 1989 Ashes tour. In a funny way I suppose I at least felt good that there was an admission from a selector that it had been a "tough" decision. I had plenty of respect for JB; he was a bloke I could talk to.

I sat home all that winter, watching it on television, watching our boys carve up the Poms ... and thinking how much I would have loved to be part of the whole thing. But as I've said, time and again, who am I to criticise? Without M.R. Whitney they went over there and won 4-nil, and you can't do much more than that. They were only the second Australian team in history to achieve such a result.

Throughout the Aussie winter of '89 the innuendoes flew thick and fast. People kept asking me if I didn't get on with Allan Border. Or had I done something off the paddock to infuriate the selectors?

But, as my mother says, out of bad there very often comes some good, and so it was this time. The controversy surrounding my non-selection gave my profile quite a boost, and I suddenly found myself in enormous demand on the speaking circuit. From the day I missed the team I was asked to attend an absolute truckload of gigs. Maybe it was the sympathy vote, or maybe it was because everyone else was away, but whatever the case it really gave me a kickalong. And, honestly, I've never looked back since. Debbie and I worked extra hard during that time; we realised that the increased focus on me was a very definite and positive opportunity for the future.

I cheered AB and the boys on from afar, and set about getting myself ready for the 1989-90 season. The winning of that Sheffield Shield competition meant a lot to me after the disappointment I had suffered, and I vowed that I would work as hard as humanly possible to make it even harder for the selectors to leave me out the next time.

There was no way was I going to spit the dummy.

Fire and Brimstone

Season 1989 marked the winter of my discontent. While the Australian team campaigned in England I was at home, pacing the floor. I would have loved to have been there. If nothing else, my disappointment focused me for the season ahead. I was determined to start the year with a real bang, to stick it up the selectors. I wanted to prove to the people who'd supported me that they were right ... that I should have been selected for England.

In NSW's first Shield match of the year, against South Australia, I took five wickets, so it was a solid start. Then we played the touring Sri Lankans in Canberra and I took six wickets in the match, bowled really well and knocked over most of their gun batsmen.

Then we went to Newcastle to play Queensland, in a match that, for whatever reason, turned out to be just about the most sensational match in the history of the world. Craig McDermott ran in first ball and flattened Steve Small's stumps with a yorker. The crowd erupted ... and then made more noise when they realised it had been a no ball.

At about that point an elderly man in the crowd had a heart attack and died. It happened right near the players' enclosure, adding to the drama of the morning. Before long an ambulance came screaming up and took him away.

Meanwhile, McDermott and Carl Rackemann were creating havoc out in the middle. They ripped through us, and before long I found myself out in the middle, with not too many runs on the NSW score-sheet. The first ball from McDermott brought a huge shout for lbw, and a shake of the head from the umpire. "Billy" McDermott and I had never really seen eye to eye (although after the West Indies tour of 1991 we became good friends. We roomed together for a time on that tour, and got to know each other pretty well). On this day it was fire and brimstone stuff.

The second ball was short. The ball had been flying all day on a lively wicket and I ducked. Bastard of a thing. It was the only ball all day that didn't get up — instead it flew through and cracked me on the left forearm.

It hurt alright, but I could wiggle my fingers, so it was no big deal.

Greg Matthews ran on with the spray and gave the arm a burst. You'll be okay, he said. Greg was 12th man for this match — he hadn't been 12th for NSW for years — and was a bit down in the dumps.

Play resumed, and the next ball brought another lbw shout. Disallowed. End of over. Off the first ball of Rackemann's next over, Phil Emery, our wicketkeeper/batsman, took a single. I took guard, then blocked a couple. Then I finally received a delivery that was pitched up, and creamed it into the covers. Shiiiiit! The pain shot up my arm; it was agony. Allan Border ran in to help and said: "Look, mate, I think you're in trouble."

"Mo" Matthews galloped back out with the can and gave me the full contents this time. Our physio, Margaret Keech, came out too.

"How are you feeling?" she asked.

"Not too good," I said.

"Well, you'd better come off."

So they took me to Newcastle Hospital and there X-rays revealed the worst. My arm was broken. Outside a small army of TV cameramen and newspaper photographers waited to intercept me. But the sister-in-charge, a large and formidable lady, wasn't having any of it. "They won't get past the door," she said. They didn't. Finally she snuck me out the back, enabling me to make a quiet exit back to the Newcastle Travelodge, where the NSW team was staying.

I found out later that, at the end of the day's play, McDermott and Rackemann had both gone straight to our dressing room to find out how I was. I appreciated that.

For that match, I was rooming with Greg Matthews in room 201 at the Travelodge. It hadn't been a great day for 201. Mo was there when I got back. "Roy," he said, "you've busted your arm and I'm 12th man for the first time in six years. I can't see much point us sitting here wallowing in self pity. Let's go out."

Something happened during that night which helped me put the thing in perspective. A bloke came up to me in a pub to pass on his commiserations. "I'm really sorry to hear the news Mike," he said. "I know it's a big disappointment — you were having such a good season. Anyhow, at least yours is going to be okay."

With that he pointed to himself. On one side he only had a malformed stump, one of those "thalidomide" arms. I just looked at Greg, and I thought: "Shit, what am *I* worried about?"

Next morning, Bob Radford of the NSW Cricket Association invited me down to breakfast to talk about insurance. He ordered four Bloody Marys to kick the discussion off. I stayed on for the day's play and then headed home to Sydney.

The pattern of the match continued. One of the umpires fell sick and had to be replaced by a local bloke. Five of the NSW team also picked up some bug, and at one stage were strewn all over the dressing-room floor. We won the game by virtue of some dubious decisions, and they complained. It was in many ways an ugly game of cricket. The pattern had been set from that opening morning, with that poor man dying in the grandstand.

The arm injury turned out to be the most painful I had ever had. It pretty well "froze" my elbow. On the day they took the cast off I was thinking I would start rolling my arm over in the next day or so. But my arm was as crooked as a right angle.

There began a painful rehabilitation process with Elizabeth Steet, my physio, who I had visited on and off over the previous eight years.

I remember saying to her one day: "You're a sadist!" She just looked me in the eye and said: "Do you want to play again this season, or don't you?"

I said of course I wanted to play and she told me in that case I should shut my mouth. She then proceeded with the task of bending my arm back to the ultimate limit. The pain was almost unbearable.

However, it worked, and I was back playing cricket later that same season, in time for NSW's final four Shield matches, against Victoria, South Australia, Western Australia and Tasmania, and the Shield final ... against Queensland.

I was still filthy on Craig McDermott and when he came out to bat in the second innings of the final (he'd only scored 2 in the first innings and I hadn't had a chance to bowl at him) I was itching to have a crack at him. Mark Taylor, our stand-in captain (Geoff Lawson had withdrawn on the morning of the final with an arm injury), knew this well enough and, soon after McDermott came to the wicket, signalled to me at fine leg. I was coming on to bowl. "You beauty," I thought, "I'm going to really give it him."

Well, you wouldn't believe it. Mark Waugh was bowling. He dropped one short and Billy promptly zacked him over the fence. Next ball, Mark hit him on the pad; there was a huge shout ... and McDermott was out!

Bugger it! "You b------, I'll get you next season," I was yelling at him as he walked out.

He turned around, pointed to his arm, and said: "One nil."

"I'll kill you, you b------," I yelled.

The mob in the Bradman and Noble Stands at the SCG knew *exactly* what was going on, and they were singing out too.

After the game McDermott and I had a beer. Not a friendly one. But a beer.

I even had a go at Mark Waugh. "You so and so ... why didn't you bowl it wide of the crease?" I complained. "I'm gonna kill you as well."

"It *is* the Shield final," was all Mark said.

We won that Shield final by 345 runs, and one of the heroes was Mark "Tubby" Taylor, who scored 127 in the NSW first innings and 100 in the second. He was, of course, by then an established star in our team, and the Australian XI. It was in the previous season that Mark had first made it into the Aussie side. The news came through when we were at a NSW team dinner in Melbourne. Journalist Greg Baum walked into the restaurant, trailed by a photographer, put a hand on Mark's shoulder and said: "Mark, I've got some news for you. You've been picked in the Australian team."

I called for champagne. "Four bottles ... no make it five!"

I can still picture the look on Tubby's face. We soaked him in champagne.

He was a bloke I didn't know much about when I made it back into the NSW team in 1986. I'd missed the 84-85 Shield season with a knee injury; hadn't played at all. I came back to grade during the 1985-86 season, and was down the coast at Kioloa, camping with Debbie (then my girlfriend), my sister Christine and her husband Dean, at the time the Shield side for NSW's sixth game of the season was picked. It was great just to be in contention for the side again, after so many months on the sideline. I was hopeful. I felt I'd done enough in the preceding weeks of the grade comp.

I remember piling the 20 cent pieces in and ringing my mother from the camp. "You're picked," said mum. It was like a re-birth, a second coming. Plenty of people had wanted to tell me that I wouldn't make it again. Now I had.

After the two-year break, it was a whole new team. Gone were blokes like McCosker, Chappell, Toohey, Dyson, Pascoe, Rixon ... all the old crew I'd started with. Geoff Lawson was out with injury. In the team were Taylor, Mark Waugh, Greg Dyer and some other young guys. Steve Waugh, who hadn't played Shield cricket when I was injured, was now in the Test side. The only blokes I knew were the remnants of the old guard — Dirk Wellham, Murray Bennett, Greg Matthews and Dutchy Holland. All of a sudden I was a senior player — and these young blokes were looking up to me.

Mark Taylor had his limitations when he came into the team, but he worked so hard on his game that he became the *complete* player. We used to call him "Stodgy" as well as Tubby. Stodgy because he couldn't play a lot of shots and Tubby because of his fat arse and huge thighs.

Another Mark — Mark O'Neill — came back into the side that year, 1985-86, and became a terrific contributor to the Blues' cause. Mark had played for NSW as early as 1982-83, but it wasn't until 1985-86 that he cemented a spot in the side. He was a bloke who was not *really* happy unless he was unhappy. We'd practise on perfect wickets and when he went into bat, no matter how perfect the pitch, one would inevitably leap off a good length and hit him on the gloves. Things seemed to happen to him. I remember a practice session in Zimbabwe in which Peter Taylor and Mark both chased a high catch. Mark tripped at the critical moment and as Taylor took the catch he trampled right up Mark's back. Peter was wearing brand new boots at the time and left a trail of sprig marks up the middle of O'Neill's back.

On another day we had him bowling his leggies in the nets. Dave Gilbert smashed a cover-drive in the next net and caught him fair in the groin. What did everybody do? Laugh, of course!

Mark O'Neill picked up a couple of nicknames, too, and both came about in a fairly convoluted sort of way. He had a terrible smoking habit. He'd cough his head off, and we'd call it spitting the oyster. As a result of a number of players having played in the Lancashire League, we shortened that to Th'oyster. You know the way they talk over there. "The umpire" becomes "th'umpire". When you go down to the pub they talk about th'ale. After a while, we were all calling him "Th'oyster". But then, in a game park in Zimbabwe in March, 1986, we found this animal called the Tessaby. Its major characteristic, we were told, was that it could run all day at 75 per cent capacity. Now, because of pair of bad knees, Mark rarely put in 100 per cent in the field. So we promptly dubbed him "Tessaby".

Mark O'Neill has the second-worst knees I've seen in first-class cricket. The only player with worse knees was the former NSW left-arm wrist spinner, David Hourn.

There's a story about Hourn — of the day he went to see the eminent orthopaedic surgeon, Merv Cross, about a chronic knee problem. Dr Cross examined his left knee at length and then declared: "I've only ever seen one knee worse than this."

"Oh yeah," said Hourn. "Whose was that?"

"Your right knee," said the doc, straight-faced.

It's a matter for very serious contemplation that Doc Cross is now comparing *my* knee with the better knee of David Hourn.

Caribbean Magic

To tour the West Indies with an Australian team had been a dream of mine almost from the day I became serious about the game of cricket. In three tough, colourful and exciting months in early 1991, that dream came true for Michael Roy Whitney. Winning a spot in Allan Border's team for the campaign against Viv Richards' famous Windies outfit remains one of the very great thrills of my life in cricket.

From a cricket point of view, it was for me a tour that began with great promise, but faded away disappointingly. I played in all five of the one-day internationals (we won the series 4-1), and the first two, of five, Tests (we lost the Test series 2-1). Late in the tour, with my Test spot long-since gone, I went for nearly six weeks without playing at all.

Yet, I can't find too much regret when I look back — despite my disappointment at not consolidating a Test spot. The tour was an adventure of the highest order as we visited those magical isles. The sights, the sounds, the tastes and the people were unforgettable.

Throughout the campaign, from mid-February to mid-May 1991, I kept a diary of the day-to-day events. In the end it ran to some 50,000 words, reflecting my impressions of the often remarkable events — on and off the field. Following are just some of the entries, one man's view of what it was like. Although disconnected at times, the daily entries add up to a valid overview of one of the most thrilling experiences available in the world of cricket.

February 19, 1991 *(Basseterre, St Kitts)*
At breakfast the other morning, Errol Alcott, our physio who also keeps an eye on our diets, had some advice for Merv. At brekkie, Merv generally has his eggs and bacon and all the trimmings, then cleans up about three plates of leftovers. Errol suggested that he should watch what he was eating, because he was already carrying a stone or so. "Listen man, I'm a road train ... not a sports car," the big bloke responded.

Nice one, Swerve.

... During our first fielding session I was catching a few of Bob Simpson's tracer bullets. Then I dropped one. As I bent down to pick it up, the next one hit me right on the arse — and I now have this tennis-ball bruise, yellow, purple and black, right on the buttock — courtesy of Simmo. I don't know whether he meant to do it, but he had a bit of a giggle about it and reckoned I should have caught the first one. Yep, I suppose I should've.

February 21, 1991 *(First day, v Jamaica, Sabina Park, Kingston)*
I took six for 42. Went through them after lunch. Billy McDermott ended up with 4-44, and I got the rest. It was only my second "six" and it's unbelievable to think that I've come all the way to Sabina Park, Kingston, Jamaica, to do that. I've taken 12 wickets now, in two games, and there's really heavy talk about me getting a berth in the first Test. I'll have to wait and see about that ...

February 22, 1991 *(Second day, v Jamaica, Sabina Park, Kingston)*
Thanks to a century by David Boon and a big stand between Mark Waugh and Greg Matthews we're very well placed indeed — Australia 6-412, against Jamaica 158.

The biggest drama of the day involved Junior Waugh, who was hit in the side of the head by their Test fast bowler, Courtney Walsh, and had to go off. When "Pretty Boy" (Mark Waugh) came back to the room it was clear he'd copped a vicious one. There's damage done to the visor, and the helmet is cracked ...

... Billy McDermott went in and drove the first ball for a boundary. Then he copped three consecutive bumpers.

Not long after, Billy copped two more Walsh bouncers. One hit him on the arm-guard and the next one went through the visor and split him above the right eye.

February 23, 1991 *(Third day, v Jamaica, Sabina Park, Kingston)*
Junior went on to score his century, and was finally dismissed, for 108 ...

The boys were more than a little fired up, and we went on and won easily, by an innings. But Billy has needed 10, maybe 15 stitches in his head. And the reason he got it? Because he bumped Walsh on the first day. You know, Michael, maybe that's a sign to think more about what you're doing, to worry more about getting wickets instead of bloody bouncing these bludgers out. You know you're going to get some more off Patterson because you bumped him in St Kitts ...

February 24, 1991 — My birthday! *(Kingston, Jamaica)*
... Let me tell you about fielding at fine leg on the fence at Sabina Park.

There's a little hill there, no more than 70 or 80 metres long, and wired off, and all the locals get there. I've had an outrageous time there over the last couple of days. I was holding hands with a little girl called Kameal yesterday. She'd put her hands through the wire, and just wanted to touch my hand between deliveries. They're talking all the time, and they're interested in all the players. Now, what's (Jeff) Thomson doing, and what about the Chappell brothers and blah, blah, blah. It's a lot of fun.

February 25, 1991 *(Kingston, Jamaica)*
The team was announced this morning for the first one-dayer — and the good news is that I've won a guernsey! I can't really believe it. I know that if I do well in this game then I'll be an enormous chance to play in the first Test ...

February 27, 1991 *(Kingston, Jamaica)*
... It's now the night after the one-day game — and we beat them! We scored 244 off our 50 overs, and they replied with 209. My figures were seven overs, none for 16, and I suppose I'm pretty happy with that. And I didn't make any stuff-ups in the field, which was good. It was a blow-out fielding down on the fence. I can tell you there was a lot of pot smoking going on, and rum drinking, and yelling out.

March 1, 1991 *(Day One of First Test, Sabina Park, Kingston)*
At practice beforehand I commented to Simmo: "I think it's a very significant game for me."

He answered: "Well, I think it's a very important game, too, and I respect you for the way you've kicked on and got back into the team."

The cricket itself added up to a strange day. They ended up reaching 264, but at one point were 6-75. At stumps we're 0-4.

I was disappointed that I had to leave the field for the last hour because I had stomach pains, and cramps in my legs. I suppose I bowled okay — 21 overs, none for 58. I was a bit unlucky, I had a couple put down — one through first and second slip and one by Craig McDermott down on the boundary at fine leg. I thought he should have taken that one, but he misjudged it.

March 6, 1991 *(Day Five of First Test, Sabina Park, Kingston)*
... It was a dismal day's play; there just wasn't anything in the game. Before the rain came yesterday and washed the whole day out it looked like being a real good Test. Today, the Windies finished at 3-334, which made our 107 first-innings lead seem pretty irrelevant. Their captain, Viv Richards,

batted on to be 52 not out and so pass Gary Sobers' record for the highest number of Test runs by a West Indian. I bowled a few overs and didn't get a wicket — and that was extremely disappointing. I was hoping I'd do well in this Test to keep the ball rolling. But we had a good time after the game, when we got together for a drink and a talk. I think everybody was disappointed because it was heading up to be such a good match.

March 8, 1991 *(Port of Spain, Trinidad)*
... Greg and I found a place called Independent Square, where there are a lot of craft shops, guys who make sandals, leather workers, people who make pots ... stuff like that. There were a lot of Rastas (Rastafarians) there and as soon as they cottoned we were with the Australian team it was tremendous. We drank some hibiscus wine and they gave us a taste of this local moonshine. It was a shocker — tasted like methylated spirits. They reckon that, after a couple of nips, you're anybody's.

March 9, 1991 *(Second Limited-overs International, Queen's Park Oval, Port of Spain)*
... We beat them easily, by 45 runs, and I was very happy with the way I bowled — nine overs, three wickets (Haynes, Hooper and Richards) for 41, and a run-out.

I had a bit of a brush with Desmond Haynes. He slogged me and I yelled out to him: "That's about the only place you're going to get to them." He was pissed off with that, and chased a wide one which he nicked to Heals. We won comfortably in the end and are now two-nil up.

March 12, 1991 *(Bridgetown, Barbados)*
... I'd like to talk about my relationship with the guys in the team. All the blue-baggers (Mark Taylor, Steve and Mark Waugh, Greg Matthews and I) get on tremendously well, as does Peter Taylor, who, of course, used to play for NSW, but now wears the maroon of Queensland. And Allan Border seems to have respect for me, otherwise I wouldn't have played all these games.

I have had a couple of set-tos with Terry Alderman, notably one last night over a really stupid issue. I think now we've pretty well sorted out our differences. If you'd suggested to me at the start of the tour that I would have had a cross word with him I would have said: "No way." But he's not playing, after being in the team for a long time now and ... maybe I've taken his spot.

Dean Jones is a funny bloke. I like Deano but he seems to just want to do well for himself. He's not a bad team man — but he's not number one. I get on really well with Ian Healy, and with Bruce Reid. He's a great guy — just goes with the flow. Boonie is the same — a very funny guy in his own little way. Geoff Marsh is a bit hard to get to know; I haven't spent a lot of time with him. Mike Veletta is a very good bloke, and I get on extra well with Errol Alcott.

Simmo. He's a bit of a strange character. The more I get to know him the more it seems to me that he tries to play people off against each other. "I'm an observer," he once said. "You don't have to be there all the time; just listen to what people say."

But, all in all, I think it's going okay. I feel like I'm fitting in ...

March 15, 1991 *(First day, v Trinidad, Guaracara Park, Point-a-Pierre)*
I'm not playing in this match, but was still witness to a funny thing that happened in the dressing room this morning. Boonie was captain for the game, and went in to the toilet before the start of play. Next thing he came bolting out of the cubicle, pulling up his jocks. He was white. "Jeezus," he said. "Have a look down the bowl."

I stuck my head in the door for a look, and there at the bottom of the toilet bowl was the biggest frog, or toad, I've ever seen. We had a good laugh about that ...

March 21, 1991 *(Georgetown, Guyana)*
I was walking through a part of Georgetown called Tiger Bay this morning with Greg Matthews, and we decided to cut up a road that would take us back onto the main street that led down to the Pegasus Hotel where we were staying. A guy approached us and asked if we wanted to buy drugs. We told him to piss off.

It was hot and Greg didn't have his shirt on. Suddenly, out of nowhere, this guy ran down the road, grabbed Greg's chain with his wedding ring on it, ripped it off his neck and bolted up a lane. The instant reaction was to chase — but around the entrance to the lane were a dozen or so black dudes. There are a lot of guns and knives in this part of the world. We just looked at each other and said: "Shiiit!"

We let them know back at the hotel and the police came. They reckoned they knew who it was and thought they'd be able to get the chain and the ring back. It was an unbelievable thing; makes you realise how spooky and how bad these places can be.

Later on, at a place called the Palm Court Restaurant, the owner, a guy called Jad Rarmon, introduced us to a guy known as "Big Daddy" — a Rasta man, who is sort of the main man in Tiger Bay, a very rough area of town. He's reputedly a very tough cookie indeed. Greg told him the story, and Big Daddy came back to us later and said he knew who had done it, that the stuff had already been sold, and that Greg would get it back.

After lunch, I went down to the police station with Greg and Jad Rarmon to see a bloke called Kit Roberts, who's head of the Crime Enforcement Unit. He had Greg's ring. Someone had produced it, apparently because they were getting a bit scared by all the pressure being put on by the police, and by Big Daddy. They reckon the other half of Greg's gold chain will be back by Saturday.

At the pool today I had an interesting talk with Richie Benaud, who's over here commentating for Channel Nine. I grabbed him for 10 minutes or so because I wanted to talk to him about bowling around the wicket. He said he thought it was a good idea as long as I bowled the right line. He said that, because the wicket here is a real plugging away sort of wicket, I should concentrate on getting on the right line and length. He seems to think I'm bowling well. We had a talk about field placings. He's not real keen about using two gullies, which is interesting because Allan Border and Bob Simpson think I should.

It was good just to talk to Richie. I hadn't had such a conversation with him before, but it was comfortable and it was good. Maybe I should have approached him a long time ago, and asked him for some advice ...

March 22, 1991 *(Georgetown, Guyana)*
Having orchestrated the return of Greg's ring and chain, Big Daddy asked us if we would like to join him for a drink one night. We were well aware by now that Big Daddy was a genuine *heavy*. He's an ex-boxer, and something of a wild man — but a likeable bloke who took a shine to us Aussies.

So tonight, Mo, Steve "Tugga" Waugh and I went down into the ghetto — to places where white men just don't go — to have a drink with Big Daddy. Go to such a place "cold" and you'd be a pretty fair chance of being shot, stabbed, robbed or mugged ... or possibly all four.

I'll never forget walking up the stairs into this bar. When we reached the top it all went quiet, and everyone in the room turned and looked at us — just like in the westerns when the baddy comes into the saloon. There was one pool table, and a bar which was completely fronted by a metal grate. At the bottom of the grate there was an opening, just big enough to pass a beer through, and to hand over your money.

This was Big Daddy's local, and we were happy to be there with him. He took us around the room and introduced us to just about everyone in the joint. When I look back on it now I'm inclined to think that Steve, Greg and I are probably the only three white men to have ever gone into that bar and had a beer, played pool and had a great time.

In fact we had a *tremendous* time. In the corner of the room stood one of those old-fashioned juke boxes, same as the ones that used to be in every Hollywood rock'n'roll movie. The records were from the '50s and '60s too, and there was this old couple there who danced to just about everything that was played.

We played the locals at pool, drank their beer, enjoyed their company, and loved their music. It was a sensational night.

March 25, 1991 *(Day Three of Second Test, Bourda Ground, Georgetown)*
We were absolutely belted, all over the ground. I went for 103 off 28, Merv, at one stage, bowled 10 overs for 70, and Greg went for a lot — he ended up with three for 155 off 37.5. Allan Border took five wickets and bowled very well — a bit flatter than Mo. Richie Richardson scored 182, Desmond Haynes 111, Carl Hooper 62 in front of his home crowd, Gus Logie 54, Richards 50. They finished at 569 — which means we have to get 221 to make them bat again. The pressure is on.

Two more catches were dropped off my bowling. One was off Richardson. I bowled him a full toss which he slashed at, but Geoff Marsh palmed it and put it down in the gully. It was a toughie. Ian Healy dropped the other, a nick that came after I went around the wicket to Desmond Haynes. I've probably had four or five genuine outs in the first two Tests that haven't been taken. I'm disappointed, but I've got to keep plugging ...

March 28, 1991 *(Day Five of Second Test, Bourda Ground, Georgetown)*
... In their second dig they only needed 28 to win, which they did comfortably, to win by 10 wickets. In the dressing room, before we went out for their second innings, I was getting my ankles strapped when Allan Border yelled across to me: "I wouldn't worry about it, Whit".

I turned to him, and said: "I was hoping you'd give me a chance to get a wicket."

"I wouldn't worry about it," he answered.

"Are you serious?" I asked.

He just sort of barked at me: "I wouldn't have said it if I wasn't serious."

I thought, oh, shit, while everybody just looked at us. We went out onto the ground, they scored the runs and that was that.

We just didn't attack enough in this Test. I thought we were apprehensive with our batting, and over-pitched with our bowling. But there were still a number of happenings that made this a memorable Test match ...

The crowd at the Rohan Kanhai stand end where I fielded was fantastic. A guy was there yesterday selling chick-peas in this hot mix, and he came over to the fence to give me a spoonful to taste. Wasn't bad! And today they brought along an effigy of one of the umpires who had given Dean Jones run out in the second dig when he wasn't run out at all.

That was a very contentious issue. Jones had been bowled by a no-ball from Courtney Walsh, but had started to walk off the ground. He hadn't heard the umpire's call, and, because of the noise of the crowd, also hadn't heard Allan Border, the other batsman, shouting at him to get back. Hooper ran up with the ball and pulled the middle stump out of the ground, and Jones was given run out. At tea Bob Simpson and team manager Laurie Sawle challenged the umpire, who had told them Jones had looked like he may have been taking a run. That was absolute crap. Deano was walking virtually at right angles to the wicket, coming off the ground. It was a very severe blow for us.

One morning, while sitting outside the dressing rooms, Mark Waugh had about half a bottle of rum spilled over him. There's this old wooden stand, the Members' Stand, a fantastic place with a lot of old photos. But if you drop a cigarette or a match it falls through the floorboards and onto those below. Junior was unlucky enough to cop a shower, after one of the members dropped his drink.

Before the fourth day's play, some kids noticed a snake swimming in the little moat that runs around just inside the boundary. Mark and Peter Taylor saw it first. I hit a ball over to that area and these little kids, who were fetching balls hit away from the practice nets, brought the snake out and bloody killed it with my bat. I said to someone at the time: "That's the only thing my bat has ever hit."

Greg Matthews picked up the dead reptile, and took it out and put it where Jeff Dujon would be standing for the first over. When Dujon went out there and saw it, he jumped a mile ... and so did Viv at first slip. We found out that Viv wasn't the Black Superman after all!

During the match, I was bounced twice by Courtney Walsh. One hit me on the forearm — thank God for the armguard — and Malcolm Marshall hit me on the tricep with a bumper. Walsh will get his. I hope I get another bowl at him; I didn't appreciate what he did.

But, full credit to the West Indies. They were hungry to win the game, and they did it. It was noted down as our worst performance in five years.

April 2, 1991 *(Third Day, v West Indies Under-23s, Arnos Vale, St Vincent)*
Four guys not playing in this match — Billy, Swampy, Mo and myself got charged $100 each for going out on a fishing trip to the bad side of the island. It was two and a half hours out, two hours back, and a super-rough nightmare — we all finished up with sore arses, wet through ... and no fish.

We had a great time, though, three days ago, on another expedition. We went out snorkelling, which was fantastic, and then to a beautiful waterfall where the boys were jumping off the top of the falls into the water. Afterwards we went for lunch at a place called the Balahulu-hulu Lodge where they had a rickety sign up the front which read: "Welcome to the Australian Cricket Team". Lunch was fantastic. I had some local dolphin, although it's not really dolphin — it's a member of the tuna family. I wasn't keen about eating dolphin, but they assured me it wasn't *really* dolphin.

April 4, 1991 *(Port of Spain, Trinidad)*
Before we left for the airport to fly from St Vincent to Trinidad we had a team meeting. Simmo really got stuck up a lot of guys, basically the whole team, saying how disappointed he was. He went through the whole saga of when he joined the team, and of all the work that had been done. He was disappointed that Waggy (Mike Veletta), Clem (Terry Alderman) and Chook Reid, who didn't play in the Test, had fallen asleep in the dressing room. Sometimes there were only one or two guys out front watching the game. He made the point strongly that there hadn't been a lot of support for the batsmen or bowlers. He then went around to everybody and asked them what their thoughts on the game were. Mo was the only one who didn't get asked — and that was really wild. We tried to thrash out a lot of things, and we all hope it's going to stand us in good stead for the next Test.

April 12, 1991 *(Bridgetown, Barbados)*
On the bus heading along Beach Road to drop a few of us off for a late-night swim, Allan announced the team to play a West Indies Board XI at Kensington Oval in Bridgetown tomorrow. The four players not in our XII are Border, Healy, McDermott and ... Whitney. For me, that was pretty shattering news. I'm definitely not playing, and the message that gives to me is that I'm out of contention for the last two Tests. I won't be playing another game of cricket until we get to Bermuda, which is three weeks away. I haven't played since the second Test, so that'll be six weeks between games. There are three one-day games in Bermuda, and I'll probably play them all, which, to me, is a joke.

One thing I can't criticise is our preparation on tour. I thought at times our practise sessions were maybe a little intense, but that's the way Bob works. We're a professional cricket team, and if he says "jump", we have to jump. It hasn't been that *physically* hard, it's just tough to get out every day and warm up, practise and do the things you have to do. And, over the last month, it's been very tough sitting in the dressing room watching the guys play — when all I've wanted to do is get out and play myself.

I thought that in the games I did play, including the one-day internationals, that I've bowled as well as I could — with the exception of a couple of spells in the Test matches where I tended to overpitch, and was driven a bit. I don't feel like I've lost form, or discredited myself. It's disappointing.

The other day someone commented about me not playing lately, and Simmo came over the top and said: "Well, he played a lot early in the tour."

That's his attitude.

April 19, 1991 *(Day One of Fourth Test, Kensington Oval, Bridgetown)*
I may not be playing in this Test, but I still thought Allan Border's speech at the team meeting last night was one of the most inspiring I'd heard from him. He's not the sort of person who comes out and struts his stuff, but he spoke really well about the job to be done in the Test

All the guys are fully aware that we have to win. Anything less than an Australian victory, and the Sir Frank Worrell trophy will be staying in the Caribbean ...

April 25, 1991 *(Bridgetown, Barbados)*
Yesterday, the final day of the fourth Test, was a really amazing day at Kensington Oval. The after-game scenes were just outrageous with a lot of West Indies partying and carrying on. The hometown victory means the series is gone — two Tests down with one to play — a situation that has really hurt all of the Australian squad.

Undoubtedly the biggest news out of the whole day was the slamming of Bob Simpson by Viv Richards at an after-match press conference. Richards really nailed him, saying that Simpson had been sledging the West Indians since 1978 when he led the Australian team over here. Richards' quotes included such statements as "he (Simpson) is a moaner and a bad loser", "he's a very sour sort of guy", and "Bobby Simpson is not my cup of tea at all."

It was amazing, really. Viv, fresh from one of the great triumphs of his career, made his feelings very clear.

It was really chaotic after the game. There were some extraordinary scenes involving the crowd and the police. Gregg Porteous, the photographer with the Australian team, was threatened and then thrown off the balcony while I was talking to him. One of the nice things that happened was that I had my photo taken with the great Wesley Hall. He seemed a real gentleman and was happy to find out that I was from Randwick, where he had played years ago.

April 26, 1991 *(St John's, Antigua)*
... This is really a tough tour — mentally and physically. The grounds are hard, and the crowds extremely parochial, supporting their teams to the hilt. Not playing these recent weeks has given me the chance to get out a bit, and I must admit I've consumed more alcohol recently than I did early in the tour. However, I've worked to keep fit. I've tried to keep my flexibility and stomach exercises going — I don't want to give the impression that, because I'm not playing, I'm not interested in what's happening. I hope that next season I can force my way back into the team, and especially the World Cup squad.

April 27, 1991 *(Day One of Fifth Test, Recreation Ground, St John's)*
At stumps we're five for 355, after half-centuries by Taylor, Border and Jones, and a stunning century by Mark Waugh.

Junior's innings was very special, the century coming in just 113 balls. I was speaking into my tape recorder when he reached his ton, and this what I said ...

"I'm running down the stairs from the press box now. Mark is 96 not out, and he's just hit Viv for a straight six. It's by far our best day on tour and we're all hoping that Junior scores a ton ... Viv has dropped a caught and bowled! Well, I don't know if it was a caught and bowled, but it was a toughie. Mark was trying to launch it straight into the sightscreen. Viv has split his finger, and he's calling for assistance. It's all happening!

"Now the 'Great One' is on strike again, on 98 not out. We're just hoping that 'Pretty' can get his 100 ... And he's got it! He's swept Richards, and it's coming down to the boundary, right in front of us. Mark Waugh makes a century in the West Indies at the Recreation Ground in St John's, Antigua."

April 28, 1991 *(Day Two of Fifth Test, Recreation Ground, St John's)*
The dressing room can be a funny place to be during a Test match, even for those players not actually participating in the cricket. It's the players' haven, a mess of bats and pads and smelly cricket stuff. Quite often, the guys who are on the bench will have had a night out and the wrap-around sunglasses will be in evidence. Every now and then someone will crash out for a while, and everyone else will look after him. If someone's coming upstairs you'll get a nudge in the arm, and quickly be awake, alert and watching the game.

It's always a real rush with five minutes to go before a break. Someone will say: "Jeezus, it's lunch in five minutes!". Then everyone will run around madly to get dinners up from downstairs, and to make sure there are drinks ready for the boys. During a Test you're not allowed to split, which is different from the other first-class games when you're often allowed to get away early in the afternoon.

We're staying in a place called the Royal Antiguan, and when we returned there this afternoon, Mo suggested he, Dean Jones and I go scuba diving. The hotel is fronted by a lake on one side, and a beach called Deep Bay on the other. The bloke from the hotel who looks after the diving agreed to take us to a wreck, out in the bay. The story of that wreck is a fascinating one. The ship was called the *Andes* and, 90 years or so ago, she sailed from Trinidad, to transport a load of bitumen to Chile. However, the bitumen hadn't been packed correctly and, a couple of days out, they discovered that it was smouldering. The captain brought the ship into Antigua, where the harbour-master ordered him to anchor out in Deep Bay — to avoid any danger to other craft. Out there, the ship's load, fanned by a strong wind, caught fire and the *Andes* sank.

It was an amazing experience to dive down to it. She's in 10 metres of water, and we stayed down for 45 minutes. We saw amazing amounts of coral and unbelievable numbers of fish. We swam in and out of the remains, being careful to dodge the rusted steel girders. It was a fabulous experience.

May 2, 1991 (*St John's, Antigua*)
... It was an unbelievable night. We stayed down on the beach, talking and drinking and celebrating the Test win until six o'clock in the morning. It was an enormous day, and night, and something I'll never forget. Obviously it would have been fantastic to play, but that was out of my hands and I was just thrilled about what happened yesterday. It was the first time in the history of West Indies cricket that the Windies had been beaten in a Test at Antigua.

The final winning margin was 157 runs, and the man of the match was Mark Taylor, who scored a brilliant second-innings 144 to go with his first-innings 59.

The Recreation Ground was just the most amazing place. There were a couple of guys there throughout the Test — one called Gravy and the other Mayfield — who got dressed up every day. On the first day Gravy got dressed up as W.G. Grace; on the second day he came in drag; and yesterday he was Santa Claus. Over in another grandstand Mayfield was trying to outdo him. They shout at each other across the ground all day, and, at tea on the second day, they had a boxing tournament. And throughout it all — the cricket, the boxing and the fashion parade — the music is blaring all the time.

This Test has been a wonderful experience, and all that's left now is Bermuda. I'm looking forward to getting home. There are a lot of things I want to do. I especially want to see Debbie who I have missed more than I could have imagined.

May 13, 1991 (*Somerset, Bermuda*)
I played in the first two of the three limited-overs matches we played in Bermuda. In the first, I was basically happy with the way I went, considering I hadn't bowled since the Guyana Test — which finished on March 28. I got a bit of carry and beat the bat two or three times an over for the first five or six overs. In 10 overs I was only hit for three boundaries. That's not too bad.

In my last game we scored 9-271 and AB got 100 of them — his first century in two years. Again, I was happy with the way I bowled — 10 overs, four maidens, none for 18. I did the job, and we were happy to win. We went out and celebrated heavily that night.

Bermuda has been a wonderful place to relax after the hectic pace of the West Indies leg of the tour. My only disappointment was that Debbie couldn't join me.

The guys were in a night club the other night and ran into an Australian bloke who is the cruise director on a fabulous new cruise liner. He invited us for a beer on board and it was really something. The boat was absolutely magnificent, worth $220 million and doing the run between New York and Bermuda.

Afterwards we took him to a place called the Oasis, and had a great night. On the way home aboard the motor bikes we were pulled up by the cops. We were, I must confess, fairly well-inebriated. The reason they pulled us up was that Errol had a cricket helmet on, not a standard safety helmet. They spotted the badge. "Oh, you're from the Australian cricket team," they said. "Well, take it easy and just head home."

With its incredible blue water and white limestone buildings, Bermuda is a striking and beautiful place. It reeks of wealth, a tax-free haven for a lot of banks and monetary institutions. The only restrictions on the sweet life are that you are only allowed one car per family, and the speed limit is 25mph.

One of the best events for us in Bermuda was the time we spent as guests at the house of the showbiz millionaire, Robert Stigwood. The place is called Wreck Hill Estate, and, at 25 beautiful acres, is the biggest lump of property in Bermuda. The boys were a little rowdy, but it was a great occasion.

On the night we met the Bermudan constabulary, Steve Waugh and myself managed to scare a year or two off the life of Peter Taylor and Mark Waugh.

Steve and I were in pretty lively form that night and even after the cops had stopped us, it was still a race to get back to the Elbow Beach Resort where we were staying. Boys will be boys! I had Steve W. on the back, and, looking for shortcuts at one stage, I steered the bike at some pace down a flight of 20 or so steps. Steve was hanging on for dear life, trying to stay with it. I reckon he almost turned into a soprano that night.

With a modicum of luck we made it back to the hotel. But the fun was not quite over yet. Peter and Mark were staying in the room two-up from M. Whitney and S. Waugh and we decided it was only fair to share some of the enjoyment with them. They had made the fundamental error of leaving their bathroom window unlatched, and I managed to climb through. Inside,

I tiptoed to the front door, and let Tugga in. It was the dead of night by now, and Mark and Peter were both fast asleep.

Not for long. Safely in the room, we launched ourselves at them. Steve jumped on Taylor and I jumped on Mark and they absolutely *shit* themselves ... they had no idea what was going on. Eventually we turned the lights on and all had a laugh about it. Okay, that was funny ... ho, ho, ho ... well, we're off to bed now. As we headed out we heard them say: "Bastards, we'll have to lock that door."

So, they locked the door, but unfortunately for them they *again* left the bathroom window off the latch. "You sneak in this time, Tugga," I said. "Open the front door and I'll meet you there."

I then ducked around the front and got the motor-bike. Stephen opened the door, and I kicked the bike over, did a wheel stand in the doorway — and then roared into the room. I was revving it furiously and the front wheel finished up on Peter Taylor's bed. You should have seen the look on their faces. There was smoke and diesel fumes filling the room, and the noise must have been awful. I was doing wheel-stands, and spinning the back wheel on the carpet. In the process I knocked the television over and the half-a-dozen glasses that were sitting on it. It was absolute chaos ... madness ... but very funny at the time. Luckily no damage was done. Fairly soon we reckoned we'd better call it stumps. Laurie Sawle and Bob Simpson were staying only a few doors down the passageway, and we weren't too keen on confronting them at that time of the night.

The next morning Steve Waugh, among some others, was more than a little seedy. Steve had his bike parked on the balcony outside the room, overlooking the beach. But when he attempted to kick-start it he miscued slightly and, in a fabulous moment, toppled gracefully — with bike — into a hedge more than a metre below.

It was a fitting end to a funny and enjoyable night.

I've spent plenty of time with Steve on the trip; we get on very well. He mentioned to me the other night he's had an offer to go and play in Queensland. On my own future, I've talked to a few people here about coming back to coach if the money was right. That would be fantastic, even if it was only for a couple of months.

May 15, 1991 *(On a flight, approaching Sydney Airport)*
... Well, almost here. It's been a long, long trip. We're 20 minutes out of Sydney and I think everybody's happy to be going home.

It's now 5.30am ... and the tour is over. It's been really good. I've had a lot of fun, and enjoyed just about all of it. The only thing I can add is that I'd love to get the chance to go back and do it all again.

Indian Summer

It was in the northern NSW town of Lismore that I had my first contact with the Indian touring team of 1991-92. NSW played them up there in their only first-class match before the First Test and I remember the occasion well for a couple of reasons. There was the wicket. Groundsmen in the bush tend to prepare wickets a little differently from blokes in the city; they like to leave a little bit in them. We had a look at this Lismore wicket on the first morning and it was fresh and steamy, with plenty of greenery on it. "Bloody hell!" screamed the batsmen, almost as one. "Check this out!"

We won the toss. A couple of deliveries into my first over I was polishing the ball madly, and I glanced down at it. The thing had a black cross on either side — which meant it was a practice ball, a second. I finished the over and then went across to Henry (Lawson, our skipper). "Have a look at this," I said. Henry called for the box of balls to be brought out ... and they were all seconds!

Inadvertently, Matt Ridley, from the NSW Cricket Association, had brought up not one, but two boxes of seconds for the match. There was nothing we could do about it. The ball swung all over the shop, and we knocked the Indians over for 209.

At a 5.45am, hours before the start of the last day of the match, there was a knock on the door of my motel room. Shaking away the cobwebs I opened up, to be greeted by a bloke named Peter Barnes, a newspaper photographer. "I've got some good news for you," he said. "You've made the first Test side."

He had a bottle of champagne with him and a couple of glasses, and wanted a photo. Soon the phone was running hot with calls from journalists and friends.

That day, despite the early rise, I went out and took 6-37. That really felt good. They had taken a punt on including me in the team, and I had responded by knocking the Indians over. We really flogged them.

Mark Waugh and Mark Taylor had also made the Test team, and that night we had a big celebration. At about 3 o'clock in the morning we were in the room of Pat Farhart, our physiotherapist, and Greg Matthews decided he'd chase up Steve Rixon to come and have a beer with us. He picked up the phone, and dialled. "Stumper!" Greg roared. "Get down here."

Almost immediately he went white. Instead of dialling room 25 he'd dialled room 27 — Australian coach Bob Simpson's room ... and Simmo was not impressed.

I ran into Simpson the next morning and he said to me: "What about that Matthews phoning me at three in the morning?"

I was sympathetic. "Yeah, Bob? Gee, I had no idea ... I was in bed by midnight."

I then drew Simpson for the trip, by hire car, up to Brisbane. I remember looking at Mark Waugh and Mark Taylor as they jumped into the other car and both had these sort of Cheshire cat grins on their faces.

I recall the Test match mainly for the bowling of Merv Hughes. David Boon took three catches off him in close, real screamers. We ended up winning fairly easily and I took a couple of wickets in each innings. I think the Indians were a bit down after the loss to NSW in Lismore, and basically they just surrendered at the end of the day.

I had a lot of respect for the individual players in that Indian team. Potentially they were a great side, but they seemed to have real problems. They were a team which never really got their act together, batting or bowling — despite the undoubted talent in the ranks.

It was the Test in which Allan Border broke Sunil Gavaskar's record for the most number of Test matches played. For an article I penned for *Australian Cricket* magazine, I asked AB a couple of questions: what the record meant to him, and why he reckoned he had played for so long. "Yeah, I am pretty proud to have broken the record," he responded. "And the reason I have played so long is that I have had very little problem with injury." That was it.

I thought I had done enough to hold my spot, but for the Boxing Day Test in Melbourne I was made 12th man. That was disappointing — but at least I had one great highlight to take out of the game. I was fielding during their second dig, and Merv bounced Dilip Vengsarkar, who miscued an attempted hook shot. I was at mid-on and the ball skied in the direction of square leg. I had 25 metres to run, while Boonie, who was fielding behind square, had about 10. I ran after the ball, but didn't think it was mine until I looked at Boonie ... and he wasn't moving at all. So I kept going. I just got there, and, with a full-length dive, took the catch — probably the best catch I have taken in my life in cricket. I was more than happy, but, back in the dressing room after the game, the main comment from everybody was: "Shit, you had your watch on!"

And I *did*. Before I went onto the MCG, I had been sitting in the dressing room with Simmo and the hierarchy. There is no clock in the viewing room, and I had kept my watch on so I could keep a check on the time for drinks, lunch and so on. The thing was still on my wrist when I went on to field. I have never been one for jewellery on the cricket field, although I used to wear a medallion around my neck in younger days. The last time I wore it, the bloody thing flew up and hit me in the gob when I was bowling. Crunch! Right in the mouth, right on a tooth. So I left it in the kitbag after that.

The second Test was another Aussie win, and a pretty relaxing game for me. Not being in the XI, I didn't have to be in bed at nine every night; Debbie was in Melbourne, and we went out and saw a couple of shows.

Bruce Reid took a truckful of wickets in Melbourne, and I was left at 12th man for the Sydney Test. But, after about four overs in Sydney, Reid ripped all the intercostal muscles in his rib cage, and I spent the rest of the match on the field. It was a hard slog. They scored a squillion runs in their dig; Ravi Shastri scored a double century and the teenager Sachin Tendulkar belted an amazing hundred. He's a marvellous young cricketer, that bloke. He barely hit a ball into the air, until the end when the tail-enders were in with him. Then, he was backing away from the fast bowlers and cutting them in the air. I was at deep third man, and someone else was at deepish cover, and he'd hit it in the gap. AB would bring me around square, and then he'd hit it fine. He knew *exactly* where they were going, even when he was slogging. It was a sensational innings, absolutely sensational.

Tragically for India, Ravi Shastri had fallen awkwardly during an earlier one-day game and was now having bad trouble with a knee. He battled on, with a runner to get to his double century. But he had done some serious ligament damage, and he didn't play again on tour. It was a crucial blow to the Indians.

We hung on to draw that Test match. The Indians had rallied by this stage of the tour, and played well in that game. But the significant events of the Test were the injuries. Shastri's set India back comprehensively — and Bruce Reid's opened the door again for yours truly.

Probably my best form that summer came in the one-day series, which involved Australia, India, and the West Indies. With due modesty I would suggest that I bowled really good line and length, and in a pattern which suited me fine. I either opened the bowling or bowled first change — and Allan would always bowl me 10 overs straight. That policy certainly puts you in a better position, because if you bowl last the slogathon is on.

Other blokes took more wickets, but as far as runs-per-over were concerned, I did the job. I conceded less than three runs an over in that series.

The game I remember best is the first match of the best-of-three finals series, against India in Melbourne, played before a crowd of 48,010. We won that game — and the single outstanding image that stays with me is of our off-spinning all-rounder Peter Taylor removing the Indian opener, Kris Srikkanth, with a real screamer of a catch at mid-off.

In Sydney in the second final the crowd was chanting "Whitney! Whitney! Whitney!" every time I grabbed the ball — and it was enormous. At a vital point in the Indian innings, our skipper decided to roll his arm over. He put me down on the fence at square leg, in front of an absolutely chockablock Brewongle Stand. The Indian captain, Mohammad Azharuddin, hit a couple of fours, and then decided that he was going to smash AB right out of the attack. He took two steps down the wicket and went *bang*. Suddenly there it was, heading my way. The crowd noise was unbelievable. I went in, but too far, then had to back-pedal. On the retreat I grabbed the ball over my head, did a backward somersault, and came up with it.

It was a huge thrill, and off went Azharuddin. But Tendulkar took up the attack, and with four overs remaining India needed 20 to win. I was still in front of the Brewongle Stand, at deep square leg when the bowling came from the Noble Stand end, and deep cover for the bowler from the scoreboard end. Steve Waugh bowled the fourth-last over from that scoreboard end, and during it Tendulkar took a step to the leg side, and sliced a big hit out in my direction. For some subconscious reason, I had already moved three paces or so in the right direction before the ball was hit. Off I went, putting in the big ones. I covered more than 25 metres and ... ooofff!! ... made the catch. On Channel Nine, Richie Benaud declared: "What a catch! ... The pressure of that catch!"

It was my third catch of the night ... and it as good as won us the game! I'd never even taken three catches in a grade game before that.

The match came down to the last over with the Indians needing 12 to win. After I took the catch off Tendulkar we were all in a huddle, and AB had said to me: "Whits, great catch, mate. Fantastic."

I said to him: "Who's going to bowl the game out?"

"You are," he replied.

Now, I'd never bowled last in one of these one-day internationals in my whole career.

"Mate, it's your bloody game," AB said to me. "You've taken three snares ... it's your night."

I remember the over well. Manoj Prabhakar, their number nine, stepped away to the leg-side and nicked one behind to Ian Healy. It was a genuine, regulation nick. There was a massive deflection, and that should have been that. But the umpire gave it not out. I couldn't believe it.

Thankfully, it didn't matter. Soon after we were carrying the World Series Cup around the SCG. My return was 1-32 from 10 overs, three catches and the incredible feeling the support of the Sydney crowd had given me. It was a special night for M.R. Whitney.

The one-day series won, it was on to the Fourth Test, in Adelaide. Two days before the game we were in the middle of Simmo's special baby, the high-ball fielding session. Simpson always grabs the outfielders in his group; Allan Border takes the slippers. In Simmo's group were the regulars, which almost inevitably means the quick bowlers, in this case McDermott, Hughes and Whitney.

We've bowled 3000 overs already in all the practice sessions, and now we have to run around the ground and take high catches to improve our stamina! With all due respect, I must say that if Bob Simpson has done anything for me, it is to improve my fielding — just through the sheer volume of catches I've taken in the outfield in his practice sessions. I have to give him that.

There we were, 48 hours from the Test, and we're doing these things called "Fungos", where Bob hits the ball over your head, and you run with the ball coming from behind you and take the catch (hopefully). I was on my last one.

"Catch this one and you're in the shed, Whit," called the coach.

Up it went. Everything was fine until the last milli-second, when I took my eye off the ball. It hit me right on top of my left thumb. I dropped the ball, looked at my thumb, and it blew up like a balloon straight away.

I headed over to Errol Alcott, the physio, and said: "Have a look at this!"

"Can you move it?" asked Errol.

I could barely manage it. It wasn't broken, but it was in bad shape. I had the ice on it all that day, then a gentle massage and some time on a machine. That night, Errol put a little brace on it, but when I woke up next morning I was like little Tommy Tucker with his finger in the pie. The thing was bloody huge.

At practice that day I could barely hold the ball. I sprayed the first few everywhere. But I wanted to be in that team. I knew that if I didn't bowl reasonably well, or if I showed pain, then I wouldn't be playing. I gritted my teeth, and somehow made it through the session. "Well," said coach Simpson, "how are you going to go, Whit?"

"It's a bit sore," I said (by now the bruise was coming out, progressing from black, to purple to yellow). "But I'll be sweet."

So, I stayed in the team, even though I was nowhere near right. The thumb seemed to get worse, despite all the treatment, and, when we attacked the Indians in their first innings (after we'd been sent in and bowled out for 145), I could barely hold the ball. I bowled shit, absolute shit. For the first couple of days it was a nightmare, really ugly. By their second innings I was coming good, and bowled a bit better — although Azharuddin gave me some stick. On a slow wicket he scored a simply awesome century.

What I remember with most pleasure is a last-wicket partnership with Allan Border of 42, in 69 minutes, in our second innings. A conversation I had with him along the way illustrates why I have such respect for the bloke. He was 90 when their spinner, Venkatapathy Raju, came on. In mid-pitch, AB said to me: "We've got this over, and then we're declaring."

The ensuing conversation went something like this:
Whitney: "What? You're on 90."
Border: "I couldn't give a shit about that."
Whitney: "Mate, why not be selfish for just once in your career?"
Border: "We've got this over — then I'm declaring."
With that, he turned, and walked back to his end.

He took a single off the first ball, which left me with the strike. And do you think I could get the bloody thing off the square? In the end I just had a slog, last ball, and holed out to mid-on. And didn't I cop a bagging!

Everyone reckoned I'd just thrown it away when AB was in sight of his first Test century in three seasons. They thought I'd just had an indiscriminate slog. When we reached the dressing room the sarcasm was dripping. At least half the blokes in the team were making comments along the lines of: "Oh, nice batting, Whit."

AB cut the thing dead, silenced the room. "We were coming off at the end of that over," he explained. "Full stop. Get off his back."

Thank God he said it.

We eventually won the Test, despite Azharuddin's heroics, by 38 runs. In the wash-up the runs that Border and I had put on were crucial. It was a great win. But let me tell you about the atmosphere in the Australian camp on that fifth and final day ...

After the stretching and warm-up session, which Errol Alcott ran, Bob Simpson called us into the circle. Consider the scenario — the job at hand was to bowl India out on a fifth-day Adelaide wicket, and win the Test match. It wasn't going to be easy.

That thought was foremost in all our minds when the coach gathered us together and dropped his bombshell.

"Well, we've picked the team for the Fifth Test," he began. "I just thought I'd tell you before the start of the day's play that Geoff Marsh and Mark Waugh have been dropped."

Twelve jaws simultaneously hit the grass. Geoff and Mark were there in our midst. My own first thought was: "Shit! How bad is the timing of that!" It was no morale-booster, I can tell you.

The vice-captain gone, and so too one of the most talented players any of us has ever seen. A couple of bad digs and they'd flicked him. It was only 12 months before that Mark Waugh had made his Test debut on the Adelaide Oval, in the fourth Test of an Ashes series, and made a century.

Straight afterwards we had this fielding practice thing where Errol gets at one end and Simmo at the other, and they call "keeper" or "bowler" and you have to fling them in or underarm them to the designated end. Poor Mark Waugh just couldn't throw the ball right — he kept throwing them over the top.

Our captain was ropeable. Geoff Marsh had been his vice-captain for five years. Now, suddenly, he was gone. If AB had been consulted on the decision, he certainly hadn't agreed with it.

Back in the dressing room, five minutes before we were due out on the field, Paul Reiffel, the 12th man, was towelling down after a shower, before putting on his whites and taking his seat to watch the boys play.

AB snapped at him: "Get your bloody whites on."

"Yeah, I'm just towelling down," said "Pistol" Reiffel.

"Get your whites on NOW; you're going on with the team," roared the skipper.

We all wondered what the hell was going on. Well, Allan made Geoff Marsh take the team onto the field that last morning. As we were walking out he was on the phone, dialling Perth to speak to Laurie Sawle, the chairman of Australian selection committee. I had never before seen AB display the sort of emotion he showed that morning. It was half an hour or 40 minutes before he joined us on the field of play.

We were booked to leave Adelaide that night, and fly to Perth to get ready for the fifth Test, to start three days later. In the dressing room after our fourth Test victory, while we were all getting changed, and packed, AB remained in his whites. By the time we were all in our blazers and ready to get on the bus, he was still in his whites.

"I might see you there," he said to me.

"You *might* see me there?"

He was furious. "Stuff 'em," he said. "They can all get stuffed."

We left without him, all of us, I think, understanding his position, and believing that Allan had done the right thing. They'd sacked his vice-captain and flicked Mark Waugh, who AB holds in the highest regard. Of course he was going to be angry.

On the trip to the airport, Simmo stood up and made an announcement explaining why AB wasn't with us, and referred to "childish behaviour" at one stage. Then off we went without the captain. I couldn't believe the timing of that announcement in Adelaide ... still can't.

It was a day and a half before AB joined us in Perth. The newspapers, of course, relished the drama. But he was there to lead his team out in what turned into a Test match I'll never forget.

I took 4-68 in the first innings, and 7-27 in the second. It was the first time that I'd ever taken 10 wickets or better in a match. It was a huge game for me — and I won the man-of-the-match award.

One wicket stands out from all the others. At 1-90 in their second innings, their number three, Sanjay Manjrekar, was looking ominously good. I have a lot of respect for the way he plays the game, and I've always considered him a very good player — even though he perhaps hasn't achieved all that he should have. As I walked back to my mark I was thinking — if I can just get Manjrekar out, that's going to put a hole in their batting.

As I approached my mark, I pictured this delivery going down middle and off, hitting the seam, and leaving him. I pictured him nicking it, straight to Ian Healy. Well, you wouldn't believe it. Next ball ... clunk ... exactly how I had pictured it. Manjrekar, caught Healy, bowled Whitney. I've use mental imagery from time to time, but, boy, it has never worked that instantly or well before. I dismissed their great all-rounder, Kapil Dev, as well in that second innings, for a duck, with a little in-dipper that caught him in front. I was excited about that, but a bit sad, too.

I thought, the Australian public is never going to see this bloke out here again and I've knocked him over for a globe in his last dig.

It was in that match that Kapil Dev took his 400th Test wicket, knocking over Mark Taylor in the second innings. He joined Richard Hadlee in the very exclusive over-400 wickets club.

My 7-27 should have been 7-23. Azharuddin jammed down on one that came off his foot, and it shot through the slips for a boundary. Umpire Tony Crafter gave the batsman four runs for it and I said to him: "What are you doing to me, TC? It was four leg byes."

About eight balls later Crafter gave Azharuddin out lbw. This time I said to the ump: "Thanks very much, mate. That'll do me."

I remember a nice thing that Geoff Marsh did after that game. To me, Swampy was an excellent player — but most of what he had was heart. He was a bloke who used every ounce of his ability. Despite the great disappointment he must have still been feeling after his sacking, he took the time to come down and congratulate us. While he was there, he tapped me on the shoulder and said: "I bet you didn't know this, Whit?"

"Know what?" I asked.

"Your figures today were the best ever by an Australian bowler against India. Congratulations."

That night I had a few beers with my room-mate from the time I spent with the Australian touring team of 1981, D.K. Lillee, and celebrated what had been a memorable game for me. It was more than a decade between my Test debut and my best bowling performance in Test cricket. To be able to share my success, in some way, with the great Dennis Lillee made the experience that much sweeter.

The World Cup

During the Great Adventure of the 1992 World Cup, which was conducted in Australian and New Zealand, we played Zimbabwe in Tasmania. I remember the game well because I made something of a ... shall we say ... *goose* of myself in the dressing room before the game, and in the process did chronic damage to the well-established "intellectual" image of the fast-bowling fraternity.

Ever since I started playing cricket at something of a serious level, I have always made it a habit to write my name on the inside of my shirt collars. Cricket dressing rooms are almost always shit-boxes, and there's a terrific chance, anywhere and everywhere, of losing gear. So, I label my stuff, and hope that will improve the chances of me hanging onto it.

Before the Zimbabwe game I was sitting next to Dean Jones, scribbling away on my shirts. After a while, Deano tapped me on the shoulder and asked: "What are you doing?"

"Oh, just writing my name on my clothes like I always do," I replied. "I write my name on them so they don't get mixed up with everyone else's gear."

"Well, I'll give you a tip," said Deano. "Have a look at the back."

I turned the shirt over and there, right across the back in huge letters, was the name ... WHITNEY.

Needless to say, I didn't live that one down for the rest of the tournament. My fast-bowling cohorts were entitled to be filthy on me.

Playing in the '92 Cup on home soil was a great buzz. I think all of us had a sense of history in the fact that the South Africans made their reappearance in cricket's international family in that tournament. My memories are fragmented, but mainly of tough, enjoyable competition, big crowds, and a mix of fierce rivalry and the mateship of shared experience among the teams. But for the Australian team the Cup proved a major disappointment.

Going in on a questionable preparation, we didn't fulfil expectations, and copped flak from coach Bob Simpson and the media along the way.

THE WORLD CUP

Bookmakers had installed Australia as Cup favourites, ahead of Pakistan and England, but we rarely looked like living up to that rating. Australia had been comprehensive winners of the triangular World Series tournament which preceded the Cup, running up a 7-2-1 scoresheet against India and the West Indies.

That Series was a beauty for me. I finished with 12 wickets at an average of 25.56, and a runs-conceded-per-100-balls rate of 49.15 per cent — second only to Curtly Ambrose among the regular bowlers. But the promise given by the Australians in that tournament was never fulfilled in the World Cup that followed.

Together with Merv Hughes and Mark Taylor, I missed the first game, against New Zealand in Auckland. My main recollection is of sitting in the stand and watching Dipak Patel, an off-spinner, open the bowling for the Kiwis. Martin Crowe and his New Zealanders had come up with this theory about using spinners to open the bowling in the one-dayers. The tactic worked, and they beat us that game, and pretty thoroughly outplayed us.

Before the game against New Zealand we played a warm-up fixture against an Auckland XI, at the University of Auckland. We'd all come off a round of Test matches and first-class games and hadn't played a one-dayer for a while. There was talk in the press about how bad our preparation was for the World Cup — and there was more than a little substance in that. Traditional first-class cricket is a game of vastly different shape and colour from the limited-overs version. So the game at Auckland Uni. was a struggle from that point of view — but more so from another. I'll never forget the wind that howled down the ground that day. It was up around 100km an hour all day — and guess who had to bowl into it? Most of the time I doubted I was going to get to the stumps.

In Sydney, I had the (dubious) pleasure of helping welcome the South Africans back into the fold. I say dubious because they thrashed us, reaching our meagre 9-170 with 13 balls, and nine wickets, to spare. Afterwards, I presented the ball that was hit for the winning run to their skipper Kepler Wessels. I knew how big a thrill it must have been for him to represent his native country against his one-time adopted land — and to win. He's a bloke I always respected as a very tough competitor, and he was a star in that comeback match, too.

I walked off the field with him at the end of that game, and threw him the ball. "Here you go, Chopper," I said. "This is for you."

He was very appreciative. There has always been some mutual admiration between the pair of us. Before he left Australia, bound for home, he told me once that he had plenty of respect for the way I played the game. Coming from him, a real tough cookie, that meant something.

Whether it was the preparation or what, we never really got a roll on in the tournament. The Pakistanis beat us in Perth and for them that was the springboard that sent them all the way to the winning of the Cup. By the time we finally hit our straps we were relying on other teams being beaten to give us any chance of making it. Basically, clutching at straws.

It was a hectic time. In Sydney we stayed at a hotel in The Rocks. The hotel was fine, but I'll come clean and admit that I wasn't real keen at all about staying at a hotel while I was in my home city. Each night, when it was time to hit the hay, I'd head upstairs (I was rooming with Mark Waugh) and to all intents and purposes turn in for the night. But, at about 11.30 or so, I'd sneak out and get the keys from a porter to one of the team vans, and drive home to the Eastern Suburbs, and sleep in my own bed, with Debbie.

I'd be up at seven the next morning, shoot back into town in the van, give the porter his keys, head up to the room, join the boys for breakfast — and then head off to the game. Those that knew what I was up to didn't say a word about it. And those that didn't know ... well, it didn't hurt them.

The routine certainly did me no harm. I had a very good World Cup — in fact, of all the bowlers who sent down at least 30 overs in the competition, only Patel conceded less runs per 100 balls than I did. And that's what one-day cricket is about for a bowler — keeping it tight and economical.

What I did through the Sydney leg of that tournament might be seen as "wrong". But the fact was I wanted to be with my wife, and I reckoned it made sense for me to stick to the routine that worked for me as a NSW player. I fulfilled my obligations to the team 100 per cent — except that I slept elsewhere.

The Cup was a great exercise in co-ordination. I remember the fun they had trying to organise the official team photos. The pix were done on a Navy frigate out on Sydney Harbour, and that was a happy day — if a bit chaotic. I was delighted to see all my old pals from Zimbabwe, and all the other international teams.

Another old pal, Ian Botham, was bowling when I came in to bat against England at the Sydney Cricket Ground. I blocked the first couple, then he pitched one up which I drove through the covers for four. The crowd went wild. The next one, of course, was short and up under the ribs, but I managed to bunt it around the corner for a single.

After the match, which England won by eight wickets with Botham man of the match, he came into the room and we were kidding around. My batting prowess was under some discussion.

"Good shot, Whit," said "Beefy" of my drive for four.

"Thanks Beefy, thanks for the half-volley mate," I said loudly.

"Half-volley!!" said Botham in mock surprise. You've got to be joking haven't you ... you hit it on the *up*!"

There was raucous laughter in the room.

In fact, as the replays showed, I *had* hit the ball on the up — just like a real batsman. I genuinely thought I'd half-volleyed it which probably gives an indication of how much I know about what I'm doing when I'm out in the middle with a bat in my hand.

Bob Simpson gave us a real razzing after the South African match, which we had lost so badly. He sat us down and flew into us, telling us how poorly we'd played and how disappointed he was. He got stuck into some of the blokes about them not looking after themselves, that they'd been out on the town, and so on

Funnily enough, the night of his little talk the boys *really* went out on the ran-tan, with the exception of me. I wasn't being a goody-goody or anything — it just happened that I was home with Debbie.

There were mutterings of discontent about the coach's blast. There was a mutual feeling within the team that our preparation had been pretty damned inadequate — and that we weren't really entitled to be copping heavy flak for not producing peak one-day performances. We travelled to Brisbane the following day, and Simmo gave the team another serve up there.

There was bickering in the press as to why Merv Hughes and Mark Taylor had been picked in the squad, and Simon O'Donnell left out. O'Donnell was a world class one-day player, with bat and ball, and was showing good form in the domestic Shield competition. There was certainly a solid case for having him in the team — and that's not to say Merv and Mark aren't good one-day cricketers. But the fact was that they only played one or two games each, and were basically passengers.

I remember a great line from Merv in Melbourne. At training, Simmo told him he was playing in the match against the West Indies.

"Bullshit!" said Merv. "You're joking aren't you Simmo? I'm not playing ... you'll ruin my f------ holiday!"

Merv was kidding, of course — but what he was saying was basically true.

He'd been having a fine time tripping around with the team, without actually playing. But he had played in Brisbane, against India — a game we won in the most exciting finish of the tournament. It was a match that had a simply incredible finish. From the final ball of the match, and with nine wickets down, India needed four runs to win. A bloke called Javagal Srinath lofted a catch off Tom Moody out to Steve Waugh, who made many metres to get to the ball — but then spilled it, just inside the boundary. Waugh recovered quickly, fired the ball back in — and Srinath was run out, with his partner Venkatapathy Raju in sight of the stumps as he chased the run that would have tied the game.

There was cheering for Australia that day, and especially after that frenzied finish. But, sadly, there wasn't enough of it in the World Cup of 1992. We kept our best performance to last, when we beat the West Indians in Melbourne, and so denied them a place in the semi-finals. I took four wickets in that game, good wickets too — Richie Richardson, Keith Arthurton, Gus Logie and Carl Hooper — but the effort was for next to nought, as our previous efforts had left us without enough points to reach the semi-finals.

While Pakistan, England, South Africa and New Zealand went off to fight for one-day cricket's biggest prize, we Australians went our separate ways. For the NSW and WA players, that way was to Perth, for the Sheffield Shield final. For NSW, this was a match of special significance, as Henry Lawson had indicated it would be his final first-class game.

We Blues were determined to send him out a winner, but it wasn't to be. The West Australians finally prevailed, after a fantastic game of cricket, by 44 runs. For me, the game was a good one — 2-71 in the first innings, and 7-75 in the second — but giving my captain an appropriate farewell would have made it so much better.

As I headed back to Sydney for a well-earned break, I knew that, without Henry at the helm of the NSW battleship, future cricket seasons just wouldn't be the same, especially for me.

True Blue

I might be a knockabout product of sport's modern era, but I have a wholesome respect for cricket's history and tradition. I never tire of hearing stories of the deeds and exploits of the great players of yesteryear. During games at the Sydney Cricket Ground I made many a long trip up the steps of the Noble Stand to the press box, to sit alongside and chat with that famous bowling legend, the late Bill O'Reilly.

As a New South Welshman, I am excited by stories of O'Reilly, Keith Miller, Arthur Morris, Neil Harvey and other greats of the post-World War II years. And of the old champions, Sir Donald Bradman, of course, and Stan McCabe, Charlie Macartney, Bert Oldfield, Alan Kippax and Arthur Mailey.

New South Wales is gloriously rich in cricket lore and tradition. You feel it and literally eat it each time you pass through the SCG members' turnstiles, make your way into the old Members' Stand and walk through the door leading into the home dressing room. When I am sitting by a locker, tying up my bootlaces, or reaching for my blue NSW cap, I can't but wonder just who was it doing the same thing three, four, five decades earlier. Was it Ray Lindwall ... Richie Benaud ... Alan Davidson? Even Victor Trumper?

Playing for the Blues has been a tremendous buzz for me — the highlight of the last 14 years of my life. Tugging the blue cap over my head, stepping out through the SCG players' gate, hearing the noise and the cheers of the Sydney crowd ... I will take these memories to my grave.

In this chapter I will list a personal "Hall of Fame", chosen from the NSW players with whom I have played.

To start at the top end of the batting order, we had not one but two outstanding pairs of openers in my time — Rick McCosker and John Dyson, and Steve Small and Mark Taylor. Both duos must rank among the most successful pairings in the long history of NSW cricket.

McCosker and Dyson were both extremely sound technical players. I will always remember how comfortable the rest of our team felt when they opened the innings. So confident in fact that on one occasion Trevor Chappell, next batsman to go in, was still in no more than his jockstrap as the first delivery was bowled. There seemed no hurry. Rarely was one of the openers back in the shed before we had a useful score on the board.

McCosker played until 1984 and I was privileged to see some of the best of his cricket at state level. They called him "Rick the Snick", but I saw him play some fantastic knocks. His concentration was faultless, he played superbly on the legside, and he rarely failed to punish anything loose. And he had a good technique against short-pitched bowling.

He never flinched. And besides being a class act at the crease, he was a splendid captain. In my early days I couldn't have had a better man in charge. He always settled us down, was never upset and never blew up his men. In 1982-83 he engineered our victory in the Sheffield Shield final in Perth, ending a long drought of NSW failures in the West. I enjoyed my time playing under him.

Dyson had his critics, who labelled him dour and slow. I remember on a trip to Perth a scribe calling him a "corpse in pads". He was a batsman who was very difficult to dismiss and who had unbelievable powers of concentration. He was more an accumulator of runs than a hitter of the ball and he never got flustered or annoyed against the quick bowlers — even when he got "sledged". NSW used him in the sturdy anchor role. He would batten down one end and quietly accumulate the runs.

In more recent times, NSW has had the all left-handed opening partnership of Small and Taylor. How different was "Jack" Small from Rick McCosker and John Dyson. Scorer of just on 4,000 runs in the Shield, Small was a pain in the neck to opposing sides because he could open them up with the most adventurous and daredevil shots in the business. He made his intentions felt from ball one, and was one of those guys who was going to get out real quick or amass a lot of runs very quickly. Jack played the tough guy at the crease and he would wear a few deliveries on the body without taking a backward step. He worked hard on his fitness and wielded a three-pound bat, ensuring that when the ball was hit, it stayed hit. We called his bat "the railway sleeper with a handle".

You couldn't say Jack Small was a *great* player. But he was a damn good one, with a very unusual technique (he was able to deliberately smash balls through the off side that really had no right to go there) — and a prolific scorer of runs for NSW. Jack got plenty of those runs just on heart; he hung around at 36 or 37 years of age and gutsed it out against the young blokes who were really trying to stick it up him.

At the outset of their association, "Tubby" Taylor was a comparatively subdued player, just content to occupy the crease. But in the years that followed he developed an enormous array of shots. He is blessed with a fine temperament, and doesn't worry if he plays and misses. He just sets himself for the next ball. His technique is excellent against speed, adequate against spin and if he continues to progress in Tests he is destined to become one of the all-time greats. Small and Taylor certainly made an interesting pair!

In 1992-93, another opening batsmen emerged who I think will turn out to be every bit as good as McCosker, Dyson, Taylor and Small. I'm talking, of course, of Michael Slater. I haven't played that much with "Slats", but he is someone I just have to mention in this chapter because I think he is going to be an absolute champion. His attitude, his dedication and his technique are all superb, and the way he moves his feet is just outstanding. He's one of those guys who has entered the first-class game and come to grips with it very quickly. He's going to be a real gun.

Two number-three batsmen stand out — Trevor Chappell and Trevor Bayliss. Trevor Chappell was a very underrated player, spending his representative years very much in the shadow of his famous brothers, Ian and Greg. For all that, he was a fine athlete who had the ability to consolidate if we lost an early wicket, or get on with the scoring if we were on top. His value to NSW was strengthened with his medium-pace bowling. He was certainly an early innovator of the slower ball that has become such a part of the game, and especially the one-day game, in the last decade. The critics talk of Merv Hughes, Steve Waugh, and Simon O'Donnell, but "T.C." had a slow ball years before those fellows had thought about it. And he used it to tremendous effect. I saw him take a lot of wickets and when you consider he was one of the slickest fieldsmen around, you realise his value to the Blues. In the covers or anywhere close he had tremendous hands and could throw down the stumps with unerring accuracy.

Bayliss wasn't without fault in his technique. He was prone to the nick and he could lose his wicket to the hook, but when on fire he was an exciting player to watch. He took over the number-three role in 1989-90, when neither of the Waugh brothers wanted it, and in that one season piled up nearly 1,000 runs. The big bonus was that he scored his runs quickly. He would smack the ball around and play shots from the start of his innings. He decimated some attacks, was a mobile fielder and a specialist in the gully. And he could bowl deceptive "anythings" — medium-pacers with some off-spinners thrown in and a good change of pace.

Following Bayliss in the middle order were the Waugh brothers, Steve and Mark, the inspiration of Blues cricket. Glorious shot-makers, geniuses in the field and highly-capable seam bowlers, they could take control of a match, at Shield or international level. Steve's policy has always been to go onto the attack irrespective of the situation and in this respect he differed from Mark who can be a little more circumspect. But just as effective. I can remember NSW in dire trouble in Brisbane in 1988-89, having lost four for 29, before Steve came out, joined Greg Matthews and both finished with hundreds.

Mark is certainly a classical stroke-maker and anything directed on middle or leg stumps is fruit for the sideboard. He can hook brilliantly, but the cut shot is his favourite and he has told me that nothing gives him more satisfaction than leaning back to a short-pitched ball, middling it and sending it spearing past point to the boundary. His foot work is impeccable and he can be devastating against spin, lifting the ball into the unguarded outfield spaces with ease.

As a bowler, Steve has developed a slower ball which he lets go with his fingertips pointing down the wicket and the palm pointing to the sky, so the ball comes right out of the back of the hand but not in a leg-spin action. With the seam straight he extracts both slow cut and swing. Like Mark, he has unbelievably slick hands and he can make the most difficult catch look a formality.

Before the Waughs arrived on the scene, Peter Toohey was a fine strokemaker for the Blues and a smart fielder. I've witnessed him take some great catches in the gully. A lovely guy to play cricket with, he never had a bad word for anybody. One of the best hookers or pullers I've ever played with, anything short of a length was severely punished. I remember particularly a class innings he played in Melbourne in 1982-83. He scored an absolutely superb hundred, but in the scorebook his brilliance was overshadowed by Steve Smith who had piled up a mammoth 263.

That season was, of course, the year we won the Shield final in Perth. At the end of that season, Rick McCosker stood down as NSW captain, and his replacement was Dirk Wellham. To say the least, Dirk has been a controversial cricketer. Not only has he played Shield cricket for three states (NSW, Tasmania, and Queensland), he has captained all three, with varying levels of success, in an unusual career. I must say he was one of the best captains I played under. As the Blues skipper, he knew his players and understood their personalities, and was therefore able to relate to everybody. His field placings were always spot on as, almost always, were his bowling changes. He wasn't a flamboyant run-maker, more a quiet accumulator, but he scored 90 in a pre-lunch session at the Gabba one day in one of the best knocks I have seen. A good worker of the ball and smart judge of a single, he scored over 8,000 runs in first-class cricket. In the field, he was quick off the mark, excellent close to the wicket, and had a good arm from a short distance.

One of the many fine batsmen to play under Wellham was Mark O'Neill, who was, sadly, in many ways an unfulfilled talent. Bill O'Reilly was one good judge who confidently predicted Test honours for this son of the former Test star, Norman O'Neill. Being a Test player's son is always an extra burden to carry, but I guess it's part and parcel of having a famous sire. At the crease, Mark seemed to move late to the ball but his timing was excellent and in an inspired period in 1985-86 he scored centuries on the trot in Adelaide, Brisbane and Sydney. Thrilling innings they were, too. O'Neill made many valuable runs for NSW when the going was tough, and had a great sense of humour to go with his runs.

In Mark O'Neill's last season for the Blues, 1990-91, a young left-hander called Michael Bevan produced a remarkable sequence of run-scoring that suggested he was destined for high honours. Anybody scoring five centuries in six games has to possess enormous talent. Coupled with his batting prowess, he is a fitness fanatic and a good mover in the field, a keen chaser with a powerful throwing arm. And he can bowl, too, with left-arm seamers or "Chinaman" deliveries.

But batting is his forte and he is one young man not frightened to go out and play his shots. Inventive, too. When the speed men try to bounce him I've seen him calmly lean back, angle his bat, and neatly steer the ball over the slips' heads to the boundary.

Michael Bevan is one of the "young guns" who will take the Blues through the '90s. Seasons before, when I first came into the NSW side, batting about number seven or eight was Graeme Beard, an all-rounder with a great attitude to the game. He was a cricketer who could pull an innings around, take inspired catches at slip or bowl out a team with his probing seamers. I saw him grind out 30 or 40 runs to save many a batting situation for our state. He could steady the lower order at a time when you were five or six wickets down and wondering if the tail was going to capitulate. His right-arm seamers moved both ways with a bit of swing thrown in, and, at the tail end of his career, he developed into a versatile and extremely effective off-spinner.

I have played with a lot of class spinners, and would have to include Bob "Dutchy" Holland in this list of top NSW players. Dutchy was a tremendous guy, admired by team-mates and opponents alike. If I could sound one note of criticism, I thought he didn't bowl his wrong 'un enough. He had another, less well-known nickname — "Pops" — because he was a bit older than the other players and could land a ball on a handkerchief — all day. He could bat a bit, too. I batted with him in one game in Brisbane where he went on and scored a half-century. He was pretty happy too!

Of all the spin bowlers I've seen in action in the Shield, few have been better than Murray Bennett. He was a left-arm orthodox finger-spinner who often seemed to have the ball on a string. On reflection, it was disappointing he didn't play more games for the Blues. He had a couple of injuries, lost a bit of form and had work commitments. Murray was also a more than adequate late-order batsman, good enough, in fact, to open the innings for his club, St. George. Always smiling, he was, like so many of the men I am mentioning in this chapter, a top team man.

At his best, Murray joined Greg Matthews and Dutchy Holland in a three-pronged spin attack that proved lethal on the Sydney turning decks of the early and mid-1980s. Greg has been a golden player for NSW. At 10 minutes to six, when there's a few weary backsides trailing the ground, he has always been the guy bouncing around, urging: "Let's get some more."

He was more of a batsman than a spin bowler during the early '80s, but knew if he wanted to play for Australia he needed to work hard on his bowling. Greg's career has had plenty of ups and downs, but you could never count him out. If he failed to take wickets he was just as likely to bob up with a big score. For NSW, he continues to take wickets, especially on the turning Sydney pitches, where a lot of interstate spinners have failed to prosper. You still have to bowl on the right spot, which Greg has done consistently and patiently. With so much energy he has always been a great mover in the field and can handle any position, especially slips. An extrovert, I think he's been one of the best things to happen to Australian cricket, especially in the mid '80s when our national team was on a bit of a downer and he came in and gave the side a fresh look. Very dedicated, he loves to talk about cricket, about statistics and older players. Greg Matthews remains a real bluebagger at heart and one of my best friends in the game. We have roomed together for many years.

Peter Taylor first came into the NSW team in 1985-86, as Bennett and Holland were nearing the end of their careers. Taylor was a very good all-rounder, but mainly in the side as an off-spinner. His technique was different from Greg Matthews'. He used to fire them in and turned out to be a top one-day player, as he was extremely hard to get away. A tremendous fieldsman, who held a bagful of slip catches, completes the picture of Peter Taylor.

When it comes to wicket-keepers, I can choose between Steve Rixon, Greg Dyer and Phil Emery — all stalwarts for the Blues.

Of all the keepers I played with, including Rodney Marsh, Steve Rixon was the best. As NSW's first choice behind the stumps from 1974 until 1985, he was the complete keeper, fantastic at handling the quick bowlers. I can still visualise him, when I was younger and letting them fly wide down the legside, diving full length to pick up the ball in one glove and flicking it back to the slips. All in one natural movement. Then he would spring straight back up, brush himself down and be ready for the next one. Yet he got his nickname, "Stumper", from his ability to whip the bails off when keeping to the spinners. He certainly relished those days when New South Wales had three spinners in operation. He was an aggressive, gutsy batsman, too. Stumper was a great help to me, using the drink breaks to pick me up on any faults, such as my right arm falling away, and he always had an encouraging word if you were dragging your butt after a hard day. He could fire a rocket too.

Greg Dyer, Rixon's successor, was a very capable custodian who played Test cricket for Australia. But I don't think we saw the best of him. In 1988-89, just months after controversially losing his Test spot to Ian Healy, he was unceremoniously dropped from the NSW team captaincy, a savage blow that still astonishes a lot of people. He went from being Test keeper to a grade keeper, just like that.

I remember when Greg Dyer was so unceremoniously dropped from the NSW team, they picked this guy called Phil Emery, who I had heard very little about. But I liked the guy from the start, and found him to be an excellent gloveman. He's a big guy, which is a little unusual for a keeper, but has worked tremendously hard on his fitness and reached the stage where he now holds the top two positions on the list of NSW keepers with most dismissals in a single season. And he's a more-than-capable left-hand batsman who has played more than a couple of crucial innings for the Blues.

When we come to the speed men, I have a special place for Lenny Pascoe, who had a lot of heart and bowled aggressively all day. Even before I first reached the NSW XI, I had heard stories that he raced in and tried to bowl at 100 miles an hour, but by the time I made my debut Len had developed a very good outswinger, a useful off-cutter and could bowl a very dangerous bouncer which he exploited a lot. He would roll up his sleeves, which indicated he meant business, and the angrier he got, the faster and better he bowled. Few fast bowlers are like that — usually they lose it when they lose their temper. You could wind Len Pascoe up and he'd bowl all day.

When I first played for NSW, the pace bowling trio was Pascoe, Whitney and ... Lawson. From that first appearance on, I looked up to Geoff Lawson with respect and admiration. From early in 1989 until the end of the 1991-92 season he was my NSW captain and in that time he displayed a great attitude that so often brought the Blues success. He was criticised from time to time (if we lost) for leaving opposition teams realistic targets to win. But that was the game NSW played and the way "Henry" Lawson played the game. As a fast bowler he was outstanding. Some have forgotten that in his younger days he had genuine pace and was a bowler who could intimidate the best batsmen with his bouncer.

In my mind, Henry was the true professional. He didn't drink or smoke and he never knocked his body around. Courage was his trademark. In 1985, he shrugged off back problems that would have finished off a lesser player. In 1988 he suffered a broken jaw against the West Indies, yet played in the Shield match against South Australia in Adelaide only a few weeks later. He couldn't open his mouth and just breathed through his nose. When he batted, the South Australians tried to bounce him out, but Henry hit a gutsy 71. His record is amazing, the first bowler to take over 300 Shield wickets for NSW. Henry, in addition, was very good in the field, a keen chaser and equipped with a good throwing arm.

And he has been a great friend to me.

Into the '90s, Henry and I were joined in the NSW side by Wayne "Cracker" Holdsworth. On his day, Cracker can be absolutely devastating. He's one of those crazy quicks; when he's on fire he can really rip through a side, bowling as fast as anyone in Australia. But when he bowls badly he bowls two lengths — too full, and too short. What his bowling has needed is the ability to step back and take stock. If you're going for a few runs you have to come back half a metre in pace and say to yourself: "Hang on, I just have to get my line and length right ... and build from there."

But when he's in the groove he's a sensational bowler. And a genuine character who I really enjoy playing with. Cracker is definitely fun to be around, and *definitely* one of the boys. He has a couple of party tricks I can't write about here, but the boys love them. The NSW dressing room is never a dull place when Wayne Holdsworth is about.

So, that's my personal NSW cricket Hall of Fame, chosen from the many players to wear the baggy blue cap during my career. You might ask about Doug Walters, Ian Davis and Steve Smith, but I just didn't play enough with them to choose them in my line-up.

I shared some memorable summers with these great players, and can only conclude by saying that they all did NSW cricket proud.

Hot Times in Sri Lanka

The eight-match tour of Sri Lanka in 1992 was four weeks in another world. For the travelling Aussies it was a test both of character and of physical endurance. Along the way we battled unrelenting sauna-bath heat, sickness, plus willing opposition hell-bent on bringing us to heel. At times, I struggled. A tummy bug knocked me for six early, and later a ricked neck made every trip to the bowling crease a painful and daunting experience. Much of the time I felt drained by the heat ... and I'm sure we all did.

Yet, there were things that happened on that tour that I will never forget — events of such richness they will always rank high in my cricketing memory bank. We were the first cricket team to tour the country in five years — because of the seething internal situation that has resulted from the struggles of the Tamil Tigers to win the right to create their own autonomous state.

We had police escorts and security men with us wherever we went on tour; two security men would patrol the floor on which we are staying in our hotels; two more were posted permanently outside the lifts, scrutinising every arrival. The security was ever-present, and always strong. The country was in an edgy state; and I can remember while we were there the Sri Lankan army lost 10 of their highest commanding officers, up north where the civil war with the Tamil Tigers raged. The last team to tour before us, the Kiwis, had decided to cut short their tour when bombs exploded near their hotel.

Throughout the tour there was a sense of unease. But the hairs still prickle on the back of my neck when I remember some of the special things that happened.

How could I ever forget the first Test, when we came back from the brink to win? Emotions ran high that day, and I can still picture our man of the match, Greg "Mo" Matthews, in the dressing room afterwards, his head swathed in a towel, sweat streaming down his face. We were all overcome by what he, and the team, had achieved.

In the town of Kandy, high in the mountains, I was privileged to watch the extraordinary annual Esala Perahera Buddhist parade. The image of a hundred magnificently bedecked elephants swaying down the main street of the town, their progress lit by the torches of hordes of dancers, will stay with me forever.

I loved the people. They looked after us beautifully. They seemed a very kind, very mellow race and it was hard to understand or even believe the reported violence taking place in the country. The Sri Lankans really love their cricket too, and we sensed deeply their affection for the game wherever we went.

The Sri Lankan tour is one I could talk about forever, but I'll confine myself to just a few of the remarkable and, in some cases, very funny happenings that occurred on tour. They will, I hope, give a glimpse of what it was like to be there.

• **Cricket, and life, in Kandy**
The wake-up call at our hotel in Colombo came at 5.30am, and we were on the bus by 6.30, to travel up into the mountains to Kandy, where we were to play the Sri Lankan Board President's XI.

Kandy is a really beautiful place, with a nice little ground called the Old Trinidadians Sports Club Ground. On a wicket with some moisture in it, and which definitely played better after lunch, we ended up making 9-278, with Mark Waugh getting 74. I had a bat at the death and faced four overs for none not out. I almost got off the mark a couple of times with a glide through the gully — but it wasn't to be.

The evening following that first day's play brought one of the great highlights of the tour. The team went into town to watch the Esala Perahera, a gigantic festival-parade which is the celebration of the bringing back to Kandy of the Buddha's tooth relic. This precious relic was the subject of a war some 400 years ago.

The parade was sensational. There must have been at least 100 elephants in it, all of them magnificently dressed up and accompanied by hundreds of dancers, carrying flaming torches. Chandra, our liaison officer, organised for us to get viewing spots out on the street, joining people who had paid 1500-2000 rupees ($50-$70 Australian) for the privilege. We had a great view. I can recall Mo saying it was one of the most spectacular things he had seen in his life, and I wouldn't argue with that.

The weather closed in next morning, and we battled through a bloody awful day's cricket. After declaring at our overnight score we were on and off the ground most of the day. There was a buzz for me early on, though. I took a wicket with the last ball of my first over — first blood on the tour for big Roy.

After a day of trooping back and forth to the wicket they finished at 1-74. The run-ups made it a real struggle for we bowlers. They were saturated. I worked three or four different angles, switching virtually every ball so that I didn't land in the same soggy footmarks. We played with this strange sort of meshed ball, with a quarter seam on it. But, surprisingly, the wicket played quite well.

At the end of the day my back was stiff and sore, and Errol Alcott did some work on it. Afterwards, we headed up the hill from our hotel to a function they put on for us. There was pork on the spit, and chicken and beef — a regulation sort of Asian barbecue with some salads. I think everyone went pretty carefully, as the fear of stomach trouble always loomed.

On our rest day we headed to town, firstly to the Botanical Gardens, which house the largest palms in the world. They're absolute monsters, towering up to 50 metres tall. Then, our interest sparked by the carnival the other night, we visited the temple where the tooth relic is kept. Some of the guys had to put sarongs on, as you're not allowed in there wearing shorts. Nearby was a smaller temple which houses the stuffed remains of an elephant named Rana which apparently carried the tooth relic around for 50 years or so in the annual parade, and is something of a legend.

Downtown, I had the luxury of a haircut, shave, head massage and face massage, which cost me 50 rupees, less than $2 back home. Mo slung the bloke 100 rupees for doing a good job. We drew a large crowd of curious onlookers — biggest I've ever had for a haircut. They don't get too many Aussie cricketers in Kandy.

At night we had the first gig organised by the tour social committee (Damien Martyn and me). With the help of some of the security guys, and having splurged $30 or so on rockets, bungers and star-showers, we set the scene with a spectacular fireworks display. Then we took to the card tables, playing some acey-deucey, a bit of drop and some poker. The journos joined in and the big winner on the night was Malcolm Conn, of *The Australian*, who cleaned up on the last hand and took away 17,000 rupees (around $450) — not a bad night's work.

With the rain playing its part, the match finished in a draw. They batted pretty well. Atapattu got 64 not out and Mahanama 82, almost all the runs from angled deflections on either side of the wicket. Anything full and they struggled to punch it away. I finished with 3-53 off 24 overs. I was stiff and pretty drained at the end of the game. The heat and humidity had taken their toll ... but it was a positive start to my tour.

- **Hangers-on?**

I mentioned the security men who were our permanent shadows on tour.

With easy-going Mark "Junior" Waugh, it took a little while to sink in who all these extra blokes hanging around were.

One morning I was sitting next to Junior on the bus when he nudged me: "Gee there are some hangers-on in this game, Whit, aren't there?"

"Yeah," I said. "Yeah, there are."

Mark glanced back over his shoulder at the four security guards who were travelling with us.

"What about these four blokes from the Sri Lankan Cricket Association," he said. "Before long they're going to be wanting autographs and tickets to the games and all the rest of it."

I thought to myself: Mate, are you fair dinkum, or what? I mean, everyone *knew* they were security guards. Or did they?

I called one of the guards down, got him to turn around, and lifted up his jacket. The pistol (all of them were armed) bulged in its holster. We had a good look, and then the bloke went and sat down again. That was that.

There was silence for another five minutes or so, then Mark nudged me again. "Mate," he said, "why on earth would the guys from the Sri Lankan Cricket Association carry guns?"

Batsmen ... they're a bit of a worry!

• The First Test

On a wicket that had a seaming look about it, we were sent in to bat, and eventually got rock'n'rolled for 256. I made 13, which was my highest Test score, but more important than that was the 49 I helped put on with Ian Healy. We finished up just three runs short of the record last-wicket stand against Sri Lanka — 52 by New Zealand's Warren Lees and Ewen Chatfield. They bowled well, especially the seamers, and we were always struggling.

The Sri Lankans came out and promptly turned the game into some sort of slaughter. Their batting was just awesome — and three of their guys scored hundreds. Gurusinha batted for a long time for his 137, and it was a real good solid dig. Ranatunga got 127, chancing his arm throughout, but striking the ball very well. Then Kaluwitharana, the wicket keeper, who was making his Test debut, came out and scored one of the best centuries I've ever seen. The bloke was a bit of a smarty but, notwithstanding, he played beautifully — hitting the ball so crisply.

There we were, 291 behind, and our turn to bat again. The guys responded to the challenge and for only the third time in Test cricket history every batsman reached double figures. I managed 10 not out, putting on 40 with Shane Warne for the last wicket — making the Australian last-wicket partnerships worth 89 for the game. I was pretty happy with that. We totalled 471 and, on the last day of the match, they needed 181 to win.

And you know what? We knocked them over! It was just the most

HOT TIMES IN SRI LANKA

phenomenal thing. The last day was a Saturday, and the ground was packed to capacity, with the expectation of a Sri Lankan win. Crowds had been poor on the first few days, but on this last day the people really rolled in to see the last rites delivered ... or so they thought. They arrived armed with musical instruments and drums, and sang songs which I later learned were Sri Lankan victory chants.

They started well and at 0-70 were cruising. But we picked up a couple of wickets — Mahanama, caught bat-pad off Mo, and then Hathurusinghe, run out for 36. The wicket was dry, and turning. Within the Aussie side was this growing feeling that things were going to happen. It was phenomenal, one of those rare days when the momentum just builds and builds. Long before the game was over I *knew* we were going to win.

Allan Border's magnificent catch of Aravinda de Silva was the turning point. De Silva, their star batsman, had chanced his arm early and lofted one which landed just over AB's head at mid-on. Not long afterwards he played the same shot again and I can still picture Border tearing off his hat and sun-glasses as he turned and set out after the ball. The skipper got there and took a magnificent catch full stretch. I'm sure the game turned on that one moment.

The pressure on their batting that day was unbelievable. It was the old story — how inexperienced players can crumble when the pressure is really on. Kaluwitharana, who had scored that brilliant century in the first innings, was a classic example. He came out and hit one cracking boundary — and then Mo bowled him clean through the gate. Right then, I thought the game was over. We finally knocked them over for 164 and so won the Test Match by 16 runs, with Shane Warne coming on to take the last three of wickets under great pressure.

Understandably, AB classed it as one of the great Test wins of his career. Having been on the losing end at Headingley in 1981, when Ian Botham won for England an Ashes Test they should have lost easily, and a couple of others where it seemed that Australia was in control, this was one back for the skipper.

The atmosphere in the dressing room was fantastic. Cans were flying around, and up into the fans that tried to cool the room. Boo Boo (David Boon) stood up and sang his stuff, and outside he gave the Aussie chant. The crowd didn't know what to make of it all.

This great ritual of Australian cricket — or at least of modern times, anyway — is guaranteed to send chills down the spine of any cricketer, lucky enough to be involved in it. It happens only after a Test match win, or victory in a one-day series. It was Rod Marsh who selected Boon to carry the baton; Marsh had done the job for years. In the dressing room after a win such as that one in Colombo there is a tremendous air of expectation.

You glance at Boo Boo, wondering when he is going to get up. And then he does — up onto the table, and recites the following:

Underneath the Southern Cross I stand.
A sprig of wattle in my hand
A native of our native land
Australia ... YOU BLOODY BEAUTY!

Then he continues ...
"Second verse ... same as the first."

I took some photos down in the tunnel, and I'll never forget the look on the faces of some of the Sri Lankans. Sheer bewilderment, disappointment, shock — they were just three of the emotions. Some of them were crying openly. They had the Test in hand, then lost it in two sessions of play.

Mo received the awards for man of the match and bowler of the match, and it soon became apparent how much it meant to him. Unlike the Sri Lankans there was no disappointment, just sheer joy. I remember walking over to him, and kissing him on the forehead.

• **The Bogey Man**

We had the distinction of playing the first game for quite a time at a place called Matara against a Southern Districts Invitation XI. The game was played between the first and second Tests. There had been awful trouble in that part of the country. Locals told us a story of how, a while before, the rebel group had captured the mayor and a number of dignitaries and executed them ... on the cricket ground ... where we were playing. Understandably there had been no cricket there since that incident, and it was a considerable honour to be part of the game's return to the region.

Matara is a truly beautiful place, much of it on the water, and provides some extraordinary sights. At low tide, you can see fishermen walk out and plonk themselves on poles that rise out of the sand. When the tide comes in you see groups of them line fishing, way out in the water, perched on the poles.

Coconuts are one of the major local crops and the trees are lashed together with ropes. The guys who pick the coconuts scamper across the ropes from tree to tree knocking down the coconuts. It saves them from having to go up and down from tree to tree.

I will always remember the match we played there because of a funny experience, involving a young quick called Dulip Liyanage. We had played against him at Kandy, and he had done pretty well. There was even some talk of him being picked for the Tests.

Young Dulip batted eight or nine. He was a big strong kid, still a teenager. I had picked up a couple of wickets by the time he came to the crease, and when he arrived I was getting advice from the boys along the lines of: "You'd better give it to this kid, Whit ... let him know what it's all about."

As I was walking back I was saying to myself: "I'm going to stick it up this bloke. He's a Test chance — he's in with the big boys."

I gave him a bouncer first ball, and it reared nicely and caught him high on the ribs, under the right armpit. The ball rolled down to Ian Healy, Dulip was rubbing the wounded spot and the boys were saying to me: "C'mon Whit ... give it to him."

The second ball was short and rising too. Dulip managed to get a glove on it, and it trickled down to fine leg. As he was running up the wicket for the single, I stopped in my follow through, right up close to him and, with a finger pointing skywards, snapped: "You'd better watch out, champ, the next one is going straight up your nose."

As we walked back towards the bowler's end, he was a couple of metres ahead of me. I heard him say something to the umpire. Then he stalked away, laid his bat down and started to rip off his gloves.

I thought to myself: Oh, shit. I've got a live one here. He's going to have a go at me!

He dropped the gloves onto his bat, then started to take his helmet off. Things were looking pretty serious. Dulip then went over and said something else to the umpire. Then the umpire gave him a handkerchief, with which he started to wipe his face. The hold-up was a minute or more now and I walked up to the umpire and asked: "What the bloody hell is going on?"

The umpire looked across and said: "I am very sorry Mr Whitney ... but Dulip thought you said he had a 'bogey' on his nose."

• The Second Test

On the day before the second Test, we had a humungus practice session. It was very, very hot, but we had a long warm-up, a huge net session and then went to the Khettarama ground for some fielding. A lot of the boys thought it was too much. There was genuine concern that if we were called on to bowl on the first day of the Test we would be jaded. Tony Dodemaide weighed 88 kilos before the session; when we returned to the dressing rooms he hopped on the scales, and was down to 84. I lost three kilos — from 95.5 to 92.5.

At night, we got together for the traditional pre-Test dinner. This one was a beauty — a barbecue around the pool, with shish kebabs, lamb chops and little chicken sausages. A standard team meeting — very standard — a couple of relaxing beers, and I crashed.

The Khettarama Stadium, where the match was played, is very good by the standards of the sub-continent. We lost the toss and were dobbed in. Before long at all we were in massive trouble at 5-109. The five included three bat-pads. Tommy Moody was given out early to one he reckoned he missed by probably a bat width. From this perilous position, Mo and Deano resurrected the cause. Deano was almost run out before he scored, and dropped when only one, but by the end of the day was 77 not out, and at 5-177 we were looking a little healthier.

I basically spent the day in the dressing room, watching the guys bat, and agonising. I'd become pretty pally with the guys in the security force who were looking after us, and I chatted to them through the day. I got on well with most of the local people here because I tried hard to make inroads into the language and to learn about the place.

That night I went for a feed with Tubby and Billy McDermott, and we had a real good talk. Mo was one topic for discussion — how he has the unhappy knack of antagonising people. Like when he was batting in this Test ...

We'd been told that we couldn't change our shirts on the field. At one point Mo actually ran off the field in his full batting kit, walked into our dressing room, and changed his shirt. The whole process probably took three minutes. Simmo, and AB in particular, were really pissed off.

"Why does he have to do things like that?" they asked.

It was an antagonistic act, but Mo just doesn't seem to think about those sort of things. Afterwards, he wonders why all the fuss, why it's cost him.

I asked Greg about it later and he said that, one, his shirt was absolutely filthy from diving to make his ground; and, two, he felt we needed to slow the game down and try and make them lose their rhythm. And, might I say, it *was* productive for the team. The partnership with Deano finally realised 72 runs and Greg finished with 55.

Different strokes for different folks!

My memories of this second Test are dominated by two things — the rain that punctuated the game, and the number of lbw decisions against us, particularly on the second day. Resuming on the second day, three blokes were absolutely fired — Dean Jones, Ian Healy and Craig McDermott. It was an absolute disgrace. I was fired after that as well — making it four lbws out of the last five wickets to fall.

At the end of the Test a couple of the journos did their sums and worked out that we'd lost 13 wickets via lbw decisions, and the Sri Lankans had lost three. The ball had swung around and seamed a lot in all the matches we played. That should have made it more difficult to get an lbw. But the local umpires just kept putting their fingers up. Innuendoes about the umpiring were flying in the media, but, to our credit, we said nothing.

I took one wicket in the first innings — bouncing out Gurusinha. I also dropped an absolute sitter of a caught-and-bowled chance given by Hathurusinghe, a bloke who plays it tough. We exchanged some words. I was very disappointed with myself.

On the last day they needed 286 to level the series, but ultimately the game just fizzled out to a disappointing draw.

Before we bowled on that last day I dived to take a catch in the warm-up and hurt my neck. Bob Simpson was hitting high balls at the warm-up and I dived for one, and actually took this amazing catch. But I fell awkwardly, and ricked my neck as I hit the ground. I felt it first of all as a dull pain in the middle of my back, but by the end of the day's play, I was in real pain. The bloody thing was sore for a long time after, even though Errol Alcott worked on it every day. It felt like it just needed a good crack to get everything back into place.

There were times on the tour when I had never felt so wasted physically. I remember AB saying to me during the third one-day game: "I've never seen you look so drawn after five overs."

That day, as I found throughout the tour, I was struggling to get air into my lungs. Sri Lanka was the most difficult place I ever played cricket in.

In the days before the third Test, I had real problems with my shoulder blade, and back. At practice before the Test was due to begin, I was getting pains flicking down my arms, and I had to rule myself out. Even when I returned to Australia it wasn't any better and for a long time I had to live with the flashes of pain that ran down my left arm every time I bowled.

The final Test was interrupted by rain, and my main memory as a spectator is of Greg Matthews getting 57 in the first innings, and 96 in the second. His second innings was just sensational. He really saved the game for us. Funny thing — we won that Test series one-nil, yet we could so easily have been beaten 3-nil if it hadn't been for the occasional brilliant individual performance. Allan Border scored 106, his first Test century for a long time, and that really added some emotion to the game for us. Right at the other end of the scale, unbelievably, Mark Waugh recorded his second successive pair. Can you comprehend that? A batsman of Waugh's calibre getting four ducks in a row against guys who were not regarded as world-class bowlers.

The odds would be about a million to one, I reckon. Cricket, as they keep telling us, is a funny game.

A Break in my Testimonial Year

In the beautiful NSW South Coast town of Berry, on a September morning soon after returning from the Sri Lankan tour, I said to Debbie: "My arm is bloody killing me. I don't think I'm going to be able to play." We were staying with my sister and brother-in-law, en-route to Bowral, where I was to take part in a State trial match the following day.

The legacy of Simmo's catch in Colombo, in the taking of which I'd badly ricked my neck, was now really biting deep. The pain had moved to the top of my shoulder, and it ached constantly. However, when I made it to the ground the next morning, I got the sniff of the game — and ended up playing not one, but *two* 50-overs matches that weekend. The pain was at a level at which I could just about keep going, with severe discomfort. It got no better, and no worse.

For the first few weeks of the season, I continued to have regular stretching and manipulation, physio and chiropractic treatment. But nothing seemed to help and gradually it began to deteriorate, to the stage that after four Mercantile Mutual Cup 50-overs games, and a Shield match against Victoria, I was living with pain 24 hours a day. At night I would toss and turn as the shoulder nagged away at me. No matter where I was, or what I was doing, I was never comfortable.

It was a demanding time in my life. My testimonial year had kicked off, and functions were in full swing. We had a huge launch at the Cricketers' Club in Sydney, and my diary was full of the reminders of upcoming meetings and functions.

The pain that was my constant companion was the one negative. It now ran from my shoulder, the length of my left arm and into the middle of my back. We had a match scheduled against WA in Perth in the middle of November, and a couple of days before I went to see Nathan Gibbs, a sports injury specialist who is the resident doctor with the NSW and Australian rugby league teams. Nathan and I had played rugby league together as kids.

A BREAK IN MY TESTIMONIAL YEAR

Nathan reckoned I had a nerve problem, and may have injured a disc in my neck. He gave me the name of a doctor in Perth, Ken McGuire. When we reached the WA capital, I visited McGuire, and subsequently had a CAT scan. This showed I had a "bulging" disc. The bulge in the disc was pressing on a nerve. Every time I bowled the disc was rubbing against the nerve, and getting more inflamed. They told me that if I kept playing, and the disc ruptured, I would be in serious trouble. The message was that if that happened to me I would never be able to play cricket again.

We made a decision — that I would play the upcoming game, and then go into hospital the morning after the last day's play and have a steroid injection into the disc and nerve.

With the help of a great pal, Noel Patterson, a Perth-based chiropractor (and genius!), I made it through the game — and successfully. I underwent constant manipulation and stretching through the four days — and came up with five wickets in the first innings and three in the second. I was delighted with the way I bowled and the fact we won the match — which was a considerable bonus.

The hospital procedure had to be done early, as I had a lunch-time testimonial function booked for that day. I was in hospital by 7.30am, where they gave me a mild anaesthetic and then the injection into my neck. By 12.30, I was at lunch, and an hour later on my feet addressing the gathering, which included, among others, D.K. Lillee. It was a huge gig, yet it seemed unreal that I had been in hospital, in pain, that morning — and here I was having a ball.

The treatment was spectacularly successful. My troubles seems to evaporate that very day. I am immensely grateful to all my expert friends — Nathan Gibbs, Liz Steet, Noel Patterson and the others — who contributed to keeping me on the paddock in the early part of what was a hugely important year for me.

Then came a downer. I made the first Australian one-day team against the West Indies, but we turned in a shocker in Perth, and were flogged. I'll never forget that game. I doubt if any Australian cricket team has ever been given more hostile treatment by a "home" crowd. Every Australian player who fielded on the boundary was ridiculed and abused. Blokes had rubbish thrown at them and there were spectators spitting, if not exactly *at* players, then certainly in the general direction of them. The spectators' attitude was motivated by the absence of any local players in the Australian XI. We didn't play well ... but we didn't deserve what we got. It was an absolute disgrace, and I've probably never been as disappointed on a cricket field in my life.

Ian Healy and myself copped most of the flak. Healy is a great competitor, a good bloke, and a very good cricketer. However, whenever he was in the action, the chant went up: "We want Zoehrer! We want Zoehrer!" Heals was booed onto the ground, booed off the ground, jeered at and had things thrown at him. But Ian Healy, like everyone else in the team, has absolutely no control over who plays in a match and who doesn't play. It wasn't *his* fault he was out there ahead of the local hero, Tim Zoehrer.

I had plenty of problems when fielding down on the fence. Fruit and empty cans rained over the fence from time to time, and the mob gave me plenty. To make matters worse, the West Indians belted us all over the ground, and the end of the game came as something of a relief.

Afterwards, we all slumped in the dressing room, not really believing what had happened. I remember Allan Border commenting that it was the worst crowd behaviour he had ever experienced in Australia. "Christ! You don't even get a serve like that when you play at Sabina Park, Kingston," said the skipper.

We had the word "Australia" plastered across the front of our shirts, but that night we didn't feel very Australian.

I missed the first Test, in Brisbane, but was picked for the second, at the MCG. And that was a great thrill. Fantastic. The Boxing Day Test in Melbourne is special in any season, and this was my third one. I was rapt in being there; Debbie came down to Melbourne for the game, we stayed in a lovely hotel and had a fine time.

For me, the best thing about that Test was that I made my highest score — 13 not out — and hooked Curtly Ambrose to the boundary, well, for three anyway. As we walked off the ground, Curtly said to me: "You know, man, when you're an old fellow you will be telling them about the day you hooked Curtly Ambrose."

I looked (up) at him and replied: "Curtly, don't worry about one day — I'll be telling them all tonight!"

I took a wicket in each innings — the left-handed Brian Lara's both times. Over the course of that season, I knocked Brian over on a number of occasions. I had this theory about bowling to him left-arm, over the wicket, into his pads. In both innings in that Melbourne Test I got him with balls that curled in really late with the arm. In the first innings, one hit the seam, jagged in as well, and trapped him plumb lbw. In the second, another one moved into him, and he flicked it off his hip to short leg, where David Boon took a magnificent catch.

I felt, during this Test, that AB didn't give me a lot of opportunities. I only bowled 13 overs in the first innings and 10 in the second, and it was very disappointing. I was feeling great about being there, about being in the team — but I wanted to bowl more.

It was the match in which Shane Warne came into his own. In their second dig, he took seven wickets and bowled the Windies out, and we won the Test. After a draw in Brisbane, we were one-up. Shane just couldn't believe what he'd done.

Not long after that first Test, we had played the West Indies in a day/night international in Sydney on a wicket that was saturated. It was a disgraceful track. The curator, Peter Leroy, has copped some flak now and then over the state of the ground. When I first started playing cricket at the SCG in 1980, the outfield was like a billiard table. The wicket by then had begun to lose the bounce and pace it had been renowned for for many years.

Over recent years the ground has looked worse each cricket season. Where once there was beautiful couch grass, there are now different grass varieties, and the SCG looks nowhere as near as pleasing to the eye as it once did. Recently, however, they have re-turfed the entire outfield and the hope is that the ground will return to what it once was.

They re-laid the wicket a couple of years ago, but it didn't make any difference. It's still a turner, as it was throughout much of the '80s, but I'm not bagging anyone for that. NSW have performed extremely well at the SCG in recent times, and the reason for that is that we have had a plethora of very good spinners over the past decade. For the wicket to be slow and turning has not been a drawback for us at all.

However, I do sometimes think there's too much technology involved these days. Out at the SCG there are machines that tell you just about everything you thought you might need to know about creating perfection in a cricket ground.

Yet for that day/night match, the bloody wicket was wet. We couldn't believe the state of the pitch, but we won the game, so the punchline was good.

Soon after, we played Pakistan in a crazy one-dayer in Hobart. That was a freak of a game which ended with one of the Pakistanis, Asif Mutjaba, hitting Steve Waugh for six off the last ball to tie the match. After the game I went into the Pakistan dressing room, and the boys were into it. They were drinking Sambucas, Cascade beer, and just about anything that was around. Under the captaincy of the great Imran Khan, things had been much quieter in the Pakistani room. But with his retirement, things had clearly become a lot more relaxed.

It seemed a little strange to see them hoe-ing into the booze. One of their leading players had invented this game called "The Statue of Liberty". He would dunk an index finger in a Sambuca, light it, and hold it above his head — while sculling the rest of the liqueur!

Before the Boxing Day Test, NSW had travelled to Adelaide to play the Centenary Sheffield Shield game. That was a marvellous experience, preceded by a memorable Centenary dinner at which I had the opportunity to talk at length with former champions like Bill Johnston, Ian Johnson,

Davo, Neil Harvey and, for an unforgettable 15 minutes, the Great Man himself, Sir Donald Bradman. Four days later, we won a terrific game when we brought off a run-out with three balls to go. I took one of the best catches of my life in this match, snaring a good mate of mine, the old warhorse, Peter "Sounda" Sleep. I caught him way, way back, in front of the scoreboard. It was a huge hit that looked as if it was going for six for sure. But it dropped about half a metre inside the fence, and I hung onto it. It turned out to be a crucial moment in a desperately close game.

For the third Test in Sydney, starting on January 2, 1993, I was relegated to 12th man. I was disappointed with that but in a strange way it worked out well for me. January 4 had long been scheduled as the date for a black-tie testimonial dinner at the Australian Jockey Club Centre at Randwick Racecourse, and, as it turned out, I sold a vast amount of testimonial gear while I was on 12th man duties. People were knocking on the dressing-room door, and buying ties, T-shirts and tickets to the dinner. Simmo reckoned there was no way I would have had time to play the game as well as do all that.

Ironically Brian Lara, who I had had the better of in Melbourne, scored 277 in the Windies' only innings of that Test. I kept mentioning I reckoned the right-armers should bowl around the wicket and into his pads, but the Australian bowlers only tried it for a limited number of overs.

Probably my only criticism of Allan Border's captaincy is that he is sometimes not flexible enough. Don't for a minute get me wrong; the bloke has done a marvellous job for Australia. But his way is to hit on a plan, and stick with it. He's not a skipper who takes a lot of risks, although in the years since 1989 he has become a lot more adventurous.

I have always believed that in cricket you must be very constructive in your thinking. Under AB, when I bowl, or one of the quicks bowls, the two major decisions he makes are do we have a short leg — which we always do — and do we have a third man — which we sometimes do and sometimes don't.

Allan's fairly static approach to field setting has been the fundamental cause of the differences between him and Greg Matthews. Greg is a bloke who likes to set his own field, and I remember well a brush between the two of them in Guyana in the West Indies in 1991. "I'll set the field and you f------ bowl," said Border to Matthews.

Mo has been a fantastic bowler for NSW, but at Test level his record is not so good. The thing is, all the captains that he's played under at Shield level — Rick McCosker, Dirk Wellham, Greg Dyer, Geoff Lawson, Mark Taylor and Phil Emery — knew how to best use Mo; how to massage him to get the best out of him.

They'd always give him half a yard of rope in the business of field setting, and because they did that he was always very productive for them.

Sometimes the bloke does some strange things, although to him they're not strange at all. I might be out at square leg, some 50 or 60 metres from the bat and he'll want me to move two paces to my left. Two paces! But if I don't move the two paces it upsets his concentration.

The way it works within the NSW team is that Mo still goes through the captain when he's changing the field — so the skipper doesn't lose any sense of authority — but the field set is basically the one that Greg wants. We understand that if the bloke is relaxed then he's going to bowl well, and, if he bowls well, he's going to be a great strike weapon for us.

The Mike Whitney testimonial night on January 4 turned out to be a thoroughly memorable occasion for me. To have almost 1000 people rise as one to applaud a career in cricket was almost overwhelming. It was a very, very humbling experience.

I still can't quite come to terms with the amount of hard work that went into that night, and the year in toto. My testimonial committee — Steve Rixon, Steve Devlin, Wayne Martin, Lyall Gardner and Phil Tresidder — did a magnificent job, while my wife and best friend, Debbie, put in an unbelievable effort in organising that black-tie night almost on her own, along with a tonne of other work.

It was a super night. Allan Border came up at one stage to say that he goes to hundreds of dinners but that he had never enjoyed one more. The principle of testimonial events for professional sportsmen has its critics. My view is that in almost every case they are thoroughly deserved. A sportsman or sportswoman has, after all, only a limited life in the sporting field they have selected. Inevitably, they have worked single-mindedly and doggedly to develop their skills — and those skills very often bring great pleasure to the people who watch them. Few have a superannuation scheme to provide a golden handshake when it's all over. In cricket, we have a retirement fund, but the reality of that is that unless you play a lot of Tests, you're not going to make too much out of it.

I think the thing I enjoyed most about my testimonial year was being able to meet again the people who have brushed up against my career in some capacity over the years.

It was a fantastic time for me.

After the Sydney Test — a draw — we headed to Brisbane for the next one-dayer against the Windies. I get on well with the 'Gabba. Until they removed the dog track that surrounded the playing area in the 1993 off-season, the ground was on the small side and gave the batsmen good value for their shots. But I had always enjoyed bowling there, and experienced reasonable success.

The game ran its course as one-dayers do, and reached the exciting stage where M. Whitney, last man in, was required at the crease with nine balls to go and six runs to win.

Tim May nudged a single, and I took my guard against the fast bowler, Kenneth Benjamin. First ball, Benjamin sent down an attempted yorker that was about shin-high. It was heading down the leg-side and I shaped to flick it on. The ball, however, had different ideas, and after catching the inside edge landed right on top of my left foot. Ouch! From there it ran away towards fine-leg, and we scampered through for a single.

At the bowler's end, I was doing the running-on-the-spot bit, flexing my toes, and trying to get my foot going. I wasn't thinking that it might be broken, but the bloody thing was hurting alright. Tim and I had a mid-wicket conference. We decided that he had to take a single off the next ball. It was the last ball — and it appeared the off-spinner, Carl Hooper, would be bowling the final over. There was no argument that Tim was a much better chance of hitting Hooper for a boundary than I was.

So, Benjamin's last ball. May blocked it into the covers and took off. So did I. But I only got about a third of the way down the wicket when Tim hollered: "No!" As I planted my left foot to turn I could feel it *click*. I spun around as quickly as I could and headed back, but too late. Richie Richardson fired the ball to Gus Logie, who ran me out by about a metre. They'd won the game and all I had to look forward to was the long walk.

When I returned to the dressing room, I looked for Errol Alcott. "Shit, that hurt!" I told him. By this time, it was really starting to ache. I got the gloves and pads off, then my boots and socks, and there in the middle of the old left foot was a nasty little lump. Errol called in the Queensland Cricket Association doctor, Tom Dooley, a bloke who sports the nickname of "Hang Down" (as in *Hang Down Your Head, Tom Dooley*). Tom had a bit of a look and a feel and declared: "Mate, that's broken."

"Piss off, Tom. Get outta here," I responded. "I don't want to hear that kind of crap."

Errol took a more common-sense view, and organised for me to go across to the Mater Hospital, which is just at the back of the ground.

I was sitting there with all these thoughts going through my head: "I hope like hell it isn't busted ... that's the last thing I need ... Six days after the big dinner, and with plenty more to do ... I'm in good shape to play all the one-dayers ... then there's the tour of England ... the chance to finally make up for 1989."

I was sitting there thinking, and fiddling with my second toe, and it was making this clicketty-click noise. Later I discovered that was caused by the bones nudging against each other. "Errol," I said. "Can you hear that clicking?"

"I don't think you'd better do that," he warned.

A BREAK IN MY TESTIMONIAL YEAR

They X-rayed me before long, and after a while a bloke came in and said: "Do you want the good news or the bad news?"

"Give me the bad," I said.

"Well, it's pretty badly broken," he replied.

"Okay, what's the f------ good news?" I asked.

"There ain't none."

We all laughed. We had to.

Errol consoled me. He's a good pal to all the players, and I think their hurts are his hurts. He's a real pro.

They encased the foot in a big plaster, stuck a heel cap on it, gave me a pair of crutches, and dispatched me into the night. We took a cab back to the hotel, and it was a quiet trip. I was shattered, absolutely shattered. I was almost 34 years of age, edging towards the finish of my career, and now this had happened. I needed to be on the paddock, not hobbling around on crutches, if I was to achieve what I wanted out of the remainder of my career.

In fact, I beat the boys back to the hotel, but there were some phone calls, and I received a telegram from AB, who had gone back to his Brisbane home.

"Keep your chin up," it read.

I felt really good about that. I have a mountain of respect for the bloke. He's had a tough job, real tough — and he's had to carry the can for an enormous number of things. There were times when he absolutely carried the team. I couldn't hold him in any higher regard.

I rang Debbie, my sister and my mother — and resisted an offer from Mo and Peter Jackson, the Australian, Queensland and North Sydney league five-eighth, to join them for a drink at the Brisbane Rowers' Club. I didn't feel like talking. I grabbed my diary and put my leg up.

I'll admit the thought crossed my mind — that this could be the end. I studied the diary hard that night, working out dates in six ... seven ... eight weeks' time when I might make a comeback — dates that would still give me time to make a claim for that England tour.

The trip home from Brisbane was a real struggle in more ways than one. The other blokes had headed on elsewhere, and I was on my own, trying to juggle luggage and crutches and a bloody sore foot. When I battled off the plane in Sydney, there were three reporters and three cameramen waiting to intercept me. Suddenly the lights were on and the microphones were under my nose. It was the first time in my life as a professional sportsman that I felt the media were intruding into my life. I really didn't want to talk, but they persisted. Eventually I pleaded: "How about a bit of privacy, guys?" Still one camera kept whirring. I spun on the bloke and said: "Listen mate, if you don't turn that camera off I'm going to stick it right up your arse." Or maybe I said "down your throat". It was a pretty strong statement from a one-legged bloke. I eventually did a couple of quick interviews downstairs — but I was feeling pretty low, and really objected to the intrusion that morning.

The esteemed orthopaedic surgeon, Merv Cross, referred me to a doctor named Kim Slater who was an expert on feet. He had some more X-rays taken, and then gave me a choice in two. The first was the full plaster cast. Result — out for the rest of the cricket season. The second was to have a plate inserted, with four screws joining the bones. Possible result: back in eight weeks.

While he was explaining, I was doing the mathematics. Eight weeks would get me back on the paddock for two Shield games, against South Australia and Victoria, plus the final — if NSW made it. My decision was made.

The next morning I turned up at the Castlecrag Private Hospital and they stuck a six-centimetre steel plate in my foot. When I was released the next morning, I headed straight off on a magic mission, to see Kevin Dalton, more commonly known as the "Magnet Man". Kevin reckoned that the use of a magnet would speed up the healing process by 50 per cent or so, so I borrowed a big one off him, and off I went. On the same day I was knocking on the door of my physio, Liz Steet. I was ready to do the hard yards ... that's what I call it ... ready to start straight away on what I knew would be a painful rehabilitation process.

The battle began. My big toe and second toe had gone numb, because the doctor had had to cut a nerve to get at the break. I was told the feeling would eventually come back. I bought a special boot from Kim Slater, for 60 bucks, so I could get around a bit better, and have a little bit more protection for the foot ... sort of half-hop around the place.

The first week I was home was a nightmare. Debbie took it for a while before she snapped and really ripped in to me.

"Wake up to yourself," she told me. "Snap out of it and get on with your life."

And you know what? Suddenly, everything opened up for me. It's often the way that opportunity can come out of misfortune and it sure happened to me. In my testimonial year, I was suddenly in enormous demand on the speaking circuit. I was injured, and available, and the offers started coming in. Then John Gayleard, from Channel Nine, rang: "Would I like to join the commentary team for the fourth and fifth Tests?"

Would I!

For one thing, the offer gave me the chance to stay involved, however tenuously, with a Test series I had been a part of. But more than that, the commentary opportunity, and all the other invitations that came in, were a catalyst for me to start thinking about what I was going to do A.C. — after cricket. For all of us in sport there's a morning when we wake up with the realisation that it's all over. A morning when we have to face up to beginning what is virtually a new life. For more than one reason, I jumped at the chances offered to me at this time.

Meanwhile I worked away on the injury. I started a swimming program, and started on sit-ups and upper body work. In my mind was the goal of playing in the match against South Australia.

During the fourth Test in Adelaide the stitches came out of my foot. What a game that was. My first in the commentary box — and the smallest winning margin in the history of Test cricket. The West Indies' one-run win over the Aussies was one of the great ones, and climaxed in Craig McDermott's dismissal, caught by keeper Junior Murray off Courtney Walsh, after Billy and Tim May, who scored 42, had added 40 runs for the Test's last wicket, and all but won the game for Australia. How tough a call was that final out for NSW umpire Darrell Hair? The ball, pitched in short, had flicked Billy's helmet and *then* the glove, before going through to the keeper.

For that Test, and the fifth Test in Perth, I was over the moon about being part of the Channel Nine team. I was there with men such as Richie Benaud, Ian Chappell, Greg Chappell, Tony Greig, Bill Lawry, David Gower, Michael Holding. The minimum number of Tests that any of them had played was Tony's 58. I had played 12. Yet, there I was, in the box with them.

Everyone on the Nine team treated me generously, and helped provide for the "new chum" an atmosphere of warmth and friendship. Tony Greig and Ian Chappell were particularly helpful in steering me through, and it was a real thrill to work with them.

The swimming therapy gradually started to become more enjoyable. I'd never really been much of a swimmer; I'd been a surfer, but never a bloke who swam laps and laps. I kicked off swimming at the Sydney Football Stadium pool, but that became very boring and I said to Debbie one day: "Let's go down to Clovelly and I'll swim a couple of laps there."

Clovelly is one of the more unusual of Sydney's beautiful ocean beaches in that it has a long and deep "inner harbour", protected from the surf. I had built up to swimming about 500 metres a session by that time, and figured I'd swim out to the rock wall and back at Clovelly, a distance of about 500 metres. But when I dived in, the water was absolutely crystal clear, and I soon came to realise that the sea life that abounds in that "pool" is phenomenal. There are bream, whiting, flathead and a huge blue groper that has lived there for many years, usually accompanied by a mate about two-thirds his size. I was really carried away looking down at the sea-life, and finished up swimming four laps — and doing it easily — because my mind wasn't really on the grind of the swim itself. I was captivated by all the things I could see.

Throughout my rehabilitation, a bloke named Tim Wharton, from Sydney's Channel Seven, followed me around, putting together a feature story on my fight to get back to cricket. He ended up winning a NSW Cricket Association's Award for the piece he produced.

After eight weeks of agony, despair and only forlorn hope, I came back and bowled in the nets one afternoon, then played in a one-day grade game at Coogee Oval. I bowled 10 overs that day, and took two wickets, at around four runs per over. My pace was okay, but I lacked rhythm. We lost that game, the final of the one-day competition, to North Sydney, but the feeling of being back on the paddock again was fantastic. That night the foot blew up like a balloon and I thought I was in trouble again. The swelling, was, however, just something I needed to get used to. From that game, until the end of the season, every time I ran, my foot swelled. Funny things, feet. You don't give 'em a thought until something goes wrong — then you realise how much you need them!

On the strength of my one-day grade return, the Shield selectors picked me for the match in Melbourne. I had missed the SA game; I just wasn't ready for it. To bring me straight back against the Vics was a fabulous vote of confidence of which I was greatly appreciative. However, I only took one wicket in the game — that of Simon O'Donnell. He hit a brilliant 86 in their second dig, but I got him with a slower one that hit the seam and moved a bit. He nicked it and was caught behind.

I was happy with that wicket, and delighted to be back. But the match rammed home to me the fact that I was a long way short of peak fitness. We won the game, on the back of a magnificent performance from Cracker Holdsworth, to shoot to the top of the table — and thus get the bonus of staging the Shield final on our home patch.

The big question was ... would I get a game? Holdsworth and first-season quick Glenn McGrath were going great guns, and we were bound for the turning wicket of the SCG. I couldn't remember NSW going into a game there without at least two spinners. In my own mind I knew I had to play if I was to be any chance at all of going to England. It pretty well came down to our left-arm "Chinaman" bowler, David Freedman, or me — and there was much speculation in the press.

It was an awkward one for the selectors, and I spoke to three of them — Neil Marks, Steve Bernard and Alan Campbell — and gave them my view that they must set sentiment completely aside when they were picking the team. I wanted to play, of course, but I made the point to them that they must pick the team they believed could win the match.

We were to play Queensland, and on the morning of the match we went out, as always, to warm up, have a look at the wicket and talk about the job at hand. It was then they announced the team — and I was in it. This was a terrific vote of confidence in me, and piled on some pressure, too. It was a five-day match, and we were now a bit skinny in the spin-bowling department — something which could have been very significant in the match's final stages.

As it turned out, we won easily. We bowled first and I had their opener, Trevor Barsby, dropped two or three times in the slips before I finally had him caught behind, after I had switched to the other end. Barsby was to be my only wicket for the game. I thought I bowled pretty well, but I still lacked the rhythm and match fitness I had before the injury. You can huff and puff around the block; you can swim hundreds of laps of the pool; you can pump weights and run the treadmill in the gym — but nothing you can do compensates for actually bowling in a game.

Thanks to brilliant performances from Wayne and Glenn, I didn't even get a bowl in the second innings of the final. After the Maroons had totalled 311, we crawled to 341, and then, after lunch on the fourth day, they came out and were all out for 75! — with Cracker getting seven, and Glenn three. It was one of the most inspirational sessions of cricket I had ever played in. We needed just 46 to wrap up the Shield, and managed nine of them before stumps. As we walked off the ground, at the end of the Queensland second innings, Greg Matthews put an arm around my shoulders and said: "In all the Shield matches we have played together can you ever remember an innings in which *neither* of us got a bowl?" I couldn't.

On that day I saw the shape of things to come in NSW cricket, and realised that the fast bowling future of the team was in great hands. It wasn't that I was obsolete *quite* yet, but there were some young punks coming up who were really starting to do the business.

We had a few beers that night, but not too many. The match still had to be wrapped up next morning. And we did it without too much pain, with Adam Gilchrist and Michael Bevan knocking over the runs. Unfortunately Jack Small was not at the wicket to be part of it, as he had fallen the previous afternoon, caught in the gully as he smashed at one in characteristic fashion. It was a shame, because it was Jack's last innings for NSW.

Jack and I shared the same corner of the SCG dressing room. They called it the "Old School". I said to him after he had been knocked over: "Are you going to miss it?"

"Yeah, of course I'll miss it," he said. "But I'm not going to miss the f------ bruises."

It was as big a thrill as ever to win the Shield, and especially in its centenary year. They held the presentation out on the ground, and I spared a thought for the Queenslanders. They've been positioned to win the thing plenty of times but for some reason they always stumble in the straight, as they did in this match.

The presentation over, I was held up briefly on the field, doing a television interview, and was five minutes behind the others in getting back to the dressing room. When I walked back in, it was as quiet as a graveyard, with players and officials just standing around.

I had a bottle of Resch's Real Ale in my mitt and yelled at them: "C'mon you bastards, we've just won the Sheffield Shield Final!!" I shook up the bottle, and there was beer spraying everywhere.

As I let fly with the beer spray, I looked around the room — and realised that the Governor of NSW, Rear Admiral Peter Sinclair, was standing there with the NSWCA President, Alan Davidson. At this stage most of the bottle of beer that I had sprayed high into the air was suspended over the Guv, and descending rapidly. There was nothing I could do, except stand there, mouth agape.

When they turned, Davo had the shittiest look on his face and I thought to myself: you're in a bit of trouble here, son. Attack being the best form of defence I walked up to His Excellency and said: "Geez, I'm sorry Guv, I didn't realise you were in the room."

"Michael, don't worry about it. You've just won the Sheffield Shield," he said.

We had a bit of a laugh, although Alan Davidson's was somewhat forced.

Later Davo had a quiet word with me about the incident. Unfortunately he had been wearing a bone-coloured suit, and the beer stains were clearly visible on the shoulders. The Governor was better dressed for such an event — in a dark suit. This was the only time Alan Davidson ever growled at me. I love the bloke; he has been fantastic for me throughout my career.

(The Great Beer Drench has become an infamous moment in NSW cricket history. It received more than a few mentions when the Governor hosted a cocktail party for the NSW team to kick off the 1993-94 season.)

One event remained in that cricket season. The naming of the touring team to England. I received the news early, from a mate of mine in Melbourne, that I hadn't made it — and the phone call sort of softened the blow when the side was officially announced. My hat was in the ring, and I would have loved to have made it, but, frankly, I would have been surprised if they had picked me.

I thought they picked a good side, although I felt sorry for a couple of young blokes — Michael Kasprowicz from Queensland, who had bowled magnificently through the year, although tailing off just a little near the end, and WA's Justin Langer, who had batted three and then opened the innings in the last two Tests against the West Indies. He showed real quality, and tonnes of courage in the way he gutsed it out against Ambrose and company, and then toured New Zealand and played in three Tests there.

However, the real mystery to me was the non-selection of Greg Matthews. Over all the years there have only been three guys in the history of Australian cricket who have taken 50 wickets and scored 500 runs in an Australian first-class season. The champion South Australian, George Giffen, who played all his cricket well before the First World War, did it twice, and so did the famous West Indian, Gary Sobers, when he was out here playing for South Australia in the early '60s. Mo Matthews had done it twice too, in the last two seasons — yet he wasn't rated good enough for the tour.

However, the selectors pick the team they think will do the best job, and I'm not about to argue with them. After all, the team they picked won four Tests to one!

Calling the Shots

In England, in the northern summer of 1993, I joined the fourth estate, conscripted by Channel Nine for their commentary team for the last three Ashes Tests. If I couldn't make AB's team, well, this was the next best thing.

I paid my own fare for the privilege of joining the tour, a plane fare for M. Whitney not being in Nine's budget. My wages were 250 pounds per day for the days I worked — 15 of the 42 days Debbie and I were in England. It was in no way a financial bonanza; Deb and I had to cover all costs on the days I wasn't working — accommodation, car hire and so on. But I was delighted to be there — to have the chink of an opportunity open up for me in the field of cricket commentating. If I had said no to the invitation, I might never have been asked again.

One of the first telephone calls I made on arrival was to Bob Simpson in Leeds. I was keen to keep fit, and to get ready for the next season after my disjointed 1992-93 campaign, and I asked him if I could have a roll-over with the boys in the nets. He said yes, and I was most appreciative of Simmo and AB giving me that chance. But, before I linked with the team for some practice sessions, I first of all had a little explaining to do ...

Back home I had written a piece for the Sydney *Telegraph Mirror*, on the theme of "Give Cracker a Go". In the article I had called on the tour selectors to give Wayne Holdsworth his chance. I had discussed Paul Reiffel and Brendon Julian — how neither had set the world on fire on the tour — and made a few observations from afar on the pair of them.

On arrival in Leeds I sought out both Reiffel and Julian and told them what I had written. I wanted to be fair dinkum with them; I didn't want the story sneaking back to them second-hand, and cause ill-feeling. Basically, I had only spelled out the way things had been for both of them to that point.

The day after, Reiffel went out and took 5-65 in his first Test in England. It's amazing how quickly you can be made to eat humble pie! Bloody good luck to him. He grabbed his chance by the throat and shook the life out of it. I had always thought that "Pistol" was a good trier — a good, steady fast-

Confined to the grandstand, in Albury, a week after my arm was broken by a ball from Queensland fast bowler Craig McDermott, in a Shield match at Newcastle, early in the 1989-90 season.

All pics News Limited

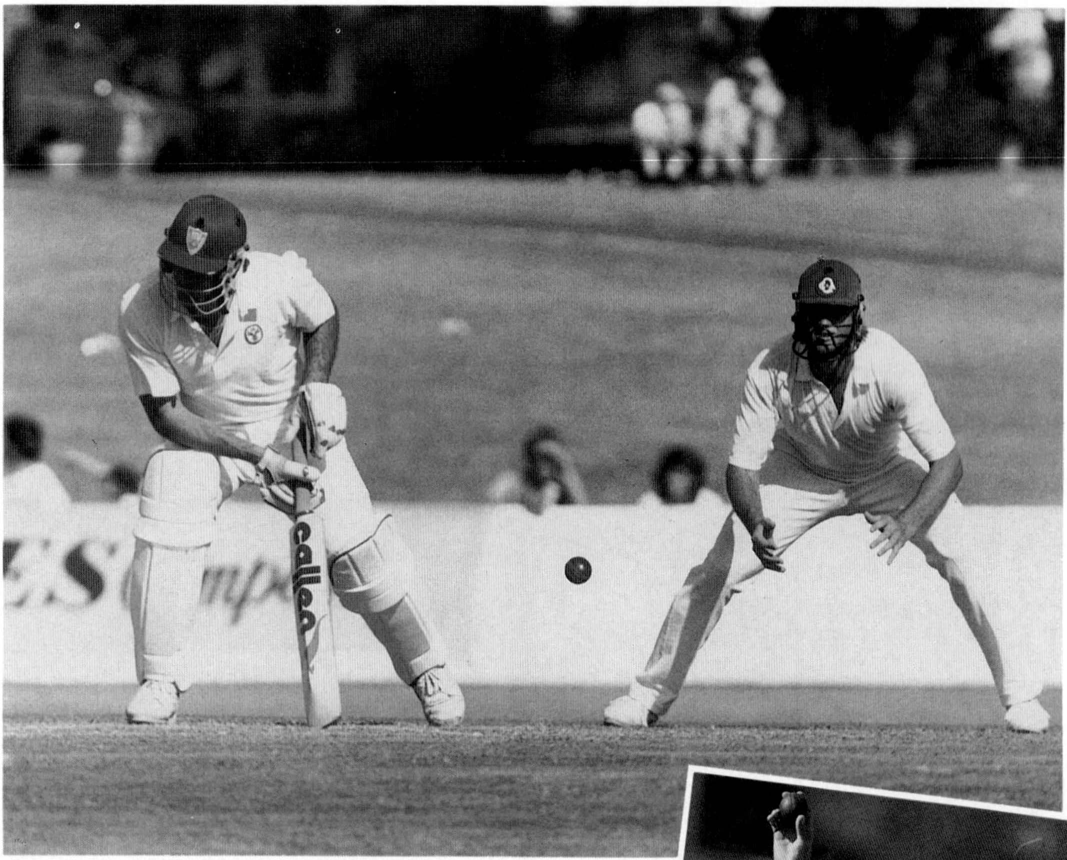

Above: The fateful moment when the arm was shattered. The short leg is Glenn Trimble.

Below: It took a while for the seriousness of the injury to reveal itself. I batted on for a short period, but then called for the physio, who advised me to leave the field. The other people are (left to right) Greg Ritchie, Margaret Keech (physio), Peter Cantrell, Phil Emery, Greg Matthews.

Right: The injury left me with no alternative but to practise in unorthodox ways.

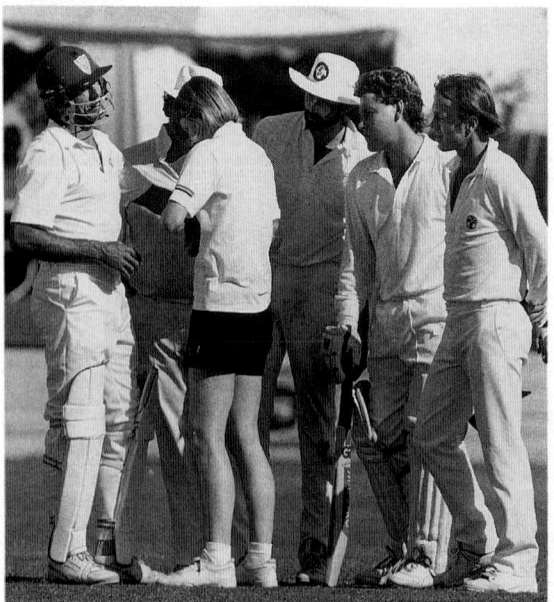

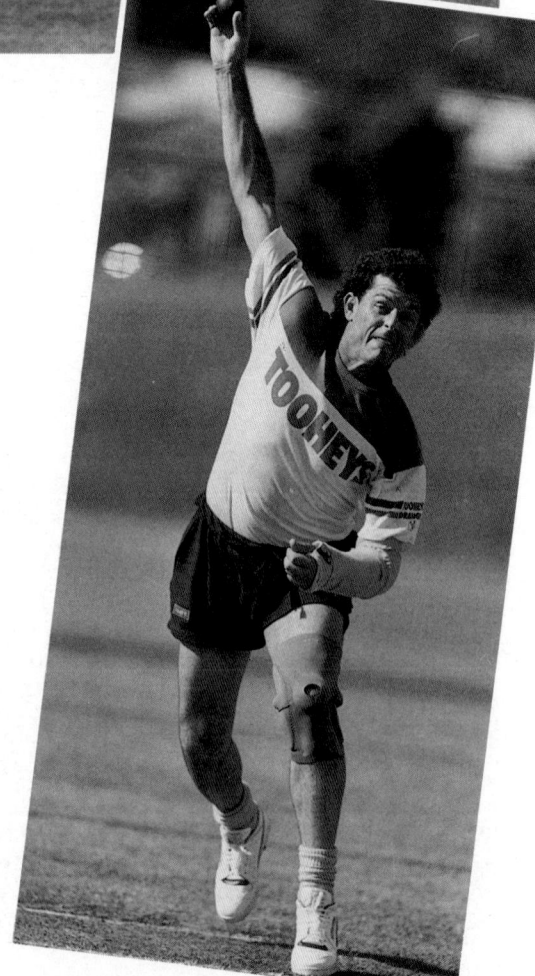

By season's end, 1989-90, I was back on the paddock and able to hoist the Sheffield Shield high after our decisive win over ... Queensland. The photo below shows the Blues team after the presentations. Back row (left to right): Trevor Bayliss, Adrian Tucker, Steve Waugh, Greg Matthews, Peter Taylor, Mark Waugh, Wayne Holdsworth; Front row: Mark O'Neill, Steve Small, Phil Emery, Mark Taylor, Geoff Lawson, Mike Whitney.

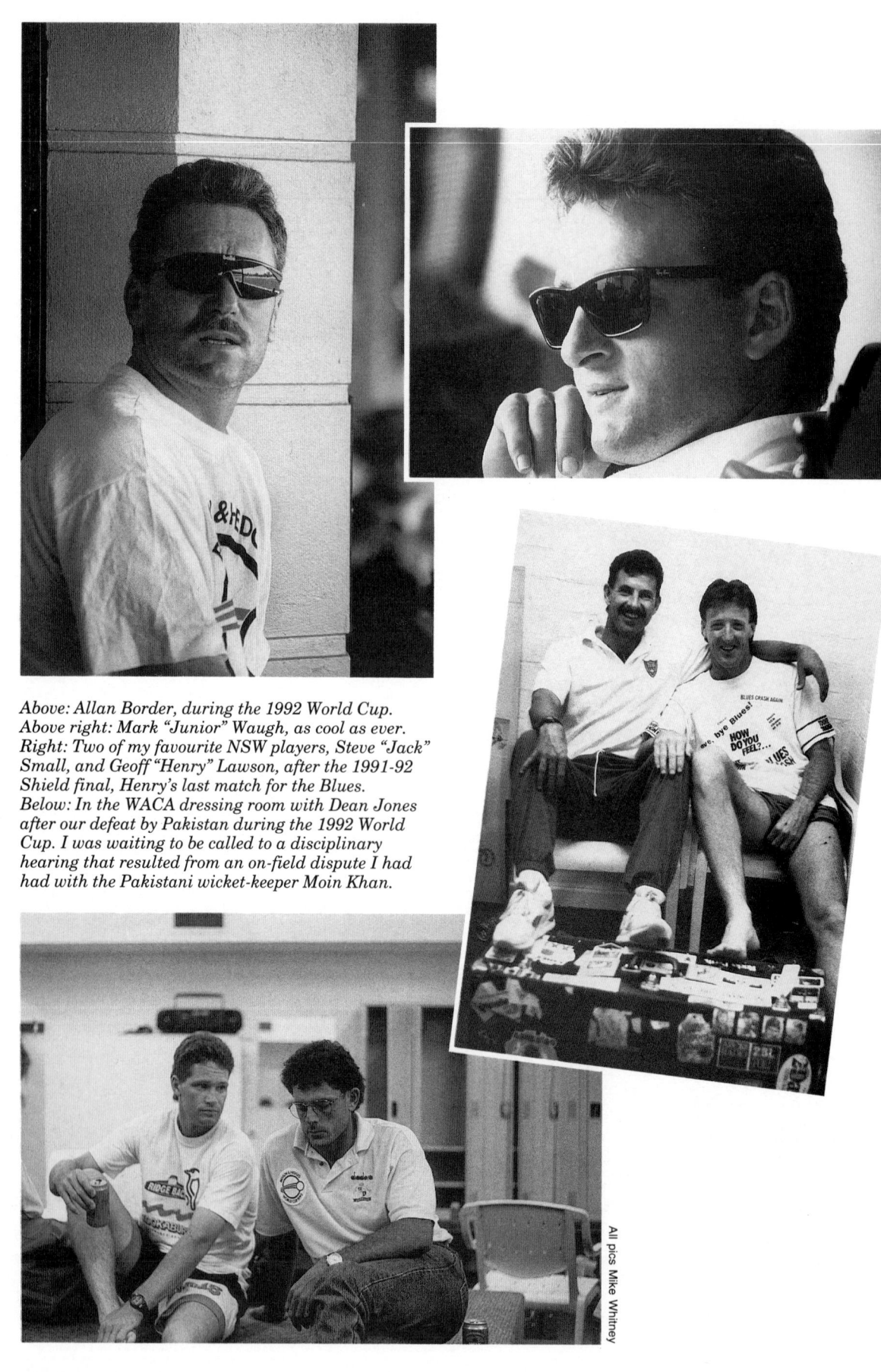

*Above: Allan Border, during the 1992 World Cup.
Above right: Mark "Junior" Waugh, as cool as ever.
Right: Two of my favourite NSW players, Steve "Jack" Small, and Geoff "Henry" Lawson, after the 1991-92 Shield final, Henry's last match for the Blues.
Below: In the WACA dressing room with Dean Jones after our defeat by Pakistan during the 1992 World Cup. I was waiting to be called to a disciplinary hearing that resulted from an on-field dispute I had had with the Pakistani wicket-keeper Moin Khan.*

All pics Mike Whitney

Top: Steve Waugh, a very special player. Above left: the unmistakable image of Greg Matthews. Above: AB with cricket's new face of the '90s, Shane Warne. Left: Craig McDermott, Mark Taylor, Errol Alcott's son Adam, Errol Alcott, Shane Warne and Tom Moody in Kandy, Sri Lanka. The guys were dressed in sarongs because they were not permitted into a local temple wearing shorts.

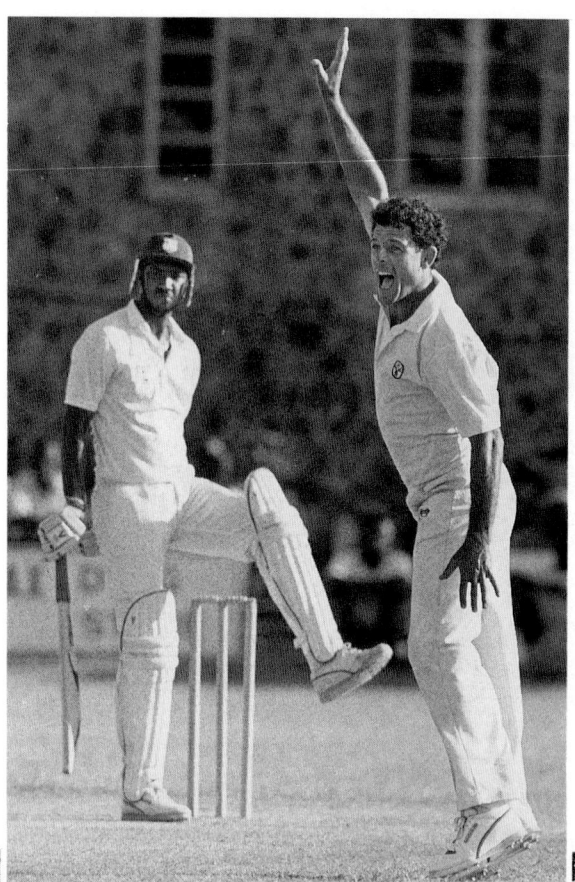

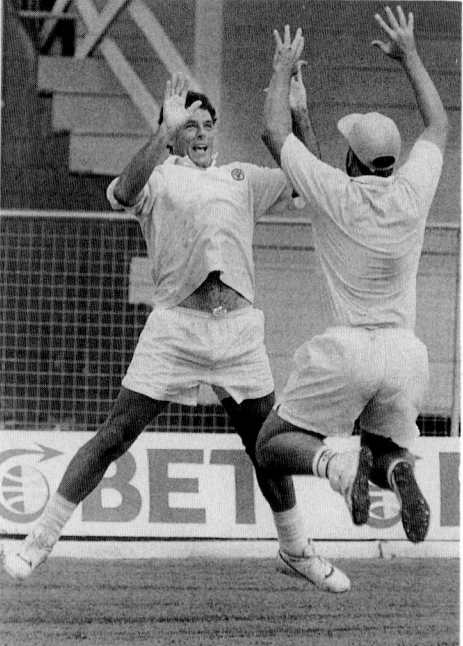

Images of the 1991 Australian tour of the West Indies. Left: Appealing for lbw against Robert Haynes in St Kitts. Below: High-fives with Mark Taylor after completing a fielding drill, and winning the side bets, in Barbados.

All pics Gregg Porteous

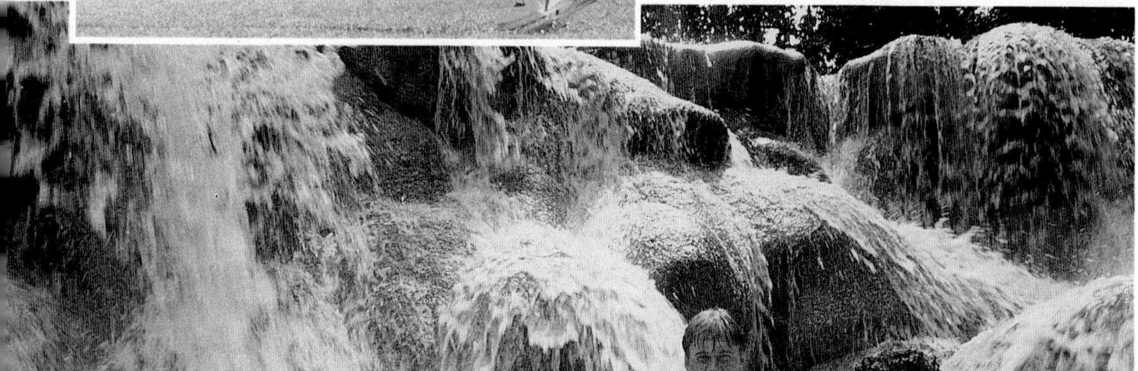

Above: Enjoying the local environment in Jamaica during the rest day of the first Test. The players are (left to right): Ian Healy, Steve Waugh, Peter Taylor, Bruce Reid and Mike Whitney.

All pics Gregg Porteous

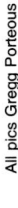

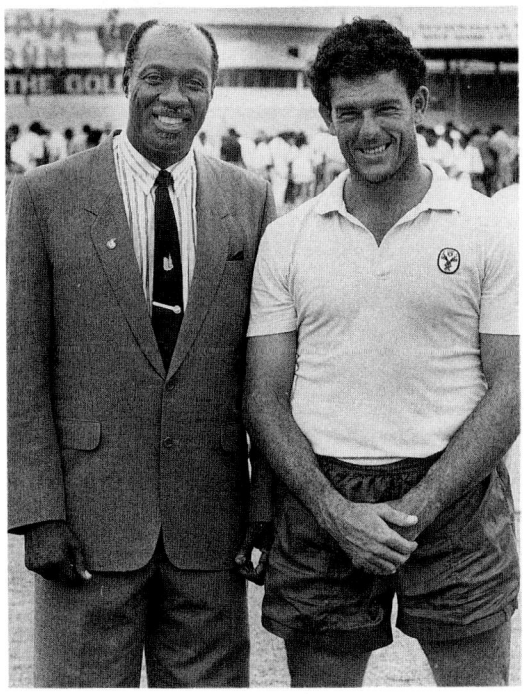

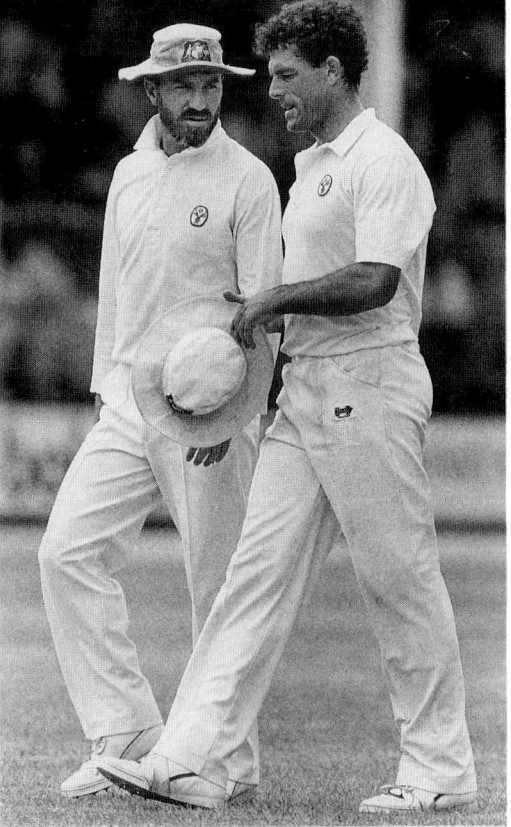

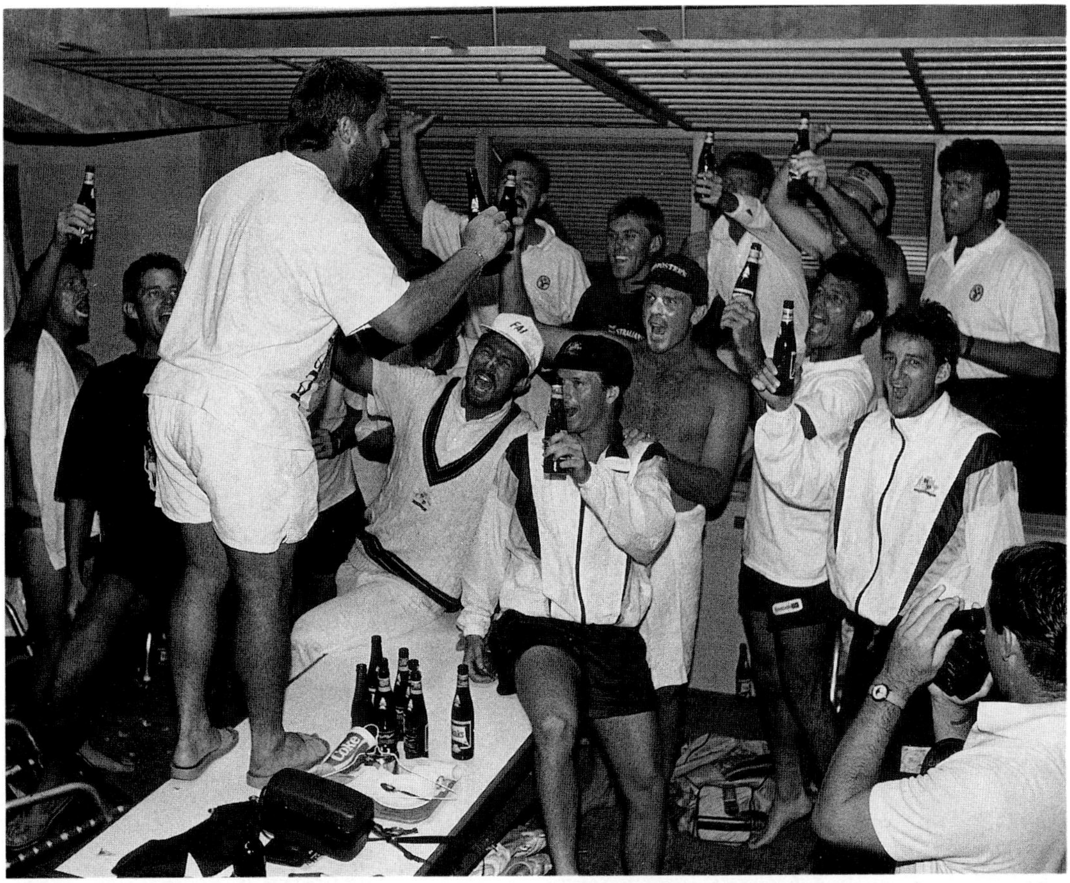

Above: David Boon leads the celebrations after our win in the fourth one-day International, in Barbados, that clinched the five-match series.
Below: With the fast-bowling legend, Wes Hall.
Right: With "Mo" Matthews after a fruitless over during the second Test in Guyana.

Left: The cricket gear of Allan Border waits to be taken to the middle for another long innings.

Below: Bowling for NSW against India at Lismore in 1991-92. The follow-through is a little more controlled than in my earlier years!

Below: Test team physio Errol Alcott, with his son Adam in the botanical gardens of Kandy. Below right: What the Australian dressing room at the MCG can look like while a Test is in progress.

Congratulations after my catch of India's Sachin Tendulkar in the second World Series Cup final match of 1991-92. The Australians are (left to right): Allan Border, Geoff Marsh, Mark Waugh and Tom Moody.

Above: One of the main talking points to come out of Australia's World Cup clash with Pakistan in Perth in 1992 was my confrontation with Moin Khan. The incident started when he sledged me after an appeal for a catch behind off their leg-spinner Mushtaq Ahmed had been disallowed. I didn't like what he said, and told him so, and the thing reached the stage where the Pakistan captain, the great Imran Khan, had to come between us. At a hearing later, Moin claimed he didn't speak English. I knew for a fact that wasn't true.
Left: With the legendary Ian Botham during practice before the Australia-England World Cup match.
Right: A mix-up with Craig McDermott in the match against South Africa. This picture pretty much sums up Australia's World Cup. We were rarely at our best.

News Limited

This photo was taken after I took my seventh (and the innings' last) wicket of the Indian second innings of the fifth Test of the 1991-92 series. My bowling figures — 7-27 — were the best of my career.

Left: The humidity and heat in Sri Lanka are such that sometimes any possible method must be used to get the cricket gear dry.

Above: Greg Matthews gets a haircut in Kandy.

Below: Our tour, in September 1992, was the first to Sri Lanka by an international team since the New Zealanders of 1987. The passion and fervour the Sri Lankans have for their cricket was there for all to see.

All pics Michael Whitney

Above: One of my favourite cricketers is Merv Hughes. I share his love for the game, and admire his guts, his ability, his character ... and his ability to win over the fans.

Right: There's nothing I can teach Mark Waugh about batting ... but maybe there's a thing or two I can demonstrate when it comes to playing the didgeridoo.

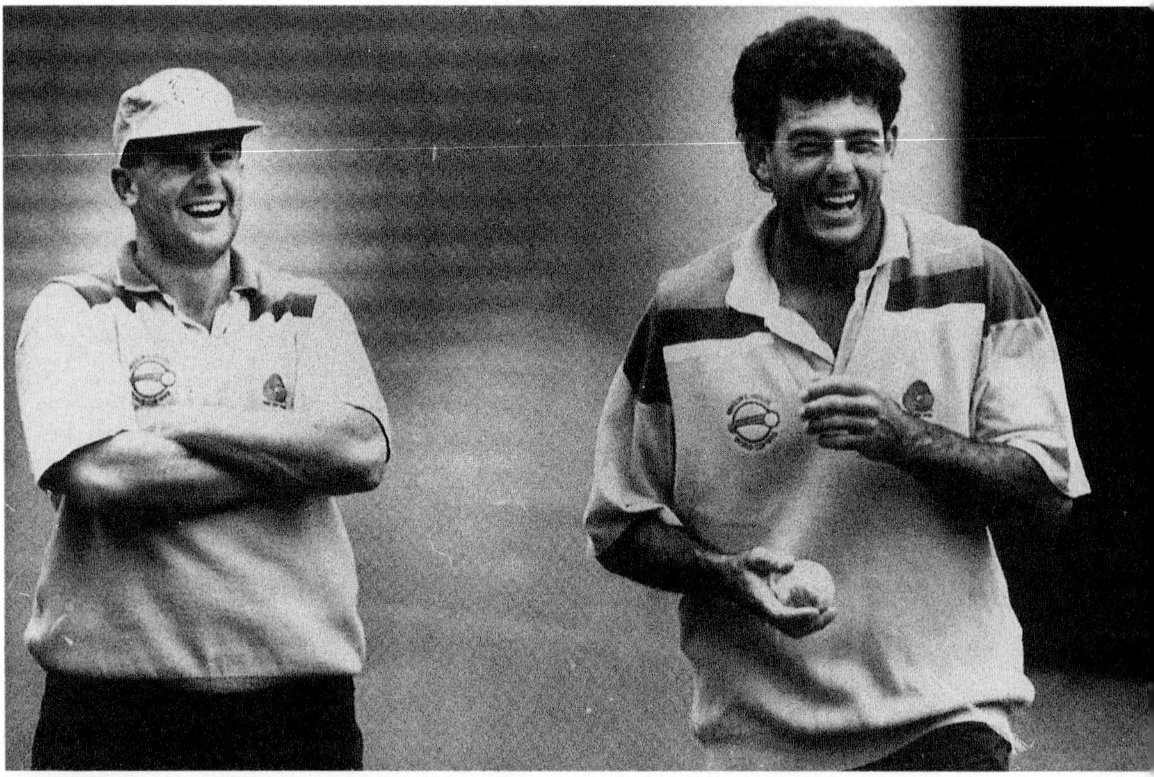

News Limited

News Limited

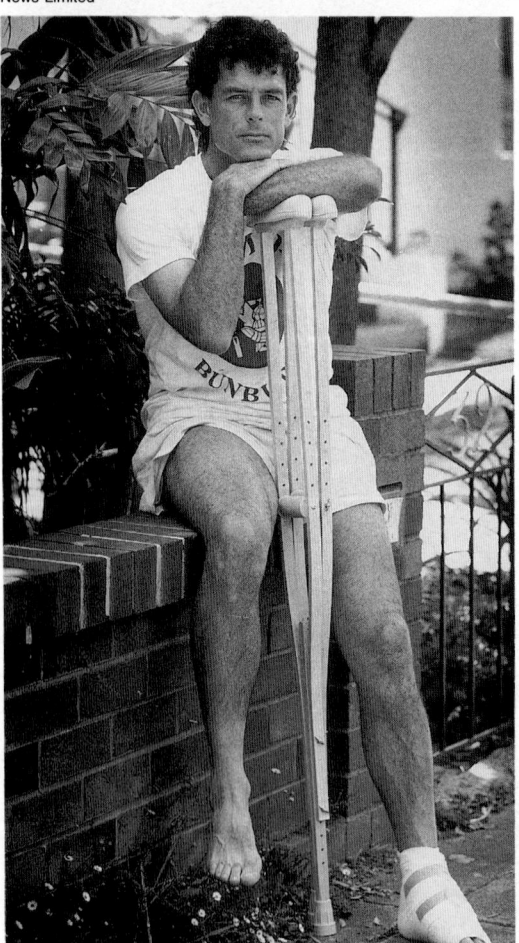

Above: Sharing a laugh with Mark Taylor during the 1992 World Cup. I was enjoying life in the Australian side ... but, less than 12 months later, the broken foot (left) I suffered wrecked my chances of going on the 1993 Ashes tour.
Below: With funnyman Andrew Denton, on the set of his ABC-TV sports show, Live and Sweaty.

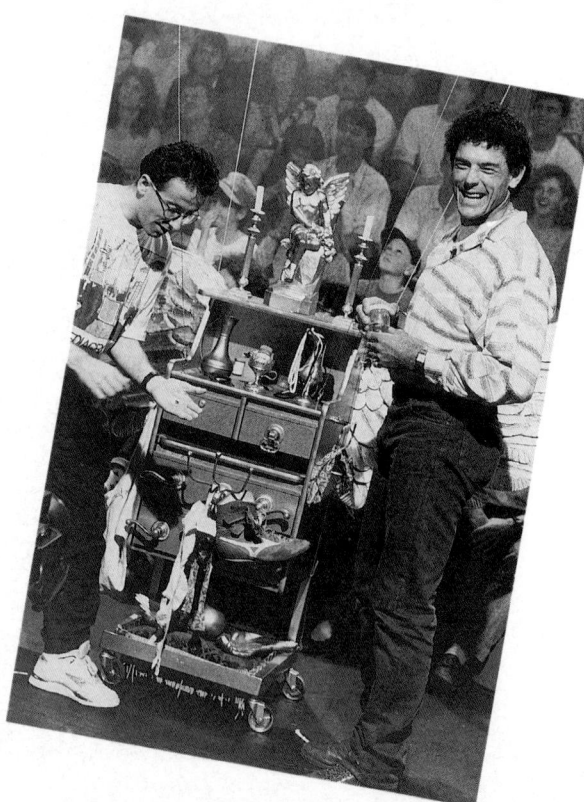

Left: Even though I missed selection in the 1993 Ashes side, I went over to England to call the cricket for Channel Nine. While there I was co-opted to bowl some overs in the Australian nets.

Below: While in England, Debbie and I, and two friends, were involved in a potentially disastrous accident, after a steel bar smashed into the windscreen of our car while we were driving down the motorway to Manchester. This photo shows the damage caused. Fortunately no-one was hurt.

Below: One of the heroes of the Ashes series was Michael Slater, who is one of my very favourite cricketers. When he returned from England he was married in his hometown of Wagga Wagga, and I was lucky enough to be among the guests.

One of the new stars of NSW cricket is Richard Chee Quee, a young batsman of Chinese descent, who plays for my club, Randwick. Before the start of the 1993-94 season, the Blues' sponsor, Reschs, organised a team photo in which all the players dressed up as Santa Claus. However, the sight of a Chinese Father Christmas was too much for me, and I just cracked up.

medium bowler. But in the Leeds Test he moved the ball both ways off the seam, and the Poms couldn't cope with him.

With me in my new commentating role, watching from the Channel Nine box at the Kirkstall Lane end at Headingley, the Aussie batsmen really took England's attack apart. Border a double century, Boon a century, Steve Waugh 157 not out — it was a slaughter.

I enjoyed calling and watching the game thoroughly. During the match I had a long talk with the former great English paceman, Bob Willis, who was doing some guest commentary work with Nine, which reminded me just how long it had been since my Test debut. He was the first genuine fast bowler that I faced in my career. Twelve years ago — a long time back. He's a super bloke — a subdued sort of character — but a very nice man.

It was great to get the chance to bowl in the nets. On the first four mornings of the Test I bowled anywhere between half an hour to an hour. It was good to see my mates again — the Waughs, Mike Slater, Tubby Taylor, Ian Healy, Cracker Holdsworth, big Merv ...

There was some discomfort for Debbie in Leeds, because of the "rules" which govern such things as Ashes tours. She and I stayed at the Holiday Inn, where the Australian team was based. It became a very awkward situation because the players' wives were not allowed to stay in the same hotel as the players until after the fifth Test. In fact, they were not even permitted in the foyer of the hotel, which I find pretty amazing. But that's the way it is, and that's the way it's been for as long as I can remember. This time the team threatened to fine me because I had my wife in the bar where they were drinking after the game. "Bloody fine me then," I said. "I'm not on the tour."

I have plenty of respect for the team rules — but the fact was that I *wasn't* part of that team. I was on media duties, and my wife was going to be with me, wherever I stayed. It was an uncomfortable situation, although there was no great drama.

While we were in the south of England, Debbie and I visited a little town called Whitney-on-Wye — for obvious reasons. Further north on our travels, on a trip from Fleetwood to Manchester, something happened which gave me a huge shake-up. I was with a great pal, Harold Wilkinson, travelling in his Honda to Old Trafford, where we were going to watch the second day's play in the Australia v Lancashire match. Debbie and Harold's wife Lynn were in the back of the car. We were zipping along at about 120kph in the middle lane when a truck which was ahead of us, on the inside lane, flicked up a metal bar from the roadway. The bar hit with enormous force on our windscreen, smashed it into a million pieces, and finished up in the car — embedded in the dashboard. We were lucky to survive. The bloody thing could have come straight through and decapitated Harold or me. The accident was a testimony to the value of laminated windscreens, and the braking ability of the Honda. We managed to stop and get off the road pretty quickly.

It was a genuinely shocking incident, and it's amazing neither of us was seriously hurt. We were cut a little from the flying glass, but it could so easily have been fulltime for Michael Roy Whitney.

At Edgbaston for the fifth Test, I saw some superb cricket. The Aussies were in full flight: Mark Waugh scored a brilliant double — 137 and 62 not out. Paul Reiffel took 6-71 this time (I wish I could take that article back!). Ian Healy hit a gallant and crucial 80, and the spinners, Shane Warne and Tim May, snared five wickets each in the second dig.

Commentating is the next best thing to playing, but with me it doesn't *yet* rank with being out there in the middle. There are some funny sidelights in the commentary box. A lot of people don't like Geoff Boycott; they reckon he talks too much about himself. Dennis Lillee calls Boycott's style the "optometrist's talk" — "*I* did this and *I* did that." They reckon "Boycs" is super-tight with a quid, too. Wouldn't shout if a shark bit him. I must say he's always been quite okay with me.

In that English summer I got on well with everyone — even Greg Chappell who had been one of the few people in the world I genuinely disliked. I've come to realise I didn't understand him properly — and probably he didn't understand me. He's a quiet bloke, but he's got this nice dry sense of humour.

Going back to Fleetwood during the tour was like going home. It was hard to believe that it was all of 12 years ago that I played there. The feeling of friendship and welcome certainly hadn't changed. The memories came flooding back of my time there, and they are just about all good ones. After all I played my first Test match while I was based at Fleetwood. That's gotta be special!

I find myself much on the same wavelength as people from that part of the world. They are working people, strugglers, very much akin to the folk around Matraville where I grew up. They were happy to meet Debbie. After all, when they knew me I was young and crazy. Now I was married, and maybe just a little less crazy.

I went back to Littleborough, too — where I played in 1983 — to watch the team play one Saturday afternoon, and visit the club afterwards. Debbie and I made a point of going to see a lady named Vera Dearden, who used to own a pub in Littleborough called The Ox and Plough. The boys used to call it "Thox and Huff". Vera's son Chris is an old pal of mine, scorer of the most runs for Littleborough, a season's guest with my club, Randwick, in 1983-84, and a great bloke. I lived at "Thox and Huff" during my stay in 1983, and Vera was unbelievably kind and generous. She wouldn't take a penny from me for rent, and she gave me all the food and drink I wanted. Deb and I made a pilgrimage to Haslingden too, where I played in 1990. My memories of that chapter in my cricket career are a little less boisterous, albeit happy ones, compared with my sojourns at Fleetwood and Littleborough. At Haslingden I was a little older, a little wiser ... and I was married. The memories there are more of good cricket and good people — and a little less of grog and parties.

One of my best memories of Haslingden involves ... my batting. I'll never forget it. We were sent in on a terrible wicket against Rishton in a second-round cup match, and before long at all were 5-50. I was batting number seven, and as I went out was thinking: "They must reckon it's all over if *I'm* batting seven." Peter Sleep, the South Australian and ex-Australian all-rounder, was the opposing professional, and was bowling well. I plugged away for a while with a bloke named John Entwhistle, but after he had scored 30 or so he copped a lifter, edged it, and was on his way. In came this 17-year-old kid, Neil Grinrod, playing in only his second or third game.

"Just hang in there," said the old pro at the other end.

I belted a couple of boundaries, then a couple more. In quick time, or so it seemed, I had 50 on the board. Shiiiitt!! It was my first 50 in a proper league game, and in the crowd they took up a collection. Down the other end, Grinrod was building in confidence, and he smacked Sleep back over his head for a boundary. To cut a long story short, we batted out our allotted 46 overs, and put an all-time Haslingden record of 115 for the eighth wicket. At the end of it I was 93 not out, and we had both given P. Sleep some stick.

I don't think he forgot young Grinrod in a hurry.

Going back in 1993 to where I had played my English league cricket was like stepping back in time. Nothing seemed to have changed. At such places you get a great sense of the timelessness of the game of cricket. In each town the team was out on a Saturday afternoon, playing the summer game, as they had for countless years past.

I found the task of being a cricket commentator a challenging experience. Channel Nine's John Gayleard and Brian Morelli counselled me to stay animated, to stay "up" and cautioned me not to be lulled into becoming too laid back by the approaches of Richie Benaud and Ian Chappell. They particularly warned me about the last session at the end of a tough day.

Richie is the doyen, and has his own unique style. That style very often is *quiet*. I was alongside Richie in the box when David Boon scored his third Test century of the tour, at Headingley.

"What a great hundred," I enthused. "A fantastic occasion for David Boon. There's no doubt he's one of the best batsmen in the world, and I'm sure you'd agree with me Rich."

There was dead silence. Play continued, the next ball was bowled and only then did Richie pick up the microphone. "And that's the end of the over. It's 5-473," he told the viewers.

A somewhat chastened Mike Whitney decided then and there that that would be the last time he'd try to put words into the mouth of the great Richie Benaud.

In the sixth Test at The Oval I was doing a session with Ian Chappell when one of the Australian batsmen drove Angus Fraser down the ground. Ian was flicking through some papers. He picked up the mike and said: "That's a long chase by Devon Malcolm down to the boundary ... and a good throw back to the bowler's end."

I had a look, and did a double take; it wasn't Devon Malcolm, it was Graham Gooch! I started to laugh, and was still laughing when I picked up the microphone.

"Ian, there aren't a lot of similarities between Devon Malcolm and Graham Gooch, and that looked more like Graham Gooch to me," I said.

In my earpiece I could hear laughter from Brian Morelli, the director in the outside broadcasting van. Instantly Morelli had the two players brought up on the split screen — Malcolm, the black man, built like a brick outhouse and Gooch, white, moustachioed and with hunched shoulders. It was a light moment, a bit of fun amid the seriousness of Test cricket.

The thing that really surprised me about the commentary business was the paltry nature of the commentary boxes in England. At the three Tests I helped cover they were just scaffolding with a few planks of wood on each side. I'm sure people at home have this perception of the commentators sitting there in big leather armchairs, sipping a martini and tasting the smoked salmon. It's not like that at all. Lunch arrived on plastic trays and was pretty ordinary, to the point where we had our Girl Friday, Lesley, ducking out to buy some rolls, or something a bit more tasty.

The boxes were big enough only for those actually working. When you weren't on air you had to stand outside in the weather. The amazing thing is that Channel Nine can bring a super deluxe coverage out of the primitive facilities they are given. The commentary boxes at Australian grounds are much better.

I had some success with the man from Ladbrokes, who would come up to the box now and then and give us odds on anything we might want to have a wager on. The Ladbrokes people were pretty keen to see D.K. Lillee too, and get back some of the cash he had won in 1981, when he'd backed England at 500-1 to come back from an impossible position and win the third Test and they had! Coming in to Australia's first innings in the last Test at the Oval, Ian Healy was quoted at odds of 33/1 about being Australia's top scorer. Most of the regular batsmen were too short for me to worry about backing, but Heals had scored an 80 and a century on tour, and I figured 33/1 were pretty succulent odds. At stumps on day two, he was 39 not out, and I needed him to get another 32 to pass Mark Taylor, who at that point was the innings' leading scorer. Australia were, however, eight wickets down. The next morning, Heals, with fabulous support from Warne and May, pressed on and, with a lofted drive off Steve Watkin, went past Mark. I was in the dressing room at the time, whooping and hollering. Three hundred and thirty quid ... Beauty!

Healy had an outstanding tour. He's a very impressive cricketer these days. His batting has improved dramatically — and his glove work throughout the English campaign was exemplary.

On the day he scored his runs at The Oval, I'd had a trundle in the nets, then a shower in the Aussie dressing room. I was in there when Shane Warne got out. When he came in he was spewing about the decision and hurled his bat from one side of the room to the other. The bat ricocheted off his kit, and cannoned into Bob Simpson's bad knee. Simmo really blew up and gave Shane a serve. It was a very funny incident, but everyone was holding back. You don't laugh at Simmo. Tim Zoehrer was in the most trouble; he had his head under a towel, trying to keep the laughter in. The coach stood up and hobbled out of the room, and seconds later there was this tremendous explosion of laughter. About five minutes later, Simmo came back, and everyone was straight-faced, deadly serious. Shane apologised, and Bob gave him a gobful. "You know how I hate that sort of idiotic behaviour," he snapped.

The Oval Test was a cracking game, and for once the England selectors picked the right team. If we think it's political here, it's nothing compared with over there. Unless you come from what they call the "Home Counties" — Surrey, Middlesex and Essex — you're well behind the eight ball. Blokes like Matthew Maynard and Steve Watkin, from unfashionable Glamorgan, should have been given a go much earlier in that series.

The appointment of Lancashire's Michael Atherton as the new English captain after the fourth Test, in place of Graham Gooch, may have appeared to be something of a vote of confidence for the north. But, with due respect to Atherton, he is a university man, who fits pretty comfortably into the stiff-upper-lip, old-school-tie syndrome that plagues English cricket. His selection as captain wasn't *too* radical.

I was at Edgbaston the day the ground announcer broadcast the news that Ted Dexter, the chairman of English selectors since 1989, had resigned. I'd say at least half the crowd stood up and applauded! The old school tie thing still pervades English cricket, and until they shoot out some of these old boys at the top — blokes who are still thinking about cricket in the 1960s, not the 1990s — then they're not going to do any good.

Their big fast bowler, Devon Malcolm, was a good case in point of a bloke who should have been called into the '93 Test team much earlier than he was. Errol Alcott told me that the last Test, the only one in which Malcolm played, was the first time he'd had to start working on our guys' fingers. The Poms had been playing these fairly gentle seamers all summer, and no-one was getting hit on the hands. Now Malcolm had brought a bit of speed and aggression into the joint. Talking to Errol, and watching the way he works within that Australian squad, made me realise how fortunate we are to have a bloke of his calibre in the ranks. I'm sure no-one in world cricket knows more about cricketing injuries than Errol and, that apart, he's a great bloke to have around on tour because of his affable and personable nature.

The genesis of Errol's unusual nickname of "Hooter" is of some interest. Errol came to cricket from a rugby league background, with the Cronulla-Sutherland club in Sydney. In a match early in his cricket involvement, Errol was querying the scheduled time of a forthcoming tea-break. "What time does the hooter go?" asked Errol, using the football vernacular. From that day onwards, he was simply "Hooter".

For most of the '93 Ashes series England plumped for reasonably good county bowlers who just weren't up to Test level. One of them, the English-based Aussie, Marty McCague, made something of a goose of himself in the nets at Headingley one day. McCague came over to Mark Waugh and told Waugh that he was batting scared. Shane Warne, who overheard, promptly told McCague to "f--- off, and stay in England." It was an insane thing for McCague to do. The Aussies came out at Headingley and belted the crap out of him, with AB getting his unbeaten 200, Steve Waugh 157 not out, and David Boon 107. McCague, who talks with a Pommy accent after a couple of summers over there, was a fairly desperate selection by the Poms. A part-timer for WA who really only made the team when blokes like Terry Alderman or Bruce Reid were missing, he was still ranked good enough to be rushed into the England XI with indecent haste.

The Poms just couldn't get it right. How about Headingley? They picked four seamers there, and we picked two spinners — and the track turned square! But at The Oval, England picked a good team, won by 161 runs, and thoroughly deserved their belated success. But the bottom line to the whole tour was that Australia outplayed them just about all the way. There was strength right through that Aussie team.

Boon 555 runs for the series, Mark Waugh 550. Fantastic! I thought Mark had a tremendous series. His 137 at Edgbaston after Australia had been 4-80 was an innings of the highest order, a real milestone for him. Tubby Taylor totalled 428 runs for the six Tests, continuing as cricket's quiet achiever. Unfortunately for Taylor, the couple of hundreds he scored early in the tour somehow faded into the background as the general run glut continued.

Young Michael Slater got 416 runs but probably could have done better. I had a good yarn with Slats one day over there and he told me that he got to the point where he was starting to believe what the press were saying about him — and he started to play the way people expected him to play. He was attempting to play his shots all the time, and hook and pull whenever possible. But he's a great player, that kid — a lovely young bloke with great footwork, a hunger for runs and a ready acceptance that he has to work hard.

Steve Waugh — another great tour of England, AB's double century, Ian Healy's runs and glovework ... the list of contributors in the Australian team is a long one. And the bowlers. Big Merv, Reiffel, May ... and Warne.

That one young bloke, Shane Warne, through all that he achieved, has dramatically changed the attitude in England, and in Australia too, about leg-spin bowling. Back home, at my cricket camps after the tour, I suddenly had a whole army of young kids who wanted to bowl leg-breaks.

I like Shane; he's a vibrant young bloke and he knows where he's going now. A couple of summers ago he was a little misdirected and overweight. I believe he has now realised there is a great and prosperous future for him in cricket — and he's prepared to pay the price. In England in '93 he bowled some absolutely *insane* deliveries — balls that would have been good enough to dismiss Don Bradman. Or maybe not on second thoughts; Bradman would probably have worked them down through the gully.

What about that Merv Hughes! Bloody hell. The bloke has a heart like a lion, and his 200 Test wickets are testimony to that. You know, he arrived back in Australia after the tour to be told he has some dead bone in his knee, and will be out until Christmas or longer. The reason he had that was that he bowled on one leg throughout the English summer, and shouldered the major share of responsibility after Billy McDermott went home because of illness. He's phenomenal, Merv — a great team man, a bloke of enormous spirit, and a champion bowler.

To me, England '93 was a special summer. I had a taste of something that I hope might one day become part of my working life. I saw countless old friends, went fly-fishing in Devon (caught nothing), won a "Batsman-of-the-Game" award (scoring 50 in a benefit match played in the beautiful Kent countryside), and kept fit by bowling in the nets to my Aussie colleagues. Away from cricket, there was camaraderie and nostalgia and long and happy nights of friendship and fun. Watching from Nine's shaky scaffolding, I enjoyed every moment of the cricketing contest as a far superior Australian team for the most part laid waste their English opposition.

I would loved to have been officially "on tour" with AB and his boys ... but, as things turned out, my summer of '93 wasn't half bad.

Best of the Best

To name with any certainty the top 10 fast bowlers of my experience is, of course, impossible. But I've never been one to shy away from a challenge, so I'm going to give it a go. The problem is there have been *so many* outstanding quicks scattered in and around the years of my career, some of them among the greatest bowlers of all time. How do you line them up? I have learned from plenty of them and relish the fact that I have the privilege of being a member of that exclusive club of Test fast bowlers.

The bowlers I have listed in this chapter are so different — yet so much the same. Speed, aggression, guile, a finely-honed competitive spirit — these qualities were and are universal to all of them. And yet as a group they cover the whole spectrum of the fast-bowling art, showing just how diverse that particular cricketing skill can be.

Apart from my number one — Dennis Lillee — I have not attempted to rate them in order. I have talked of the Australians first, and then the men from overseas. I'll leave it to you cricket-watchers to pencil in the numbers ...

To me, DENNIS LILLEE is the main man, the greatest of them all. I grew up in cricket in the years when Dennis was the gun, and for me, like every other fast bowler on every other park, he was the model. There were many, many things I liked about the Lillee approach, but chief among were the facts that:
- he was always extremely aggressive
- he had magnificent control
- he could adapt his bowling to all kinds of wickets.

At the height of his career the wicket at the Melbourne Cricket Ground was an absolute flattie. Sometimes down there the ball wouldn't bounce above shin high. It was a graveyard that beckoned with some menace us of the fast-bowling fraternity. And yet Dennis Lillee always took wickets down there.

When the conditions were his way, as on a Perth green-top, he was simply magnificent. Lillee was just a genuine wicket-taker, whatever the conditions. He was a fit, hard bloke — and he was an inspiration to me, along with countless others.

I count it as one of the great thrills of my career that I was able to play a couple of Tests with him.

It would be impossible for me to talk about fast bowlers and *not* talk about JEFF THOMSON. There is a general belief in cricket circles that he was very likely the quickest bowler in the history of the game. Maybe he didn't have the subtle skills of Dennis Lillee but, for sheer awesome pace, Thommo was just phenomenal. Right to his last game, the Sheffield Shield final of season 1985-86, he was steaming in, letting them rip. I'm sure many a batsman who faced him wakes — even in later years — to nightmares of that slingshot action and the whirr of a Thommo delivery scorching past the nose. He was one of the all-time greats.

GEOFF LAWSON is a great mate — and perhaps I'm a little biased in my assessment of him. But to me he was always grand-final material — a outstanding fast bowler, and a cricketer of integrity and intelligence.

Henry had a great cricket brain, and by the end of his career was regarded as being an exceptional captain and one of the most astute of cricketers. He was a fit, courageous fast bowler with nice array of skills, and a capable batsman too.

The time that I spent opening the bowling for NSW with him will always remain as one of the special experiences of my career. Henry was the supreme professional. He always looked after himself, trained hard, was always very focused on the job at hand, and was aggressive — as a champion fast bowler must be. He had a great bouncer, too — and he carried the load as Australia's premier quick in the years after Dennis Lillee retired in early 1984.

The fact that he won two or three "Man-of-the-Series" awards in Test cricket was testimony to his ability. He was a superb bowler, Henry, and I will always have enormous respect for him.

LEN PASCOE is something of a forgotten man, but, as a fast bowler, he made an enormous impression on me. He had a heart like a lion; he would run in all day, in all weather and at 5.30 in the early evening he'd still be going as hard as he was at 11am.

As a young bloke, Lenny was regarded as a tearaway, a bloke who would rip in and bowl short and really try to stick it up the batsman. But he developed more subtlety in his approach as the years went by, without ever losing that aggressive edge.

Aggressive? I think Lenny invented the word. Sometimes I think he took it to the point where he was over the top, but for me he was an important teacher. Lenny Pascoe taught me a lot about what you had to do, and what you had to expect when you became a fast bowler. Lenny lived his own message: that you had to be prepared to bowl 30 overs a day ... and still be steaming in hard at the end of it. Some people underestimated him.

I never did.

Among the Australians, it would be remiss of me if I didn't mention CRAIG McDERMOTT and MERV HUGHES, who have forged a outstanding partnership at Test level since 1991. As far as I'm concerned, McDermott is top shelf. On his day he is a class act and a genuine wicket-taker. In my view, despite the fact that he probably has many more years left in him, he already qualifies legitimately for the word "great" among Australia's fast bowlers.

When you consider that Jeff Thomson, who took 200 Test wickets, is regarded as a Test legend but is *behind* McDermott on the all-time Australian Test wicket-taking list, you get a pretty fair guideline to McDermott's qualities. Billy is a dedicated trainer and I have no doubt he will go right on with what he has already achieved in his career. He's an interesting guy sometimes as far as temperament is concerned, and he and I have had our moments. But everybody is his own man — and when things are going his way, he's awesome.

I can't say enough about Merv. I couldn't give a stuff about whether he does what he should do as a fast bowler, or what he looks like. The fact is he's already taken more than 200 Test wickets and he's earned every single one of them.

He's a bullock. He just keeps charging in. I would pick Merv in my team before I would pick anyone else. Apart from his skills as a bowler, he's a terrific team man and, while the style might look bull-at-the-gate, he's a fast bowler of skill and variety. He bowls with genuine pace, and never lets a batsman relax for an instant. Swervin' Mervyn has been a fantastic performer for his state and for his country, and will be as long as his legs maintain him in the vertical state.

And he's a good bloke to boot — one of my favourite characters. To hang out with Merv is to be part of a cultural experience. Apart from being a top bowler, Merv is particularly famous for what he can eat. He is the only guy I have ever known who can fit a whole Big Mac in his north and south. All in one go. It's phenomenal.

I went to Darwin with him in 1987 for an exhibition match, and they took us to this place where there was a sensational smorgasbord, at $20 a head. Merv was a revelation. He went back there four nights in a row, and they reckoned it was costing the little Japanese owner $100 a night to get Merv's $20. Merv wore a track to the food. I'd never seen anything like it.

Six Aussies down, and it's about time I mentioned SIR RICHARD

HADLEE. Hadlee to me was the consummate, absolute professional. It always seemed to me that everything he did in his life was geared towards being a world-class bowler. He was a great trainer, intensely single-minded about what he had to do, and for the best part of 15 years he held the New Zealand bowling attack together.

He was their killer bowler, the strike man. Almost always, he would open the attack with "seamers". Blokes like Ewen Chatfield — not that I'm about to run Ewen down, he took more than 100 Test wickets after all, and I would have dearly loved to have done that — but there's no doubt that being Richard Hadlee's partner was of enormous benefit to Chatfield, or whoever else happened to get the job. Relieved batsmen, happy to be away from Hadlee, would feel more inclined to chance their hands against the bloke at the other end.

Hadlee was a fabulous bowler. His control of line and length was second to none among all the bowlers I have seen. He could swing it like mad, and his ability to hit the seam was just awesome.

Perhaps, though, the thing I remember most about him was this: when I was growing up all the West Indies quicks who created such fear and trembling would run 50 or 60 metres to the crease. So did Richard Hadlee in his formative years. But, before long, he decided that such an approach was basically bullshit and cut his run by half. Because of his influence at the very highest level in world cricket there are now countless bowlers operating off shorter runs, and bowling as well as they are physically able.

Hadlee was the inspiration for me to cut down my run, and I believe I have been a much better bowler ever since I made that decision. With the reduced approach came more control, and I found I could hit the seam more. All sorts of things improved in my bowling.

My model was the first man to take 400 Test wickets. You couldn't possibly have a finer inspiration than that.

Now, the West Indians. I have always regarded MALCOLM MARSHALL as a genuinely great fast bowler. Malcolm wasn't all that big, but he had just about everything. For almost the entire decade of the 1980s he routed batting line-ups all over the world. He was fast, aggressive and swung the ball both ways. An absolute dynamo. Of all the bowlers to take over 300 wickets in Test cricket (he took 376), his average of 20.94 is the lowest (the next lowest is Fred Trueman's 307 at 21.57) — a phenomenal performance. He ranks very high on the list of champion fast bowlers of the modern era.

It seems logical to pair JOEL GARNER and CURTLY AMBROSE. The word that leaps to mind when considering the two of them is "awesome". Both stood around 203cm (6ft 8ins) tall, and brought the ball down from steepling heights against the luckless batsmen who faced them. Both were hard, durable men who rarely broke down, and the type of bowlers who can make life a misery for the best of batsmen.

In my view, Ambrose is a sensation. In 1992-93 in Australia he bowled his 30 overs every innings, without ever looking like breaking down. He looks wiry and thin, but he's actually very strong and sinewy. Viv Richards once told me he reckons Curtly is the strongest human being he knows. He's a tremendous bowler, is Ambrose, and capable of maintaining the pressure all day. He's one of those players who always looks like he's just about to get a wicket.

Garner, my co-star in that Tooheys ad made so many years ago, was so much the same. Talk to the guys who played against him, particularly in the days of Kerry Packer's World Series Cricket, and they'll tell you how tough he was to face. The ball would come down from that enormous height, then be leaping up at your throat. And beware the sandshoe-crusher; he was a master at that.

One spot left — and I want to give it to about eight blokes. But in assessing the great fast bowlers there is no way I could leave the great Pakistan captain, IMRAN KHAN, out of the Top Ten. He was simply a magnificent bowler — coming off those wickets of the sub-continent which seem designed to break the heart of anyone who hankers to bowl fast.

Imran learned his special skills on those wickets, and then transported them all over the world. He was superb, and something of a teacher as he showed out here when he played for NSW in season 1984-85. I may not have played any first-class cricket that season, but, because of the influence of Imran Khan, it was still a significant season in my career. On that campaign, he shared the secrets of swinging the ball "Irish", something which added a significant weapon to my own armament, and was a fast-bowling art form which reached its high point for me in the fifth Test of the 1988-89 series against the West Indies, when I took 7-89 in the Windies' first innings at the Adelaide Oval.

It used to amaze me to see Imran pick up a ball that was 70 overs old, and, in three or four overs, get it to swing half a metre both ways. To the rest of us, that old ball was ready to be thrown in the garbage bin.

In many ways he was Pakistan's answer to Hadlee — He held his country's bowling together for a long time, just as Hadlee did for New Zealand. He was an extremely fit athlete, and adaptable.

In the middle of his career he changed his action to enable him to add the outswinger to his armament. To that point, his natural delivery, and the one he relied on, had been the late inswinger. And he was the best batsman among the fast bowling greats, a genuine all-rounder and an aggressive power-hitter.

As those with a mathematical bent will have already realised, I have actually picked 11 bowlers on my list. The best I can do to bring it back to 10 is to bracket Ambrose and Garner — I'll let you, the reader, decide which one has to go.

If it was hard picking the 11 who made it — it was harder by far choosing who to leave out. At the very least the following deserve an honourable mention on the Whitney list:

- Ian Botham — one of the all time top all-rounders in the game, and the taker of 373 Test wickets.
- Michael Holding — nicknamed "Whispering Death", he was a magnificent athlete, and quick, real quick! A great man, too!
- Bob Willis — taker of 325 Test wickets and outstanding as both a competitor and a bowler.
- Kapil Dev — held the Indian pace-bowling stocks together for 15 years and became the second man in cricket history to capture more than 400 Test wickets.
- Wasim Akram — a left-armer of such quality that Sir Donald Bradman recently rated him the best left-arm quick of all time — not a bad wrap! With his whippy arm action, Wasim has all the tricks, at genuine pace. And the thing I really like about him is the fact he is an absolute master of bowling around the wicket

I am in awe of every bowler mentioned in this chapter. To get any sort of honourable membership in their club will do me forever for an accolade.

The Whitney Clan

As I admitted, early on in this book, there was a time in my life, from not long after my father died, when I went absolutely crazy. I know I gave my mother a great many grey hairs, as she strove, unsuccessfully, to have any sort of control over me.

She wouldn't know where I was. There were Friday and Saturday nights when she would be waiting up for me, while I was out for the entire weekend. Some of the things I did then were pretty outrageous and I guess I was pretty lucky at times not to get into a lot more trouble, particularly with the law. We were all very fast runners at the time.

The fact that the mother/son relationship survived that rocky period is probably the reason we are such great mates today. And, I would like to think that, through my success on and off the cricket field, I have made up for the stress I put her through.

I am still astounded by the way my mother stuck with me through those times. I never owned a car until I was 21, and when I finally did, it was not M. Whitney, but my mother who bought it for me. Despite the things that I had done! She asked me, months before my 21st, what I wanted for my birthday. There was a bloke up the road selling an old Valiant for 500 bucks. "If you want it, I'll buy it for your birthday," she said. "Go and have a look at it."

I took it around the block and if it had only had one tyre on it, I wanted that car. Mum gave me the $500. In the five years since after my father had died, she had supported me and my older sister through school. She was then, and still is, an amazing lady.

Nowadays I have a fabulous relationship with my family. I'm very close to my mother, and my sister, Christine, to the extent that if anybody makes a critical comment about them I jump on the defensive straight away. I know nobody is perfect, but we are such a tight-knit team.

My mother has provided enormous support for Christine and myself. My mother and sister are unbelievably close, more like sisters than mother and daughter. Christine now lives at Berry, on the NSW south coast about two hours drive from Sydney, with her husband, Dean, and three children, and mum spends quite a bit of time down there. She really loves her grandchildren.

Christine and I have a great relationship, though we have had our stormy times, especially in those years when I was out partying all the time. During that time I would, every so often, receive a timely gobful from Christine, reminding me I was doing the wrong thing by our mother.

I have some unbelievable memories of our early years; of the two of us getting up and singing Beatles duets to the family, and of family holidays to Forster, on the NSW north coast. Forster has a special place in the story of the Whitney clan. My family started going up there for holidays over 40 years ago, when there was virtually nothing there. Today, my father's brother and two sisters all reside there, and memories of family holidays are fresh with all of us.

Christine has backed me in everything I have done, and her support means such a great deal to me. Her husband is such a tremendous guy, and they have three beautiful children. The eldest, who was born in 1988, they named after me, while their second, a girl, they called Whitney because Christine wanted to keep the family name in their family. I still find it hard to believe that their first two children are called Michael Whitney! Their third child, another beautiful little girl, they named Amy.

My mother and sister are two of three very important women in my life. The third, of course, is my wife Debbie. Her influence on me has been extraordinary. We first met, as Debbie explained at the beginning of this book, at a New Year's party — a 1982-going-into-1983 New Year's Eve party. She was a little bit different from the run-of-the-mill girl, and a very attractive lady as well.

At first our relationship was hindered by my commitment to cricket, and by the fact that I didn't want to be tied down. Then I went to England for six months to play league cricket. It wasn't until the 1984-85 season, when I missed the entire season because of injury, that Debbie and I got back together, and not until the following year that I realised just how much she meant to me.

When I was chosen for my first Shield match of the 1985-86 season, in Perth, it was my first match for NSW in over two years. While I was away, I realised that I didn't want to be without this girl. So we moved into a flat in Coogee together, where we stayed for the next two years.

Living with Debbie brought dramatic changes. I became more organised, and saved money (for the first time in my life). My cricket improved, my approach to training became more dedicated and the big nights out with the boys became less regular. I had made a commitment to this girl, and the responsibility of that commitment had started to turn things around.

We started putting some of our incomes into a joint account. For me to do that, after the nonchalant way I had approached things in the past, was just amazing. I was actually planning for the future! Then the rent went up again. Debbie said that was ridiculous, and that we should buy somewhere. I thought: "Shit! Get involved with a mortgage? You've got to be joking!"

We ended up with a unit at Clovelly. It was a 50-year-old place that needed some work, but after we'd bought it, I felt ... safe. "Hey," I thought, "I actually own something."

I guess I would have bought some property eventually, but Debbie had brought me forward by five, maybe six years. Maybe more. Soon after we were married, which was one of the greatest things I have ever done in my life. We really haven't looked back from there. Debbie really settled me down and changed my whole focus on what I wanted to do with my life.

For the best part of a decade, Debbie has had to live with a professional sportsman, and wives do not get any accolades at all for that. And, mate, I'm telling you it is a really, really tough job. The cricketer in the partnership can be away for days, weeks, months at a time, and the cricketer's wife is obliged to handle the business while he's not there, make sure the house is okay while he's not there, pay the bills, and so on and so on. I don't care whose wife it is, they have to be doing it tough.

Debbie knows that cricket is my job, and that it is what I want to do. I know that sounds selfish on my part, but Debbie is prepared to put up with it, because one day it will finish and then we'll have a lot more time to devote to ourselves and the things we want to do.

I'm not harsh with too many people, but I sometimes expect too much from my wife. Our workload at home is quite phenomenal, yet sometimes I say to her, "why didn't you do this?", without considering that she has been up the road shopping, or she's done three loads of washing. Maybe she's painted the window out the back that I should have painted three months ago, or been organising timber and plants for our backyard and new garage we have been building. And here am I complaining that she hasn't sent a fax!

It's the old story. You're harshest on the ones you love. You have a tough day and come home tired, and a bit cranky, and they're the ones that cop the punishment. I always regret it later.

Debbie has really shaped my life. So many of the positive things that have happened to me in the past decade have occurred because of her influence. So many important decisions we have made have, in fact, been hers. We are a great partnership, even if we are not that much alike (opposites do attract!!). I'm not saying we don't have words because every couple have words now and again. But I think we really have a deep love and respect for each other.

That is by far the most important thing.

The Bottom Line

I have always felt I possess some sort of inner strength, and a desire to be successful, which I believe I was born with and I think that has come from my mother. I have to admit she is a very tough individual. She has gone through some very harrowing things in her life — no more than some in this world perhaps, but more than most. She is a very resilient woman, my mother. Very hard in some respects, very soft in others.

All my life, I've believed I am a little bit different. I don't say that with a big head. I have simply felt that there was something there a little bit special. If you believe that, you're always going to be positive in mind and attitude.

I know there have been many better bowlers than me. A lot of other guys with more skill, but probably very few that have really wanted to be there as much as I have. And I think that comes from within. You know, I don't think that you can make people want to do things. They either want to or they don't want to do them.

I have met guys who are the same height, weight, and build as me who could not bowl a hoop downhill. And then I've seen runners with that physique who would outsprint me by 10 metres. To be a fast bowler you have to be born to the job — it is not something you can learn to do. In that respect I look on it as an art, and the fact that I am a fast bowler as a real privilege. Not many sportsmen are that lucky.

The training involved in being a fast bowler at first-class level has never really been a problem. However, I will admit that as I've got older I've had to work harder at finding the time to train, sometimes simply because my life has become a lot busier in other areas, and sometimes because it's getting tougher to get motivated and get out and train. But I always manage to be there at the end of the day and I've always been fit enough to be highly competitive.

I have never been a really astute scholar. More street-wise. I might just have been a top scholar and gone to university if I'd had the ambition, but studying never really turned me on. I used to get through school without picking up a book, as my life as a teenager revolved totally around sport. Fortunately, I could pass exams without the need to study.

I can get totally caught up in things I really love and take an interest in, but if something doesn't interest me, I just push it aside. For example, I get captivated by world issues, and have always loved travel. As a youngster touring the world was such a fabulous experience and education. I am, in many ways, a free spirit, even if these days it has to be put in a box most of the time. As an Australian Test cricketer, I have achieved a certain status in the community, but that status can make it difficult to walk around with a free spirit, being a hippy, not having a haircut, wearing an earring and things like that.

Sometimes I'd like to do that, but unfortunately it doesn't fit in to the persona that I have sculpted for myself. It is very important that I care for my reputation because the community has always valued respect and tradition. Through cricket, I've learnt a lot about respecting tradition, and that respect has filtered into my outside life. I won't ever go to a gig and not wear a collar and tie, because I realise that the audience are paying me to be there and I should go with respect to them.

Travel for me meant self-education, and it has been some tutorial, as I have visited over 50 countries. I don't think I'll ever forget the places I've seen, the people I've met, the things I've done. Money could never buy those experiences. I have had a genuine hunger to get out there, learn about the world, and try to understand why people are the way they are. Why, for instance, are the people of Egypt the way they are? How do you explain Israel, the Communist states, America? Every country has its own history, its own fascination, its own people, language, dress, beliefs. In essence we are all one on this planet, yet in too many ways we aren't! We are all different! And man has been so cruel to his fellow man, far more than any other animal on this earth. No animal does what we do to each other without reason. Lions kill, sharks kill, other animals kill and they do it because they are hungry or because they are threatened. That is not the reason for our actions ... we do it for greed and power. Which I see as bizarre, and incredible. For my entire life, I have been curious to find out why.

Why is a Muslim a Muslim? Why is a Buddhist a Buddhist? I think I developed this questioning philosophy from my father, as he was a sailor when he was a young fellow and often told me stories about sailing around the South Pacific Islands and to America.

When I journeyed to India, for example, I learned enormous lessons. I learned to be very humble, and I learned patience. If you haven't been to India and seen how people live there, you really have no idea. People in Australia seem to be always complaining about where we are in the '90s, and how bad the recession is, but, while it may not be as it was in the golden years of the '60s when everybody was making a quid and everybody had a job, let's be realistic. Even when it's bad here, in comparison to many other parts of the world, it's very, very good.

If I could take an Australian to one place I would take them to India, or perhaps Bangladesh or Sri Lanka, and say, okay, you live here for 12 months with no more than a sandshoe and a galosher and then come back home and tell me where you would rather live. We have the greatest country in the world and until you go away you cannot appreciate this fact.

I mirror my fervour for travel in other areas. In fact, I can be a very thorough and pedantic person (to the point of annoyance) on some issues. My precise bookwork and record-keeping for taxation, and my passion for collecting cricket memorabilia are examples. I treasure the little things that are memories for me.

But, on the other hand, if I have a $3,000 lounge suite that breaks, well, I think: "Oh well, it's only a $3,000 lounge suite. You can always replace that."

Everything must be done right. Preparation is the key and I suppose that might have been one of the secrets to my success as a sportsman. I've always been prepared. I've always been ready on the day to go and bowl and do what I have to do.

I am careful with my money, though in some respects I'm reasonably generous. I certainly wouldn't call myself a tightwad with my cash. If someone is throwing in for somebody else or wants to buy a lottery ticket, or if someone wants to borrow 50, I seem to be one of the persons they always come to. Money is a strange commodity, and, unfortunately, it rules so many people's lives. It takes people down. They get too greedy about it.

I like to do things for people who I feel aren't as well off as me. As a sportsman, I'm something of a "target" for charities and fund-raising projects. All I try to do is as much as a can, particularly for children. I've been involved in the Christopher Robin Committee of the Prince of Wales Children's Hospital for almost a decade and I love to see the kids with smiles on their faces.

It's so ugly when anybody dies, and so much sadder when a youngster, five, 10 or 15 years, dies through illness, a car accident or something tragic like that. That troubles me more than an elderly person dying, because you know that even if you die when you are only 40 at least you've had an opportunity to witness life and have some enjoyment. But kids who meet an early death never get that opportunity. I often ask the cricketers to come up and visit the kids — that's something I feel good about. It makes me feel I'm helping someone who's not as well off as me and if that kid can go on and live a normal life because of it, that's just fantastic.

I believe I'm a forward thinker. I question a lot of things about life, the world and our existence here. I question the church. Indeed, I question the church seriously. I was born and raised a Catholic, but I question at times some of the motives of the church. It appears to me that sometimes they are not in it for the right reasons.

Religion is such a touchy subject. I have searched for answers. I have spent time in sacred places such as Jerusalem, but haven't found the answers. I still ask questions about God ... Jesus Christ ... the Bible. Religion is such an unbelievable thing in the world we live in. There are so many different religions, cults, everythings ... but all keep telling us God is coming back one day to sort it all out.

Well, mate, if he doesn't come back soon, we're going to be in real trouble.

The thing that worries me about Christianity is the fact that Christians are supposed to live under the rules and ideals laid out in the Ten Commandments. One of those Commandments states that we shall not worship false gods. Okay, that's fair enough. I can cop that. But you go to India and tell a Hindu that the cow he is worshipping and which he believes is a reincarnation of God is not the real thing. Well, he's going to tell you to get out of India because he really believes in that cow. To the extent that his family may be starving in the street but they will not kill that cow to eat it. Now I can't relate to that, but they can, and that is their belief.

But Christian rules say you should not worship false gods. So does that mean all Hindus are wrong? Does that mean Muslims are wrong ... that Buddhists shouldn't worship Buddha?

When I quiz Christian believers on this subject they say: "Oh well, really, it is all the one God but it is manifested in different ways." In that case, why are there so many anomalies? People cannot give me a straight answer about religion.

So many people are fanatical. They go to church, and look at a person, or an image of a man, on the cross, and believe that their soul is going to be cleansed. To me, that concept remains one of the greatest mysteries of the world. Are you or I going to heaven? Are we going to hell? Well, I'll tell you what I believe. I believe that when you die, you die and that's it. It's all over. We are in heaven here right now, so you may as well have a good time, because I don't believe you go anywhere. I don't believe I'm going to see my father when I die and go to heaven and I don't believe I'm going to hell. I believe that I am going back to dust.

People say — what then about the creation of the earth ... and the universe? Well, don't ask me, brother. That's too big for my mind, too big for anybody's mind. Our minds are incapable of absorbing the infinite distances of the universe. You shoot a rocket off today and it just goes forever.

THE BOTTOM LINE

Well, how far is forever? I have no idea ...

I have always regarded myself as a good communicator. I've never been short of a word, which I suppose is reflected in the fact that I have an after-dinner speaking business rolling along nicely. My communication skills have given me a lot of opportunities to go to places and meet a lot of different people. Whether it has been the Governor of NSW, a Prime Minister or a drunk on the street, I've never had a problem communicating. I pride myself on being able to talk on most levels. Communicating is the essence of life, it opens so many doors for you.

I've always liked to smile and have a good time, especially in younger days when we all used to get out, party and experiment. I feel in some respects I have an addictive personality, so I really have to keep a check on a few things. For example, drinking. When I was younger I drank fairly heavily. It was just what we did in those days. My mother said to me from time to time: "You know, you're going to be just like your father." I know now that my father was an alcoholic. He couldn't go without a drink, but fortunately I'm different. Everything in moderation. To do that has made me a much stronger person.

I have never thought of myself as a violent person, even though I got into my fair share of fisticuffs when I was a young bloke. But that was just a product of the environment I was living in, and the company of some of the young guys I knocked around with at the time. They would be keen to have a stoush if someone looked just sideways at them. But I could never think of picking up a gun or a knife, then or now.

Evil acts repulse me. Killing an animal, for instance. I've shot rabbits and that never troubled me until one day I was up on a farm near Tamworth with some friends, who asked if I would like to go shooting. We were looking for wild pigs, feral pigs. No problem, but we couldn't find any pigs so they said, "Well, why don't you shoot a 'roo?" This place had a lot of 'roos on it and I managed to shoot one in the back of the head and kill it. When I came up close to it I felt so bad about what I'd done that I haven't picked up a gun since. That poor animal, five minutes earlier hopping around the countryside enjoying itself ... and I'd taken its life away.

I'm a sympathetic person with an ear to listen to people with problems. I don't claim to be a person of outstanding morality, because there are some things I did back in my adolescent years that probably lacked morals. But I think I have attained a standard acceptable to most people. There are things I regret having done and felt guilty about the day after. You wonder why you do it. I guess it's an instinctive thing and the old primeval instincts take over. It just happens, but it doesn't make it right.

I've worked hard on my cricket. Harder than a lot of other people and that's why I've attained the success that I have. For much of my life, I never regarded myself as an ambitious person but I suppose over the last half-dozen years I started to set some pretty high goals, for my cricket and my life. I like to think of myself as being comfortable and successful, and, while I'll never be a person who walks over the top of people, I think I'm ambitious and confident enough to get in there, work hard and hope that things will fall my way.

I'm not frightened to tell people what I think or what I'm involved in. I'm a member of the ALP and have been a Labor voter all my life. That's probably a family thing. It's probably not logical to vote for the Labor party just because my father and my grandfather did, but I looked at the two parties when it got around to voting time and that was my decision. I believed in their mode of operation and their morality, so I joined the Labor party.

People have come up to me at functions and whispered: "Oh, I heard you're a member of the ALP."

And I say: "Yeah, what are you whispering about?"

And they say, still quietly: "Oh, you know people. I don't want people here to know."

And I'll say: "Bullshit, mate, what are they going to do? If they don't like it they can lump it."

That's me and that's the bottom line.

Statistics

to September 30, 1993

Michael Roy WHITNEY
Born: February 24, 1959 (Surry Hills, NSW)
Left-Arm Fast-Medium Bowler, Right-Hand Batsman

1. FIRST-CLASS CAREER

Debut: 1980/81, New South Wales v Queensland, Brisbane.

Bowling:

Season	Country	Balls	Mdns	Runs	Wkts	Avge	5	10	Best
1980/81	Australia	666	22	347	11	31.55	-	-	4/62
1981	England	1338	49	726	24	30.25	1	-	5/60
1981/82	Australia	889	28	465	9	51.67	-	-	2/33
1982/83	Australia	2537	85	1323	45	29.40	2	-	5/93
1982/83	Zimbabwe	490	25	162	12	13.50	1	-	5/29
1983	England	108	4	60	2	30.00	-	-	1/12
1983/84	Australia	498	18	271	5	54.20	-	-	2/89
1985/86	Australia	1173	43	483	22	21.95	1	-	6/65
1985/86	Zimbabwe	341	15	127	6	21.17	-	-	3/37
1986/87	Australia	1327	35	726	24	30.25	2	-	5/39
1987/88	Zimbabwe	330	15	122	5	24.40	-	-	3/67
1987/88	Australia	1742	63	762	32	23.81	3	-	5/33
1988/89	Australia	2763	110	1370	58	23.62	2	-	7/89
1989/90	Australia	1325	58	639	24	26.63	1	-	5/125
1990	England	162	5	97	5	19.40	-	-	3/46
1990/91	Australia	1554	70	708	29	24.41	-	-	4/32
1991	West Indies	900	28	445	14	31.79	2	-	6/42
1991/92	Australia	2351	84	1122	52	21.58	3	1	7/27
1992	Sri Lanka	612	31	246	9	27.33	-	-	4/34
1992/93	Australia	1686	66	818	23	35.57	1	-	5/43
Total:		22792	854	11019	411	26.81	19	1	7/27

Bowling in:	Balls	Mdns	Runs	Wkts	Avge	5	10	Best
Test Cricket	2672	90	1325	39	33.97	2	1	7/27
Sheffield Shield	14983	562	7314	251	29.14	10	-	7/75

Bowling against:	Balls	Mdns	Runs	Wkts	Avge	5	10	Best
England XI	585	21	266	16	16.63	1	-	5/39
England	468	16	246	5	49.20	-	-	2/50
India	701	21	359	17	21.12	1	1	7/27
Indians	397	16	179	14	12.79	1	-	6/37
Jamaica	216	6	78	8	9.75	1	-	6/42
Lancashire	282	13	136	4	34.00	-	-	3/74
New Zealanders	222	5	134	3	44.67	-	-	1/12
New Zealand	321	11	137	4	34.25	-	-	4/92
Pakistanis	222	8	100	9	11.11	1	-	5/66
Queensland	3137	105	1554	58	26.79	2	-	6/65
South Australia	3225	124	1665	51	32.65	4	-	5/33
Sri Lankan Board XI	264	16	87	7	12.43	-	-	4/34
Sri Lankans	510	18	275	13	21.15	-	-	4/86
Sri Lanka	348	15	159	2	79.50	-	-	1/49
Sussex	144	3	81	6	13.50	1	-	5/60
Tasmania	1977	79	869	42	20.69	1	-	5/54
Victoria	3055	126	1438	46	31.26	1	-	5/68
Wellington	204	10	90	4	22.50	-	-	3/39
West Ind. Board Pres. XI	288	11	151	6	25.17	1	-	5/114
West Indians	420	12	275	4	68.75	-	-	2/82
West Indies	834	27	424	11	38.55	1	-	7/89
Western Australia	3589	128	1788	54	33.11	2	-	7/75
Worcestershire	222	8	117	4	29.25	-	-	3/54
Zimbabweans	1161	55	411	23	17.87	1	-	5/29

Bowling in:	Balls	Mdns	Runs	Wkts	Avge	5	10	Best
First Innings	7062	259	3527	114	30.94	3	-	7/89
Second Innings	7540	270	3612	140	25.80	9	-	6/42
Third Innings	2222	86	1092	39	28.00	1	-	7/27
Fourth Innings	968	239	2788	118	23.63	6	-	7/75

Bowling, by venue in Australia ...	Balls	Mdns	Runs	Wkts	Avge	5	10	Best
Adelaide	2450	84	1311	35	37.46	3	-	7/89
Albury	126	3	63	4	15.75	-	-	2/28
Brisbane	1803	48	940	36	26.11	1	-	5/93
Canberra	198	9	75	6	12.50	-	-	3/21
Devonport	474	14	210	6	35.00	-	-	2/31

Bowling, by venue:	Balls	Mdns	Runs	Wkts	Avge	5	10	Best
Hobart BEL	294	9	151	5	30.20	-	-	3/55
Hobart TCA	249	9	126	7	18.00	-	-	3/74
Lismore	235	11	82	9	9.11	1	-	6/37
Melbourne	1774	71	820	23	35.65	-	-	4/49
Newcastle	876	35	484	19	25.47	1	-	5/39
North Sydney	204	10	90	4	22.50	-	-	3/39
Perth	2827	91	1451	50	29.02	3	1	7/27
St Kilda	204	10	91	3	30.33	-	-	3/91
Sydney	6797	278	3140	127	24.72	6	-	6/65
in England ...								
Bristol	444	17	263	9	29.22	-	-	4/86
Hove	144	3	81	6	13.50	1	-	5/60
Manchester	546	22	260	8	32.50	-	-	3/74
Scarborough	270	9	157	7	22.43	-	-	3/46
The Oval	204	7	122	11	22.00	-	-	1/46
in Sri Lanka ...								
Colombo KS	126	3	62	1	62.00	-	-	1/49
Colombo SSC	222	12	97	1	97.00	-	-	1/84
Kandy	144	6	53	3	17.67	-	-	3/53
Matara	120	10	34	4	8.50	-	-	4/34
in West Indies ...								
Georgetown	168	4	103	-	-	-	-	-
Kingston	444	13	191	8	23.88	1	-	6/42
Basseterre	288	11	151	6	25.17	1	-	5/114
in Zimbabwe ...								
Harare	1161	55	411	23	17.87	1	-	5/29

Bowling, by country:	Balls	Mdns	Runs	Wkts	Avge	5	10	Best
In Australia	18511	682	9034	334	27.05	15	1	7/27
In England	1608	58	883	31	28.48	1	-	5/60
In Sri Lanka	612	31	246	9	27.33	-	-	4/34
In West Indies	900	28	445	14	31.79	2	-	6/42
In Zimbabwe	1161	55	411	23	17.87	1	-	5/29

Bowling, for:	Balls	Mdns	Runs	Wkts	Avge	5	10	Best
Australia	2672	90	1325	39	33.97	2	1	7/27
Australian XI	1402	61	559	39	14.33	4	-	6/42
DB Close's XI	108	4	60	2	30.00	-	-	1/12
Gloucestershire	726	30	399	13	30.69	-	-	4/86
M Parkinson's World XI	162	5	97	5	19.40	-	-	3/46
New South Wales	17722	664	8579	313	27.41	13	-	7/75

Five wickets in an innings:

Wkts	Team	Opponent	Venue	Season
5/60	Australian XI	Sussex	Hove	1981
5/133	New South Wales	South Australia	Adelaide	1982/83
5/93	New South Wales	Queensland	Brisbane	1982/83
5/29	Australian XI	Zimbabweans	Harare	1982/83
6/65	New South Wales	Queensland	Sydney	1985/86
5/39	New South Wales	England XI	Newcastle	1986/87
5/97	New South Wales	South Australia	Sydney	1986/87
5/33	New South Wales	South Australia	Sydney	1987/88
5/68	New South Wales	Victoria	Sydney	1987/88
5/54	New South Wales	Tasmania	Sydney	1987/88
5/66	New South Wales	Pakistanis	Sydney	1988/89
7/89	AUSTRALIA	WEST INDIES	Adelaide	1988/89
5/125	New South Wales	South Australia	Adelaide	1989/90
5/114	Australian XI	WI Board Pres.	Basseterre	1990/91
6/42	Australian XI	Jamaica	Kingston	1990/91
6/37	New South Wales	Indians	Lismore	1991/92
7/27	AUSTRALIA	INDIA	Perth	1991/92
7/75	New South Wales	Western Australia	Perth	1991/92
5/43	New South Wales	Western Australia	Perth	1992/93

10 wickets in a match:

Wkts	Team	Opponent	Venue	Season
11/95	Australia	India	Perth	1991/92

Batting and Fielding:

* Indicates not out

Season	Country	M	Inn	NO	Runs	HS	0s	Avge	Ct
1980/81	Australia	4	2	-	4	3	-	2.00	6
1981	England	6	7	-	5	4	5	0.71	3
1981/82	Australia	6	5	2	4	3*	3	1.33	1
1982/83	Australia	12	9	4	50	28*	3	10.00	7
1982/83	Zimbabwe	2	3	1	5	2*	-	2.50	-
1983	England	1	2	1	6	5*	-	6.00	2
1983/84	Australia	3	4	-	16	12	2	4.00	5
1985/86	Australia	6	7	3	33	19	2	8.25	1
1985/86	Zimbabwe	2	-	-	-	-	-	-	2
1986/87	Australia	8	8	1	34	19	2	4.86	1
1987/88	Zimbabwe	2	2	-	0	0	2	0.00	1
1987/88	Australia	9	11	7	23	5*	1	5.75	1
1988/89	Australia	13	13	6	50	22*	2	7.14	2
1989/90	Australia	8	6	4	24	15*	1	12.00	7
1990	England	1	-	-	-	-	-	-	1
1990/91	Australia	8	7	1	51	19	2	8.50	4
1991	West Indies	4	5	2	11	6	-	3.67	-
1991/92	Australia	10	14	6	33	12	5	4.13	1
1992	Sri Lanka	4	6	4	30	13	-	15.00	1
1992/93	Australia	8	7	2	36	13	-	17.20	4
Total:		117	118	44	415	28*	31	5.61	50

Batting in:	M	Inn	NO	Runs	HS	0s	Avge	Ct
Test Cricket	12	19	8	68	13	4	6.18	2
Sheffield Shield	77	74	28	287	28*	19	6.24	31

Batting against:	M	Inn	NO	Runs	HS	0s	Avge	Ct
England XI	3	4	1	32	19	-	10.67	3
England	2	4	-	4	4	3	1.00	-
India	3	4	3	20	12	-	20.00	1
Indians	2	1	1	2	2*	-	-	1
Jamaica	1	1	-	2	2	-	2.00	-
Lancashire	1	1	-	0	0	1	0.00	-
New Zealanders	2	2	1	6	5*	-	6.00	5
New Zealand	1	2	2	2	2*	-	-	-
Pakistanis	1	1	-	0	0	1	0.00	1
Queensland	18	18	6	68	15*	5	5.67	6
South Australia	15	14	7	60	19	2	8.57	8
Sri Lankan Board XI	2	3	3	6	3*	-	-	1
Sri Lankans	3	-	-	-	-	-	-	1

Batting against:	M	Inn	NO	Runs	HS	0s	Avge	Ct
Sri Lanka	2	3	1	24	13	-	12.00	-
Sussex	1	1	-	1	1	-	1.00	1
Tasmania	11	8	1	44	19	1	6.29	6
Victoria	15	12	7	27	9	3	5.40	4
Wellington	1	1	-	0	0	1	0.00	-
West Ind. Board Pres. XI	1	1	-	6	6	-	6.00	-
West Indians	3	3	1	0	0*	2	0.00	-
West Indies	4	6	2	18	13	1	4.50	1
Western Australia	18	22	7	88	28*	8	5.87	7
Worcestershire	1	1	-	0	0	1	0.00	1
Zimbabweans	6	5	1	5	2*	2	1.25	3

Batting in:		Inn	NO	Runs	HS	0s	Avge	Ct
First Innings		41	17	131	22*	10	5.46	12
Second Innings		45	17	188	28*	8	6.71	20
Third Innings		20	8	55	13	9	4.58	8
Fourth Innings		12	2	41	19	4	4.10	10

Batting, by venue:	M	Inn	NO	Runs	HS	0s	Avge	Ct
in Australia ...								
Adelaide	10	10	3	48	19	2	6.86	5
Albury	1	1	-	19	19	-	19.00	3
Brisbane	8	8	4	28	10*	2	7.00	3
Canberra	1	-	-	-	-	-	-	-
Devonport	2	1	-	6	6	-	6.00	1
Hobart BEL	1	1	1	1	1*	-	-	-
Hobart TCA	2	1	0	0	1	-	0.00	-
Lismore	1	1	1	2	2*	-	-	-
Melbourne	9	10	6	29	13	2	7.25	5
Newcastle	6	5	1	6	4	1	1.50	-
North Sydney	1	1	-	0	0	1	0.00	-
Perth	14	19	7	52	22*	7	4.33	6
St Kilda	1	2	1	3	3*	1	3.00	-
Sydney	38	33	12	164	28*	7	7.81	17
in England ...								
Bristol	2	1	-	0	0	1	0.00	2
Hove	1	1	-	1	1	-	1.00	1
Manchester	2	3	-	0	0	3	0.00	-
Scarborough	2	2	1	6	5*	-	6.00	3
The Oval	1	2	-	4	4	1	2.00	-

STATISTICS

Batting, by venue:	M	Inn	NO	Runs	HS	0s	Avge	Ct
in Sri Lanka ...								
Colombo KS	1	1	-	1	1	-	1.00	-
Colombo SSC	1	2	1	23	13	-	23.00	-
Kandy	1	1	1	0	0*	-	-	-
Matara	1	2	2	6	3*	-	-	1
in West Indies ...								
Georgetown	1	2	2	1	1*	-	-	-
Kingston	2	2	-	4	2	-	2.00	-
Basseterre	1	1	-	6	6	-	6.00	-
in Zimbabwe ...								
Harare	6	5	1	5	2*	2	1.25	3

Batting, by country:	M	Inn	NO	Runs	HS	0s	Avge	Ct
In Australia	95	93	36	358	28*	24	6.28	40
In England	8	9	1	11	5*	5	1.38	6
In Sri Lanka	4	6	4	30	13	-	15.00	1
In West Indies	4	5	2	11	6	-	3.67	-
In Zimbabwe	6	5	1	5	2*	2	1.25	3

Batting, by position:	Inn	NO	Runs	HS	0s	Avge
No. 6	1	-	0	0	1	0.00
No. 9	2	1	3	3*	1	3.00
No. 10	33	10	122	22*	13	5.30
No. 11	82	33	290	28*	16	5.92

Batting, for:	M	Inn	NO	Runs	HS	0s	Avge	Ct
Australia	12	19	8	68	13	4	6.18	2
Australian XI	7	9	4	20	6	-	4.00	2
DB Close's XI	1	2	1	6	5*	-	6.00	2
Gloucestershire	3	2	-	0	0	2	0.00	2
M Parkinson's World XI	1	-	-	-	-	-	-	1
New South Wales	93	86	31	321	28*	25	5.84	41

Highest Score: 28*   NSW v WA, Sydney, 1982/83

First Class Bowling — Innings by Innings ...

Game	Date	Team	Opp	Venue	Ovrs	Md	Rns	Wk	Balls	Mdns	Runs	Wkt	Avge	5wi	10m	Stk/Rt	RPO	Ec/Rte
1980/81 in Australia																		
1	17/10/1980	NSW	QLD	Brisbane	15.0	2	52	2	90	2	52	2	26.00	-	-	45.00	3.47	57.78
1	17/10/1980	NSW	QLD	Brisbane	13.0	3	39	1	168	5	91	3	30.33	-	-	56.00	3.25	54.17
2	17/01/1981	NSW	VIC	Sydney	22.0	5	62	4	300	10	153	7	21.86	-	-	42.86	3.06	51.00
2	17/01/1981	NSW	VIC	Sydney	17.0	6	44	-	402	16	197	7	28.14	-	-	57.43	2.94	49.00
3	24/01/1981	NSW	NZS	Sydney	13.0	1	48	1	480	17	245	8	30.63	-	-	60.00	3.06	51.04
3	24/01/1981	NSW	NZS	Sydney	6.0	-	26	-	516	17	271	8	33.88	-	-	64.50	3.15	52.52
4	06/03/1981	NSW	TAS	Sydney	19.0	5	50	3	630	22	321	11	29.18	-	-	57.27	3.06	50.95
4	06/03/1981	NSW	TAS	Sydney	6.0	-	26	-	666	22	347	11	31.55	-	-	60.55	3.13	52.10
1981 in England																		
5	17/06/1981	GLO	SLS	Bristol	18.0	5	60	1	774	27	407	12	33.92	-	-	64.50	3.16	52.58
5	17/06/1981	GLO	SLS	Bristol	19.0	4	86	4	888	31	493	16	30.81	-	-	55.50	3.33	55.52
6	15/07/1981	GLO	WOR	Bristol	20.0	7	54	3	1008	38	547	19	28.79	-	-	53.05	3.26	54.27
6	15/07/1981	GLO	WOR	Bristol	17.0	1	63	1	1110	39	610	20	30.50	-	-	55.50	3.30	54.95
7	13/08/1981	AUS	ENG	Manchester	17.0	3	50	2	1212	42	660	22	30.00	-	-	55.09	3.27	54.46
7	13/08/1981	AUS	ENG	Manchester	27.0	6	74	2	1374	48	734	24	30.58	-	-	57.25	3.21	53.42
8	22/08/1981	AXI	SUS	Hove	19.0	2	60	5	1488	50	794	29	27.38	1	-	51.31	3.20	53.36
8	22/08/1981	AXI	SUS	Hove	5.0	1	21	1	1518	51	815	30	27.17	1	-	50.60	3.22	53.69
9	27/08/1981	AUS	ENG	The Oval	23.0	3	76	-	1656	54	891	30	29.70	1	-	55.20	3.23	53.80
9	27/08/1981	AUS	ENG	The Oval	11.0	4	46	1	1722	58	937	31	30.23	1	-	55.55	3.26	54.41
10	09/09/1981	GLO	LAN	Manchester	21.0	8	62	1	1848	66	999	32	31.22	1	-	57.75	3.24	54.06
10	09/09/1981	GLO	LAN	Manchester	26.0	5	74	3	2004	71	1073	35	30.66	1	-	57.26	3.21	53.54
1981/82 in Australia																		
11	22/10/1981	NSW	QLD	Newcastle	17.0	3	65	2	2106	74	1138	37	30.76	1	-	56.92	3.24	54.04
12	30/10/1981	NSW	W.A	Perth	28.0	4	89	2	2274	78	1227	39	31.46	1	-	58.31	3.24	53.96
13	06/11/1981	NSW	S.A	Adelaide	31.0	6	85	-	2460	84	1312	39	33.64	1	-	63.08	3.20	53.33
14	27/11/1981	NSW	WIN	Sydney	16.0	2	79	-	2556	86	1391	39	35.67	1	-	65.54	3.27	54.42
15	10/12/1981	NSW	S.A	Sydney	15.0	4	49	1	2646	90	1440	40	36.00	1	-	66.15	3.27	54.42
15	10/12/1981	NSW	S.A	Sydney	3.0	-	10	-	2664	90	1450	40	36.25	1	-	66.60	3.27	54.43
16	19/02/1982	NSW	VIC	Melbourne	20.1	6	33	2	2785	96	1483	42	35.31	1	-	66.31	3.19	53.25
16	19/02/1982	NSW	VIC	Melbourne	18.0	3	55	2	2893	99	1538	44	34.95	1	-	65.75	3.19	53.16
1982/83 in Australia																		
17	15/10/1982	NSW	W.A	Perth	29.0	6	74	-	3067	105	1612	44	36.64	1	-	69.70	3.15	52.56
18	06/11/1982	NSW	S.A	Adelaide	32.0	3	133	5	3259	108	1745	49	35.61	2	-	66.51	3.21	53.54
18	06/11/1982	NSW	S.A	Adelaide	21.0	7	62	2	3385	115	1807	51	35.43	2	-	66.37	3.20	53.38
19	12/11/1982	NSW	W.A	Sydney	27.0	7	68	2	3547	122	1875	53	35.38	2	-	66.92	3.17	52.86
19	12/11/1982	NSW	W.A	Sydney	8.0	3	27	1	3595	125	1902	54	35.22	2	-	66.57	3.17	52.91
20	20/11/1982	NSW	EXI	Sydney	19.0	4	73	1	3709	129	1975	55	35.91	2	-	67.44	3.19	53.25
20	20/11/1982	NSW	EXI	Sydney	27.3	6	60	4	3874	135	2035	59	34.49	2	-	65.66	3.15	52.53
21	03/12/1982	NSW	S.A	Sydney	25.0	3	92	2	4024	138	2127	61	34.87	2	-	65.97	3.17	52.86
21	03/12/1982	NSW	S.A	Sydney	20.0	6	70	4	4144	144	2197	65	33.80	2	-	63.75	3.18	53.02
22	18/12/1982	NSW	VIC	Newcastle	8.0	2	22	1	4192	146	2219	66	33.62	2	-	63.52	3.18	52.93
22	18/12/1982	NSW	VIC	Newcastle	24.0	6	94	3	4336	152	2313	66	35.05	2	-	65.70	3.20	53.34
23	21/01/1983	NSW	QLD	Brisbane	10.3	-	33	3	4399	152	2346	69	34.00	2	-	63.75	3.20	53.33
23	21/01/1983	NSW	QLD	Brisbane	39.0	11	93	5	4633	163	2439	74	32.96	3	-	62.61	3.16	52.64
24	28/01/1983	NSW	VIC	Melbourne	23.0	2	98	2	4771	165	2537	76	33.38	3	-	62.78	3.19	53.18
24	28/01/1983	NSW	VIC	Melbourne	7.0	2	14	1	4813	167	2551	77	33.13	3	-	62.51	3.18	53.00
25	10/02/1983	NSW	SLS	Sydney	15.0	-	54	2	4903	167	2605	79	32.97	3	-	62.06	3.19	53.13
26	18/02/1983	NSW	QLD	Sydney	9.0	1	30	-	4957	168	2635	79	33.35	3	-	62.75	3.19	53.16
26	18/02/1983	NSW	QLD	Sydney	16.0	4	40	2	5053	172	2675	81	33.02	3	-	62.38	3.18	52.94
27	25/02/1983	NSW	TAS	Hobart TCA	19.3	4	74	3	5170	176	2749	84	32.73	3	-	61.55	3.19	53.17
28	04/03/1983	NSW	W.A	Perth	25.2	4	67	4	5322	180	2816	88	32.00	3	-	60.48	3.17	52.91
28	04/03/1983	NSW	W.A	Perth	18.0	4	45	1	5430	184	2861	89	32.15	3	-	61.01	3.16	52.69
1982/83 in Zimbabwe																		
29	01/04/1983	AXI	ZMS	Harare	18.0	6	32	2	5538	190	2893	91	31.79	3	-	60.86	3.13	52.24
29	01/04/1983	AXI	ZMS	Harare	23.4	10	29	5	5680	200	2922	96	30.44	4	-	59.17	3.09	51.44
30	14/04/1983	AXI	ZMS	Harare	17.0	4	39	2	5782	204	2961	98	30.21	4	-	59.00	3.07	51.21
30	14/04/1983	AXI	ZMS	Harare	23.0	5	62	3	5920	209	3023	101	29.93	4	-	58.61	3.06	51.06
1983 in England																		
31	31/08/1983	DBC	NZS	Scarborough	11.0	1	48	1	5986	210	3071	102	30.11	4	-	58.69	3.08	51.30
31	31/08/1983	DBC	NZS	Scarborough	7.0	3	12	1	6028	213	3083	103	29.93	4	-	58.52	3.07	51.14
1983/84 in Australia																		
32	21/10/1983	NSW	W.A	Perth	34.0	7	89	2	6232	220	3172	105	30.21	4	-	59.35	3.05	50.90
33	28/10/1983	NSW	VIC	Sydney	15.0	5	37	1	6322	225	3209	106	30.27	4	-	59.64	3.05	50.76
33	28/10/1983	NSW	VIC	Sydney	10.0	3	40	1	6382	228	3249	107	30.36	4	-	59.64	3.05	50.91
34	02/12/1983	NSW	QLD	Sydney	24.0	3	105	1	6526	231	3354	108	31.06	4	-	60.43	3.08	51.39

1985/86 in Australia

35	10/01/1986	NSW	W.A	Perth	22.0	3	84	-	6658	234	3438	108	31.83	4	-	61.65	3.10 51.64
36	16/01/1986	NSW	S.A	Adelaide	33.0	7	110	2	6856	241	3548	110	32.25	4	-	62.33	3.11 51.75
37	24/01/1986	NSW	QLD	Brisbane	30.3	5	73	4	7039	246	3621	114	31.76	4	-	61.75	3.09 51.44
37	24/01/1986	NSW	QLD	Brisbane	6.0	2	7	-	7075	248	3628	114	31.82	4	-	62.06	3.08 51.28
38	21/02/1986	NSW	TAS	Sydney	18.0	4	40	3	7183	252	3668	117	31.35	4	-	61.39	3.06 51.07
38	21/02/1986	NSW	TAS	Sydney	8.0	3	12	3	7231	255	3680	120	30.67	4	-	60.26	3.05 50.89
39	28/02/1986	NSW	QLD	Sydney	23.0	5	63	2	7369	260	3743	122	30.68	4	-	60.40	3.05 50.79
39	28/02/1986	NSW	QLD	Sydney	11.0	3	15	2	7435	263	3758	124	30.31	4	-	59.96	3.03 50.54
40	14/03/1986	NSW	QLD	Sydney	34.0	7	65	6	7639	270	3823	130	29.41	5	-	58.76	3.00 50.05
40	14/03/1986	NSW	QLD	Sydney	10.0	4	14	-	7699	274	3837	130	29.52	5	-	59.22	2.99 49.84

1985/86 in Zimbabwe

41	28/03/1986	NSW	ZMS	Harare	20.5	6	40	1	7824	280	3877	131	29.60	5	-	59.73	2.97 49.55
41	28/03/1986	NSW	ZMS	Harare	13.0	2	37	3	7902	282	3914	134	29.21	5	-	58.97	2.97 49.53
42	04/04/1986	NSW	ZMS	Harare	15.0	3	41	2	7992	285	3955	136	29.08	5	-	58.76	2.97 49.49
42	04/04/1986	NSW	ZMS	Harare	8.0	4	9	-	8040	289	3964	136	29.15	5	-	59.12	2.96 49.30

1986/87 in Australia

43	29/10/1986	NSW	W.A	Perth	25.0	3	95	1	8190	292	4059	137	29.63	5	-	59.78	2.97 49.56
44	21/11/1986	NSW	EXI	Newcastle	13.0	4	31	2	8268	296	4090	139	29.42	5	-	59.48	2.97 49.47
44	21/11/1986	NSW	EXI	Newcastle	17.0	4	39	5	8370	300	4129	144	28.67	6	-	58.13	2.96 49.33
45	05/12/1986	NSW	QLD	Brisbane	29.0	3	117	2	8544	303	4246	146	29.08	6	-	58.52	2.98 49.70
45	05/12/1986	NSW	QLD	Brisbane	16.1	-	60	2	8641	303	4306	148	29.09	6	-	58.39	2.99 49.83
46	12/12/1986	NSW	W.A	Sydney	27.0	9	51	1	8803	312	4357	149	29.24	6	-	59.08	2.97 49.49
46	12/12/1986	NSW	W.A	Sydney	5.0	1	8	-	8833	313	4365	149	29.30	6	-	59.28	2.97 49.42
47	18/12/1986	NSW	S.A	Sydney	30.0	3	97	5	9013	316	4462	154	28.97	7	-	58.53	2.97 49.51
48	09/01/1987	NSW	S.A	Adelaide	25.0	1	115	2	9163	317	4577	156	29.34	7	-	58.74	3.00 49.95
48	09/01/1987	NSW	S.A	Adelaide	4.0	-	40	-	9187	317	4617	156	29.60	7	-	58.89	3.02 50.26
49	20/02/1987	NSW	TAS	Hobart TCA	11.0	3	29	2	9253	320	4646	158	29.41	7	-	58.56	3.01 50.21
49	20/02/1987	NSW	TAS	Hobart TCA	11.0	2	23	2	9319	322	4669	160	29.18	7	-	58.24	3.01 50.10
50	27/02/1987	NSW	QLD	Sydney	8.0	2	21	-	9367	324	4690	160	29.31	7	-	58.54	3.00 50.07

1987/88 in Zimbabwe

51	08/09/1987	NSW	ZMS	Harare	27.0	6	67	3	9529	330	4757	163	29.18	7	-	58.46	3.00 49.92
51	08/09/1987	NSW	ZMS	Harare	5.0	3	7	-	9559	333	4764	163	29.23	7	-	58.64	2.99 49.84
52	19/09/1987	NSW	ZMS	Harare	13.0	3	25	1	9637	336	4789	164	29.20	7	-	58.76	2.98 49.69
52	19/09/1987	NSW	ZMS	Harare	10.0	3	23	1	9697	339	4812	165	29.16	7	-	58.77	2.98 49.62

1987/88 in Australia

53	14/11/1987	NSW	S.A	Sydney	14.4	3	33	5	9785	342	4845	170	28.50	8	-	57.56	2.97 49.51
53	14/11/1987	NSW	S.A	Sydney	15.0	4	29	2	9875	346	4874	172	28.34	8	-	57.41	2.96 49.36
54	27/11/1987	NSW	QLD	Newcastle	15.0	1	58	1	9965	347	4932	173	28.51	8	-	57.60	2.97 49.49
54	27/11/1987	NSW	QLD	Newcastle	13.0	4	51	2	10043	351	4983	175	28.47	8	-	57.39	2.98 49.62
55	04/12/1987	NSW	TAS	Devonport	16.0	4	31	2	10139	355	5014	177	28.33	8	-	57.28	2.97 49.45
55	04/12/1987	NSW	TAS	Devonport	27.0	3	89	2	10301	358	5103	179	28.51	8	-	57.55	2.97 49.49
56	11/12/1987	NSW	W.A	Perth	18.0	3	40	1	10409	361	5143	180	28.57	8	-	57.83	2.96 49.41
57	18/12/1987	NSW	VIC	Sydney	25.0	5	68	5	10559	366	5211	185	28.17	9	-	57.08	2.96 49.35
58	26/12/1987	AUS	N.Z	Melbourne	33.3	6	92	4	10760	372	5303	189	28.06	9	-	56.93	2.96 49.28
58	26/12/1987	AUS	N.Z	Melbourne	20.0	5	45	-	10880	377	5348	189	28.30	9	-	57.57	2.95 49.15
59	12/02/1988	NSW	VIC	Melbourne	24.0	5	71	-	11024	382	5419	189	28.67	9	-	58.33	2.95 49.16
59	12/02/1988	NSW	VIC	Melbourne	9.0	2	23	-	11078	385	5442	189	28.79	9	-	58.61	2.95 49.12
60	24/02/1988	NSW	W.A	Sydney	16.0	2	46	2	11174	387	5488	191	28.73	9	-	58.50	2.95 49.11
60	24/02/1988	NSW	W.A	Sydney	13.1	4	22	1	11253	391	5510	192	28.70	9	-	58.61	2.94 48.96
61	02/03/1988	NSW	TAS	Sydney	26.0	10	54	5	11409	401	5564	197	28.24	10	-	57.91	2.93 48.77
61	02/03/1988	NSW	TAS	Sydney	5.0	1	10	-	11439	402	5574	197	28.29	10	-	58.07	2.92 48.73

1988/89 in Australia

62	28/10/1988	NSW	QLD	Brisbane	15.0	1	53	-	11529	403	5627	197	28.56	10	-	58.52	2.93 48.81
62	28/10/1988	NSW	QLD	Brisbane	15.0	2	52	2	11619	405	5679	199	28.54	10	-	58.39	2.93 48.88
63	04/11/1988	NSW	VIC	Sydney	21.0	11	24	3	11745	416	5703	202	28.23	10	-	58.14	2.91 48.56
63	04/11/1988	NSW	VIC	Sydney	31.0	7	91	3	11931	423	5794	205	28.26	10	-	58.20	2.91 48.58
64	11/11/1988	NSW	WIN	Sydney	21.0	3	82	2	12057	426	5876	207	28.39	10	-	58.25	2.92 48.74
64	11/11/1988	NSW	WIN	Sydney	5.0	1	19	1	12087	427	5895	208	28.34	10	-	58.11	2.93 48.77
65	25/11/1988	NSW	TAS	Devonport	36.0	7	90	2	12303	434	5985	210	28.50	10	-	58.59	2.92 48.65
66	02/12/1988	NSW	W.A	Newcastle	13.0	4	44	3	12381	438	6029	213	28.31	10	-	58.13	2.92 48.70
66	02/12/1988	NSW	W.A	Newcastle	26.0	7	80	3	12537	445	6109	216	28.28	10	-	58.04	2.92 48.73
67	19/12/1988	NSW	PKI	Sydney	15.5	5	34	4	12632	450	6143	220	27.92	10	-	57.42	2.92 48.63
67	19/12/1988	NSW	PKI	Sydney	21.1	3	66	5	12759	453	6209	225	27.60	11	-	56.71	2.92 48.66
68	06/01/1989	NSW	S.A	Adelaide	39.1	14	104	4	12994	467	6313	229	27.57	11	-	56.74	2.92 48.58
68	06/01/1989	NSW	S.A	Adelaide	6.0	-	20	-	13030	467	6333	229	27.66	11	-	56.90	2.92 48.60
69	20/01/1989	NSW	VIC	Melbourne	12.0	4	26	-	13102	471	6359	229	27.77	11	-	57.21	2.91 48.53
69	20/01/1989	NSW	VIC	Melbourne	19.0	4	49	4	13216	475	6408	233	27.50	11	-	56.72	2.91 48.49
70	03/02/1989	AUS	W.I	Adelaide	30.0	6	89	7	13396	481	6497	240	27.07	12	-	55.82	2.91 48.50
70	03/02/1989	AUS	W.I	Adelaide	20.0	4	60	2	13516	485	6557	242	27.10	12	-	55.85	2.91 48.51

Game	Date	Team	Opp	Venue	Ovrs	Md	Rns	Wk	Balls	Mdns	Runs	Wkt	Avge	5wi	10m	Stk/Rt	RPO	Ec/Rte
71	09/02/1989	NSW	S.A	Sydney	21.4	6	71	2	13646	491	6628	244	27.16	12	-	55.93	2.91	48.57
71	09/02/1989	NSW	S.A	Sydney	14.0	3	42	1	13730	494	6670	245	27.22	12	-	56.04	2.91	48.58
72	15/02/1989	NSW	W.A	Perth	15.0	1	59	1	13820	495	6729	246	27.35	12	-	56.18	2.92	48.69
72	15/02/1989	NSW	W.A	Perth	9.0	-	53	1	13874	495	6782	247	27.46	12	-	56.17	2.93	48.88
73	22/02/1989	NSW	TAS	Sydney	13.0	5	32	2	13952	500	6814	249	27.37	12	-	56.03	2.93	48.84
73	22/02/1989	NSW	TAS	Sydney	19.0	5	51	3	14066	505	6865	252	27.24	12	-	55.82	2.93	48.81
74	10/03/1989	NSW	QLD	Sydney	13.4	4	52	3	14148	509	6917	255	27.13	12	-	55.48	2.93	48.89
74	10/03/1989	NSW	QLD	Sydney	9.0	3	27	-	14202	512	6944	255	27.23	12	-	55.69	2.93	48.89

1989/90 in Australia

Game	Date	Team	Opp	Venue	Ovrs	Md	Rns	Wk	Balls	Mdns	Runs	Wkt	Avge	5wi	10m	Stk/Rt	RPO	Ec/Rte
75	10/11/1989	NSW	S.A	Adelaide	34.0	3	125	5	14406	515	7069	260	27.19	13	-	55.41	2.94	49.07
76	17/11/1989	NSW	SLS	Canberra	24.0	7	54	3	14550	522	7123	263	27.08	13	-	55.32	2.94	48.96
76	17/11/1989	NSW	SLS	Canberra	9.0	2	21	1	14604	524	7144	266	26.86	13	-	54.90	2.94	48.92
78	09/02/1990	NSW	VIC	Melbourne	15.0	5	31	3	14694	529	7175	269	26.67	13	-	54.62	2.93	48.83
78	09/02/1990	NSW	VIC	Melbourne	18.0	4	60	-	14802	533	7235	269	26.90	13	-	55.03	2.93	48.88
79	15/02/1990	NSW	S.A	Sydney	15.1	7	41	3	14893	540	7276	272	26.75	13	-	54.75	2.93	48.86
79	15/02/1990	NSW	S.A	Sydney	12.0	3	37	1	14965	543	7313	272	26.89	13	-	55.02	2.93	48.87
80	02/03/1990	NSW	W.A	Perth	23.0	5	90	-	15103	548	7403	272	27.22	13	-	55.53	2.94	49.02
80	02/03/1990	NSW	W.A	Perth	18.4	4	56	2	15215	552	7459	274	27.22	13	-	55.53	2.94	49.02
81	09/03/1990	NSW	TAS	Sydney	9.0	3	26	1	15269	555	7485	275	27.22	13	-	55.52	2.94	49.02
81	09/03/1990	NSW	TAS	Sydney	7.0	4	8	-	15311	559	7493	275	27.25	13	-	55.68	2.94	48.94
82	23/03/1990	NSW	QLD	Sydney	8.0	2	24	1	15359	561	7517	276	27.24	13	-	55.65	2.94	48.94
82	23/03/1990	NSW	QLD	Sydney	28.0	9	66	3	15527	570	7583	279	27.18	13	-	55.65	2.93	48.84

1990 in England

Game	Date	Team	Opp	Venue	Ovrs	Md	Rns	Wk	Balls	Mdns	Runs	Wkt	Avge	5wi	10m	Stk/Rt	RPO	Ec/Rte
83	29/08/1990	MPX	IDS	Scarborough	14.0	4	51	2	15611	574	7634	281	27.17	13	-	55.56	2.93	48.90
83	29/08/1990	MPX	IDS	Scarborough	13.0	1	46	3	15689	575	7680	284	27.04	13	-	55.24	2.94	48.95

1990/91 in Australia

Game	Date	Team	Opp	Venue	Ovrs	Md	Rns	Wk	Balls	Mdns	Runs	Wkt	Avge	5wi	10m	Stk/Rt	RPO	Ec/Rte
84	02/11/1990	NSW	TAS	Sydney	16.0	3	37	-	15785	578	7717	284	27.17	13	-	55.58	2.93	48.89
84	02/11/1990	NSW	TAS	Sydney	14.0	4	36	4	15869	582	7753	288	26.92	13	-	55.10	2.93	48.86
85	16/11/1990	NSW	VIC	St Kilda	34.0	10	91	3	16073	592	7844	291	26.96	13	-	55.23	2.93	48.80
86	22/11/1990	NSW	WEL	Nth Sydney	14.0	4	39	3	16157	596	7883	294	26.81	13	-	54.96	2.93	48.79
86	22/11/1990	NSW	WEL	Nth Sydney	20.0	6	51	1	16277	602	7934	295	26.89	13	-	55.18	2.92	48.74
87	20/12/1990	NSW	W.A	Perth	17.0	4	68	2	16379	606	8002	297	26.94	13	-	55.15	2.93	48.86
87	20/12/1990	NSW	W.A	Perth	19.0	5	70	1	16493	611	8072	298	27.09	13	-	55.35	2.94	48.94
88	04/01/1991	NSW	QLD	Brisbane	22.0	2	76	3	16625	613	8148	301	27.07	13	-	55.23	2.94	49.01
88	04/01/1991	NSW	QLD	Brisbane	18.0	5	32	4	16733	618	8180	305	26.82	13	-	54.86	2.93	48.89
89	13/01/1991	NSW	EXI	Albury	11.0	2	35	2	16799	620	8215	307	26.76	13	-	54.72	2.93	48.90
89	13/01/1991	NSW	EXI	Albury	10.0	1	28	2	16859	621	8243	309	26.68	13	-	54.56	2.93	48.89
90	19/01/1991	NSW	S.A	Sydney	24.0	10	50	2	17003	631	8293	311	26.67	13	-	54.67	2.93	48.77
90	19/01/1991	NSW	S.A	Sydney	13.0	7	9	-	17081	638	8302	311	26.69	13	-	54.92	2.92	48.60
91	31/01/1991	NSW	W.A	Sydney	5.0	2	20	-	17111	640	8322	311	26.76	13	-	55.02	2.92	48.64
91	31/01/1991	NSW	W.A	Sydney	22.0	5	66	2	17243	645	8388	313	26.80	13	-	55.09	2.92	48.65

1991 in West Indies

Game	Date	Team	Opp	Venue	Ovrs	Md	Rns	Wk	Balls	Mdns	Runs	Wkt	Avge	5wi	10m	Stk/Rt	RPO	Ec/Rte
92	16/02/1991	AXI	WPI	Basseterre	32.0	7	114	5	17435	652	8502	318	26.74	14	-	54.83	2.93	48.76
92	16/02/1991	AXI	WPI	Basseterre	16.0	4	37	1	17531	656	8539	319	26.77	14	-	54.96	2.92	48.71
93	21/02/1991	AXI	JAM	Kingston	20.0	5	42	6	17651	661	8581	325	26.40	15	-	54.31	2.92	48.61
93	21/02/1991	AXI	JAM	Kingston	16.0	1	36	2	17747	662	8617	327	26.35	15	-	54.27	2.91	48.55
94	01/03/1991	AUS	W.I	Kingston	21.0	4	58	-	17873	666	8675	327	26.53	15	-	54.66	2.91	48.54
94	01/03/1991	AUS	W.I	Kingston	17.0	3	55	-	17975	669	8730	327	26.70	15	-	54.97	2.91	48.57
95	23/03/1991	AUS	W.I	Georgetown	28.0	4	103	-	18143	673	8833	327	27.01	15	-	55.48	2.92	48.69

1991/92 in Australia

Game	Date	Team	Opp	Venue	Ovrs	Md	Rns	Wk	Balls	Mdns	Runs	Wkt	Avge	5wi	10m	Stk/Rt	RPO	Ec/Rte
96	01/11/1991	NSW	W.A	Perth	20.2	4	54	3	18265	677	8887	330	26.93	15	-	55.35	2.92	48.66
96	01/11/1991	NSW	W.A	Perth	19.0	4	62	1	18379	681	8949	331	27.04	15	-	55.53	2.92	48.69
97	08/11/1991	NSW	VIC	Sydney	24.0	6	52	2	18523	687	9001	333	27.03	15	-	55.62	2.92	48.59
97	08/11/1991	NSW	VIC	Sydney	22.0	1	67	2	18655	688	9068	335	27.07	15	-	55.69	2.92	48.61
98	15/11/1991	NSW	QLD	Brisbane	28.0	6	91	4	18823	694	9159	339	27.02	15	-	55.53	2.92	48.66
98	15/11/1991	NSW	QLD	Brisbane	5.0	1	25	-	18853	695	9184	339	27.09	15	-	55.61	2.92	48.71
99	23/11/1991	NSW	IDS	Lismore	19.3	4	45	3	18970	699	9229	342	26.99	15	-	55.47	2.92	48.65
99	23/11/1991	NSW	IDS	Lismore	19.4	7	37	6	19088	706	9266	348	26.63	16	-	54.85	2.91	48.54
100	29/11/1991	AUS	IND	Brisbane	21.0	2	82	2	19214	708	9348	350	26.71	16	-	54.90	2.92	48.65
100	29/11/1991	AUS	IND	Brisbane	17.2	3	55	2	19318	711	9403	352	26.71	16	-	54.88	2.92	48.67
101	20/12/1991	NSW	S.A	Adelaide	41.0	11	105	3	19564	722	9508	355	26.78	16	-	55.11	2.92	48.60
101	20/12/1991	NSW	S.A	Adelaide	2.5	-	14	-	19581	722	9522	355	26.82	16	-	55.16	2.92	48.63
102	25/01/1992	AUS	IND	Adelaide	26.2	6	68	2	19739	728	9590	357	26.86	16	-	55.29	2.92	48.58
102	25/01/1992	AUS	IND	Adelaide	17.0	3	59	-	19841	731	9649	357	27.03	16	-	55.58	2.92	48.63
103	01/02/1992	AUS	IND	Perth	23.0	4	68	4	19979	735	9717	361	26.92	16	-	55.34	2.92	48.64
103	01/02/1992	AUS	IND	Perth	12.1	3	27	7	20052	738	9744	368	26.48	17	1	54.49	2.92	48.59
104	13/02/1992	NSW	VIC	Melbourne	20.0	6	62	2	20172	744	9806	370	26.50	17	1	54.52	2.92	48.61
104	13/02/1992	NSW	VIC	Melbourne	4.0	2	3	-	20196	746	9809	370	26.51	17	1	54.58	2.91	48.57

Game	Date	Team	Opp	Venue	Ovrs	Md	Rns	Wk	Balls	Mdns	Runs	Wkt	Avge	5wi	10m	Stk/Rt	RPO	Ec/Rte
105	28/03/1992	NSW	W.A	Perth	26.0	5	71	2	20352	751	9880	372	26.56	17	1	54.71	2.91	48.55
105	28/03/1992	NSW	W.A	Perth	23.4	6	75	7	20494	757	9955	379	26.27	18	1	54.07	2.91	48.58

1992 in Sri Lanka

Game	Date	Team	Opp	Venue	Ovrs	Md	Rns	Wk	Balls	Mdns	Runs	Wkt	Avge	5wi	10m	Stk/Rt	RPO	Ec/Rte
106	10/08/1992	AXI	SLB	Kandy	24.0	6	53	3	20638	763	10008	382	26.20	18	1	54.03	2.91	48.49
107	17/08/1992	AUS	S.L	Colombo SSC	32.0	10	84	1	20830	773	10092	383	26.35	18	1	54.39	2.91	48.45
107	17/08/1992	AUS	S.L	Colombo SSC	5.0	2	13	-	20860	775	10105	383	26.38	18	1	54.46	2.91	48.44
108	24/08/1992	AXI	SLB	Matara	20.0	10	34	4	20980	785	10139	387	26.20	18	1	54.21	2.90	48.33
109	28/08/1992	AUS	S.L	Colombo KS	16.0	1	49	1	21076	786	10188	388	26.26	18	1	54.32	2.90	48.34
109	28/08/1992	AUS	S.L	Colombo KS	5.0	2	13	-	21106	788	10201	388	26.29	18	1	54.40	2.90	48.33

1992/93 in Australia

Game	Date	Team	Opp	Venue	Ovrs	Md	Rns	Wk	Balls	Mdns	Runs	Wkt	Avge	5wi	10m	Stk/Rt	RPO	Ec/Rte
110	06/11/1992	NSW	VIC	Sydney	37.0	5	122	4	21328	793	10323	392	26.33	18	1	54.41	2.90	48.40
111	14/11/1992	NSW	W.A	Perth	19.0	3	43	5	21442	796	10366	397	26.11	19	1	54.01	2.90	48.34
111	14/11/1992	NSW	W.A	Perth	27.0	9	72	3	21604	805	10438	400	26.10	19	1	54.01	2.90	48.32
112	20/11/1992	NSW	WIN	Sydney	14.0	4	40	1	21688	809	10478	401	26.13	19	1	54.08	2.90	48.31
112	20/11/1992	NSW	WIN	Sydney	14.0	2	55	-	21772	811	10533	401	26.27	19	1	54.29	2.90	48.38
113	27/11/1992	NSW	TAS	Hobart BEL	30.0	5	96	2	21952	816	10629	403	26.37	19	1	54.47	2.91	48.42
113	27/11/1992	NSW	TAS	Hobart BEL	19.0	4	55	3	22066	820	10684	406	26.32	19	1	54.35	2.91	48.42
114	18/12/1992	NSW	S.A	Adelaide	22.0	8	46	-	22198	828	10730	406	26.43	19	1	54.67	2.90	48.34
114	18/12/1992	NSW	S.A	Adelaide	24.0	5	76	1	22342	833	10806	407	26.55	19	1	54.89	2.90	48.37
115	26/12/1992	AUS	W.I	Melbourne	13.0	4	27	1	22420	837	10833	408	26.55	19	1	54.95	2.90	48.32
115	26/12/1992	AUS	W.I	Melbourne	10.0	2	32	1	22480	839	10865	409	26.56	19	1	54.96	2.90	48.33
116	18/03/1993	NSW	VIC	Melbourne	15.0	4	58	-	22570	843	10923	409	26.71	19	1	55.18	2.90	48.40
116	18/03/1993	NSW	VIC	Melbourne	15.0	4	41	1	22660	847	10964	410	26.74	19	1	55.27	2.90	48.38
117	26/03/1993	NSW	QLD	Sydney	22.0	7	55	1	22792	854	11019	411	26.81	19	1	55.45	2.90	48.35

2. TEST CAREER
Debut: 1981 AUSTRALIA v ENGLAND, Fifth Test, Manchester.

Bowling:

Season	Opp	Venue	Balls	Mdns	Runs	Wkts	Avge	5	10	Best
1981	ENG	Eng	468	16	246	5	49.20	-	-	2/50
1987/88	NZ	Aust	321	11	137	4	34.25	-	-	4/92
1988/89	WI	Aust	300	10	149	9	16.56	1	-	7/89
1991	WI	WI	396	11	216	-	-	-	-	-
1991/92	IND	Aust	701	21	359	17	21.12	1	1	7/27
1992	SRI	Sri	348	15	159	2	79.50	-	-	1/49
1992/93	WI	Aust	138	6	59	2	29.50	-	-	1/27
Total:			2672	90	1325	39	33.97	2	1	7/27

Bowling against:	Balls	Mdns	Runs	Wkts	Avge	5	10	Best
England	468	16	246	5	49.20	-	-	2/50
India	701	21	359	17	21.12	1	1	7/27
New Zealand	321	11	137	4	34.25	-	-	4/92
Sri Lanka	348	15	159	2	79.50	-	-	1/49
West Indies	834	27	424	11	38.55	1	-	7/89

Bowling in:	Balls	Mdns	Runs	Wkts	Avge	5	10	Best
First Innings	1148	38	564	16	35.25	1	-	7/89
Second Innings	555	15	282	8	35.25	-	-	4/92
Third Innings	481	20	250	11	22.73	1	-	7/27
Fourth Innings	488	17	229	4	57.25	-	-	2/55

Bowling, by venue:	Balls	Mdns	Runs	Wkts	Avge	5	10	Best
in Australia ...								
Adelaide	560	19	276	11	25.09	1	-	7/89
Brisbane	230	5	137	4	34.25	-	-	2/55
Melbourne	459	17	196	6	32.67	-	-	4/92
Perth	211	7	95	11	8.64	1	1	7/27
in England ...								
Manchester	264	9	124	4	31.00	-	-	2/50
The Oval	204	7	122	1	122.00	-	-	1/46
in Sri Lanka ...								
Colombo KS	126	3	62	1	62.00	-	-	1/49
Colombo SSC	222	12	97	1	97.00	-	-	1/84
in West Indies ...								
Georgetown	168	4	103	-	-	-	-	-
Kingston	228	7	113	-	-	-	-	-

Bowling, by country:	Balls	Mdns	Runs	Wkts	Avge	5	10	Best
Australia	1460	48	704	32	22.00	2	1	7/27
England	468	16	246	5	49.20	-	-	2/50

STATISTICS

Bowling, by country:	Balls	Mdns	Runs	Wkts	Avge	5	10	Best
Sri Lanka	348	15	159	2	79.50	-	-	1/49
West Indies	396	11	216	-	-	-	-	-

Five wickets in an innings:

Wkts	Team	Opponent	Venue	Season
7/89	Australia	West Indies	Adelaide	1988/89
7/27	Australia	India	Perth	1991/92

10 wickets in a match:

Wkts	Team	Opponent	Venue	Season
11/95	Australia	India	Perth	1991/92

Batting and Fielding:

Season	Opp	Venue	M	Inn	NO	Runs	HS	0s	Avge	Ct
1981	ENG	Eng	2	4	-	4	4	3	1.00	-
1987/88	NZ	Aust	1	2	2	2	2*	-	-	-
1988/89	WI	Aust	1	1	-	2	2	-	2.00	-
1991	WI	WI	2	3	2	3	2	-	3.00	-
1991/92	IND	Aust	3	4	3	20	12	-	20.00	1
1992	SRI	Sri	2	3	1	24	13	-	12.00	-
1992/93	WI	Aust	1	2	-	13	13*	1	6.50	1
Total:			12	19	8	68	13*	4	6.18	2

Batting against:	M	Inn	NO	Runs	HS	0s	Avge	Ct
England	2	4	-	4	4	3	1.00	-
India	3	4	3	20	12	-	20.00	1
New Zealand	1	2	2	2	2*	-	-	-
Sri Lanka	2	3	1	24	13	-	12.00	-
West Indies	4	6	2	18	13*	1	4.50	1

Batting in:	Inn	NO	Runs	HS	0s	Avge	Ct
First Innings	8	3	22	13	1	4.40	-
Second Innings	4	2	9	7*	1	4.50	1
Third Innings	5	2	35	13*	1	11.67	1
Fourth Innings	2	1	2	2*	1	2.00	-

Batting, by venue:	M	Inn	NO	Runs	HS	0s	Avge	Ct
in Australia ...								
Adelaide	2	3	1	14	12	-	7.00	-
Brisbane	1	1	1	7	7*	-	-	1
Melbourne	2	4	2	15	13*	1	7.50	1
Perth	1	1	1	1	1*	-	-	-

QUICK WHIT: THE MIKE WHITNEY STORY

Batting, by venue:	M	Inn	NO	Runs	HS	0s	Avge	Ct
in England ...								
Manchester	1	2	-	0	0	2	0.00	-
The Oval	1	2	-	4	4	1	2.00	-
in Sri Lanka ...								
Colombo KS	1	1	-	1	1	-	1.00	-
Colombo SSC	1	2	1	23	13	-	23.00	-
in West Indies ...								
Georgetown	1	2	2	1	1*	-	-	-
Kingston	1	1	-	2	2	-	2.00	-

Batting, by country:	M	Inn	NO	Runs	HS	0s	Avge	Ct
In Australia	6	9	5	37	13*	1	9.25	2
In England	2	4	-	4	4	3	1.00	
In Sri Lanka	2	3	1	24	13	-	12.00	
In West Indies	2	3	2	3	2	-	3.00	

Batting, by position	Inn	NO	Runs	HS	0s	Avge
No. 10	2	-	0	0	2	0.00
No. 11	17	8	68	13*	2	7.56

Test Career Bowling — Innings by Innings ...

Game	Date	Team	Opp	Venue	Ovrs	Md	Rns	Wk	Balls	Mdns	Runs	Wkt	Avge	5wi	10m	Stk/Rt	RPO	Ec/Rte
1981 in England																		
1	13/08/1981	AUS	ENG	Manchester	17.0	3	50	2	102	3	50	2	25.00	-	-	51.00	2.94	49.02
1	13/08/1981	AUS	ENG	Manchester	27.0	6	74	2	264	9	124	4	31.00	-	-	66.00	2.82	46.97
2	27/08/1981	AUS	ENG	The Oval	23.0	3	76	-	402	12	200	4	50.00	-	-	100.50	2.99	49.75
2	27/08/1981	AUS	ENG	The Oval	11.0	4	46	1	468	16	246	5	49.20	-	-	93.60	3.15	52.56
1987/88 in Australia																		
3	26/12/1987	AUS	N.Z	Melbourne	33.3	6	92	4	669	22	338	9	37.56	-	-	74.33	3.03	50.52
3	26/12/1987	AUS	N.Z	Melbourne	20.0	5	45	-	789	27	383	9	42.56	-	-	87.67	2.91	48.54
1988/89 in Australia																		
4	03/02/1989	AUS	W.I	Adelaide	30.0	6	89	7	969	33	472	16	29.50	1	-	60.56	2.92	48.71
4	03/02/1989	AUS	W.I	Adelaide	20.0	4	60	2	1089	37	532	18	29.56	1	-	60.50	2.93	48.85
1991 in West Indies																		
5	01/03/1991	AUS	W.I	Kingston	21.0	4	58	-	1215	41	590	18	32.78	1	-	67.50	2.91	48.56
5	01/03/1991	AUS	W.I	Kingston	17.0	3	55	-	1317	44	645	18	35.83	1	-	73.17	2.94	48.97
6	23/03/1991	AUS	W.I	Georgetown	28.0	4	103	-	1485	48	748	18	41.56	1	-	82.50	3.02	50.37
1991/92 in Australia																		
7	29/11/1991	AUS	IND	Brisbane	21.0	2	82	2	1611	50	830	20	41.50	1	-	80.55	3.09	51.52
7	29/11/1991	AUS	IND	Brisbane	17.2	3	55	2	1715	53	885	22	40.23	1	-	77.95	3.10	51.60
8	25/01/1992	AUS	IND	Adelaide	26.2	6	68	2	1873	59	953	24	39.71	1	-	78.04	3.05	50.88
8	25/01/1992	AUS	IND	Adelaide	17.0	3	59	-	1975	62	1012	24	42.17	1	-	82.29	3.07	51.24
9	01/02/1992	AUS	IND	Perth	23.0	4	68	4	2113	66	1080	28	38.57	1	1	75.46	3.07	51.11
9	01/02/1992	AUS	IND	Perth	12.1	3	27	7	2186	69	1107	35	31.63	2	1	62.46	3.04	50.64
1992 in Sri Lanka																		
10	17/08/1992	AUS	S.L	Colombo SSC	32.0	10	84	1	2378	79	1191	36	33.08	2	1	66.06	3.01	50.08
10	17/08/1992	AUS	S.L	Colombo SSC	5.0	2	13	-	2408	81	1204	36	33.44	2	1	66.89	3.00	50.00
11	28/08/1992	AUS	S.L	Colombo KS	16.0	1	49	1	2504	82	1253	37	33.86	2	1	67.68	3.00	50.04
11	28/08/1992	AUS	S.L	Colombo KS	5.0	2	13	-	2534	84	1266	37	34.22	2	1	68.49	3.00	49.96
1992/93 in Australia																		
12	26/12/1992	AUS	W.I	Melbourne	13.0	4	27	1	2612	88	1293	38	34.03	2	1	68.74	2.97	49.50
12	26/12/1992	AUS	W.I	Melbourne	10.0	2	32	1	2672	90	1325	39	33.97	2	1	68.51	2.98	49.59

3. LIMITED-OVER INTERNATIONALS CAREER

Debut: 1982/83, Australia v New Zealand, Sydney.

Bowling:

Season	Balls	Mdns	Runs	Wkts	Avge	Best	Stk/Rt	RPO	Eco/Rt
1982/83	42	3	19	2	9.50	2/19	21.00	2.71	45.24
1986/87	120	-	114	3	38.00	2/58	40.00	5.70	95.00
1987/88	360	3	242	10	24.20	4/34	36.00	4.03	67.22
1990/91	252	2	180	4	45.00	3/41	63.00	4.29	71.43
1991/92	864	24	445	18	24.72	4/34	48.00	3.09	51.50
1992/93	468	10	249	9	27.67	2/11	52.00	3.19	53.21
Total:	2106	42	1249	46	27.15	4/34	45.78	3.56	59.31

Against:	Balls	Mdns	Runs	Wkts	Avge	Best	Stk/Rt	RPO	Eco/Rt
England	180	3	121	4	30.25	2/37	45.00	4.03	67.22
India	288	8	145	4	36.25	2/22	72.00	3.02	50.35
New Zealand	162	3	111	4	27.75	2/19	40.50	4.11	68.52
Pakistan	240	7	159	4	39.75	2/58	60.00	3.98	66.25
Sri Lanka	402	6	239	11	21.73	4/34	36.55	3.57	59.45
South Africa	36	-	26	-	-	-	-	4.33	72.22
West Indies	738	12	433	17	25.47	4/34	43.41	3.52	58.67
Zimbabwe	60	3	15	2	7.50	2/15	30.00	1.50	25.00

Bowling in:	Balls	Mdns	Runs	Wkts	Avge	Best	Stk/Rt	RPO	Eco/Rt
1st Innings	1290	22	755	28	26.96	4/34	46.07	3.51	58.53
2nd Innings	816	20	494	18	27.44	4/34	45.33	3.63	60.54

By venue:	Balls	Mdns	Runs	Wkts	Avge	Best	Stk/Rt	RPO	Eco/Rt
in Australia ...									
Adelaide	240	9	123	4	30.75	2/22	60.00	3.08	51.25
Brisbane	180	5	105	2	52.50	1/30	90.00	3.50	58.33
Hobart BEL	120	6	44	3	14.67	2/15	40.00	2.20	36.67
Melbourne	408	8	220	9	24.44	4/34	45.33	3.24	53.92
Perth	330	1	266	6	44.33	2/58	55.00	4.84	80.61
Sydney	414	10	211	14	15.07	4/34	29.57	3.06	50.97
in Sri Lanka ...									
Colombo KS	102	1	67	2	33.50	2/40	51.00	3.94	65.69
Colombo PSS	60	-	33	2	16.50	2/33	30.00	3.30	55.00
in West Indies ...									
Bridgetown	60	1	39	1	39.00	1/39	60.00	3.90	65.00
Georgetown	54	-	46	-	-	-	-	5.11	85.19
Kingston	42	1	16	-	-	-	-	2.29	38.10
Port-of-Spain	96	-	79	3	26.33	3/41	32.00	4.94	82.29

By country:	Balls	Mdns	Runs	Wkts	Avge	Best	Stk/Rt	RPO	Eco/Rt
In Australia	1692	39	969	38	25.50	4/34	44.53	3.44	57.27
In Sri Lanka	162	1	100	4	25.00	2/33	40.50	3.70	61.73
In W. Indies	252	2	180	4	45.00	3/41	63.00	4.29	71.43

Batting and Fielding:
* Indicates not out

Season	M	Inn	NO	Runs	HS	0s	Avge	Ct
1982/83	1	1	-	1	1	-	1.00	-
1986/87	2	1	-	6	6	-	6.00	2
1987/88	6	2	1	5	3	-	5.00	-
1990/91	5	1	-	0	0	1	0.00	2
1991/92	15	6	5	25	9*	-	25.00	6
1992/93	9	2	1	3	2	-	3.00	1
Total:	38	13	7	40	9*	1	6.67	11

Batting against:	M	Inn	NO	Runs	HS	0s	Avge	Ct
England	3	2	1	14	8*	-	14.00	-
India	5	1	1	0	0*	-	-	5
New Zealand	3	3	1	6	3	-	3.00	-
Pakistan	4	1	-	5	5	-	5.00	2
Sri Lanka	7	-	-	-	-	-	-	1
South Africa	1	1	1	9	9*	-	-	-
West Indies	14	5	3	6	2*	1	3.00	3
Zimbabwe	1	-	-	-	-	-	-	3

Batting in:	Inn	NO	Runs	HS	0s	Avge	Ct
First Innings	7	6	22	9*	1	22.00	8
Second Innings	6	1	18	6	-	3.60	3

Batting, by venue:	M	Inn	NO	Runs	HS	0s	Avge	Ct
in Australia ...								
Adelaide	4	-	-	-	-	-	-	-
Brisbane	3	2	1	3	2	-	3.00	1
Hobart BEL	2	-	-	-	-	-	-	-
Melbourne	7	2	2	4	2*	-	-	1
Perth	6	3	-	14	6	-	4.67	2
Sydney	8	5	4	19	9*	-	19.00	4
in Sri Lanka ...								
Colombo KS	2	-	-	-	-	-	-	1
Colombo PSS	1	-	-	-	-	-	-	-
in West Indies ...								
Bridgetown	1	-	-	-	-	-	-	1

STATISTICS

Batting, by venue:	M	Inn	NO	Runs	HS	0s	Avge	Ct
Georgetown	1	-	-	-	-	-	-	1
Kingston	1	-	-	-	-	-	-	-
Port-of-Spain	2	1	-	0	0	1	0.00	-

Batting, by country:	M	Inn	NO	Runs	HS	0s	Avge	Ct
In Australia	30	12	7	40	9*	-	8.00	8
In Sri Lanka	3	-	-	-	-	-	-	1
In West Indies	5	1	-	0	0	1	0.00	2

Batting, by position:	Inn	NO	Runs	HS	0s	Avge
No. 9	1	-	6	6	-	6.00
No. 10	5	3	24	9*	1	12.00
No. 11	7	4	10	3	-	3.33

Highest Score: 9* Australia v South Africa, Sydney, 1991/92
Best Bowling: 4/34 Australia v Sri Lanka, Sydney, 1987/88

Limited-Over Internationals Bowling — Innings by Innings ...

Game	Date	Team	Opp	Venue	Ovrs	Md	Runs	Wkt	Balls	Mdns	Runs	Wkt	Avge	Stk/Rt	RPO	Ec/Rte
1	17/03/1983	AUS	N.Z	Sydney	7.0	3	19	2	42	3	19	2	9.50	21.00	2.71	45.24
2	01/01/1987	AUS	ENG	Perth	10.0	-	56	1	102	3	75	3	25.00	34.00	4.41	73.53
3	02/01/1987	AUS	PAK	Perth	10.0	-	58	2	162	3	133	5	26.60	32.40	4.93	82.10
4	02/01/1988	AUS	S.L	Perth	10.0	-	26	1	222	3	159	6	26.50	37.00	4.30	71.62
5	03/01/1988	AUS	N.Z	Perth	10.0	-	46	1	282	3	205	7	29.29	40.29	4.36	72.70
6	07/01/1988	AUS	N.Z	Melbourne	10.0	-	46	1	342	3	251	8	31.38	42.75	4.40	73.39
7	10/01/1988	AUS	S.L	Adelaide	10.0	-	53	1	402	3	304	9	33.78	44.67	4.54	75.62
8	19/01/1988	AUS	S.L	Sydney	10.0	2	34	4	462	5	338	13	26.00	35.54	4.39	73.16
9	04/02/1988	AUS	ENG	Melbourne	10.0	1	37	2	522	6	375	15	25.00	34.80	4.31	71.84
10	26/02/1991	AUS	W.I	Kingston	7.0	1	16	-	564	7	391	15	26.07	37.60	4.16	69.33
11	09/03/1991	AUS	W.I	Port-of-Spain	9.0	-	41	3	618	7	432	18	24.00	34.33	4.19	69.90
12	10/03/1991	AUS	W.I	Port-of-Spain	7.0	-	38	-	660	7	470	18	26.11	36.67	4.27	71.21
13	13/03/1991	AUS	W.I	Bridgetown	10.0	1	39	1	720	8	509	19	26.79	37.89	4.24	70.69
14	20/03/1991	AUS	W.I	Georgetown	9.0	-	46	-	774	8	555	19	29.21	40.74	4.30	71.71
15	12/12/1991	AUS	W.I	Melbourne	10.0	3	29	-	834	11	584	19	30.74	43.89	4.20	70.02
16	15/12/1991	AUS	IND	Adelaide	10.0	3	22	2	894	14	606	21	28.86	42.57	4.07	67.79
17	18/12/1991	AUS	W.I	Sydney	10.0	1	25	3	954	15	631	24	26.29	39.75	3.97	66.14
18	09/01/1992	AUS	W.I	Melbourne	10.0	-	28	1	1014	15	659	25	26.36	40.56	3.90	64.99
19	12/01/1992	AUS	W.I	Brisbane	10.0	2	39	1	1074	17	698	26	26.85	41.31	3.90	64.99
20	14/01/1992	AUS	IND	Sydney	10.0	1	36	1	1134	18	734	27	27.19	42.00	3.88	64.73
21	18/01/1992	AUS	IND	Melbourne	8.0	2	19	-	1182	20	753	27	27.89	43.78	3.82	63.71
22	20/01/1992	AUS	IND	Sydney	10.0	-	32	1	1242	20	785	28	28.04	44.36	3.79	63.20
23	26/02/1992	AUS	SAF	Sydney	6.0	-	26	-	1278	20	811	28	28.96	45.64	3.81	63.46
24	01/03/1992	AUS	IND	Brisbane	10.0	2	36	-	1338	22	847	28	30.25	47.79	3.80	63.30
25	05/03/1992	AUS	ENG	Sydney	10.0	2	28	1	1398	24	875	29	30.17	48.21	3.76	62.59
26	07/03/1992	AUS	S.L	Adelaide	10.0	3	26	1	1458	27	901	30	30.03	48.60	3.71	61.80
27	11/03/1992	AUS	PAK	Perth	10.0	1	50	1	1518	28	951	31	30.68	48.97	3.76	62.65
28	14/03/1992	AUS	ZIM	Hobart BEL	10.0	3	15	2	1578	31	966	33	29.27	47.82	3.67	61.22
29	18/03/1992	AUS	W.I	Melbourne	10.0	1	34	4	1638	32	1000	37	27.03	44.27	3.66	61.05
30	15/08/1992	AUS	S.L	Colombo PSS	10.0	-	33	2	1698	32	1033	39	26.49	43.54	3.65	60.84
31	04/09/1992	AUS	S.L	Colombo KS	7.0	-	27	-	1740	32	1060	39	27.18	44.62	3.66	60.92
32	05/09/1992	AUS	S.L	Colombo KS	10.0	1	40	2	1800	33	1100	41	26.83	43.90	3.67	61.11
33	06/12/1992	AUS	W.I	Perth	5.0	-	30	-	1830	33	1130	41	27.56	44.63	3.70	61.75
34	08/12/1992	AUS	W.I	Sydney	6.0	1	11	2	1866	34	1141	43	26.53	43.40	3.67	61.15
35	10/12/1992	AUS	PAK	Hobart BEL	10.0	3	29	1	1926	37	1170	44	26.59	43.77	3.64	60.75
36	13/12/1992	AUS	PAK	Adelaide	10.0	3	22	-	1986	40	1192	44	27.09	45.14	3.60	60.02
37	15/12/1992	AUS	W.I	Melbourne	10.0	1	27	1	2046	41	1219	45	27.09	45.47	3.57	59.58
38	10/01/1993	AUS	W.I	Brisbane	10.0	1	30	1	2106	42	1249	46	27.15	45.78	3.56	59.31

4. SHEFFIELD SHIELD CAREER

Debut: 1980/81, New South Wales v Queensland, Brisbane.

Bowling:

Season	Balls	Mdns	Runs	Wkts	Avge	5	10	Best
1980/81	552	21	273	10	27.30	-	-	4/62
1981/82	793	26	386	9	42.89	-	-	2/33
1982/83	2168	75	1136	38	29.89	2	-	5/93
1983/84	498	18	271	5	54.20	-	-	2/89
1985/86	1173	43	483	22	21.95	1	-	6/65
1986/87	1147	27	656	17	38.59	1	-	5/97
1987/88	1421	52	625	28	22.32	3	-	5/33
1988/89	2085	88	1020	37	27.57	-	-	4/49
1989/90	1127	49	564	18	31.33	1	-	5/125
1990/91	1224	57	555	21	26.43	-	-	4/32
1991/92	1415	52	681	26	26.19	1	-	7/75
1992/93	1380	54	664	20	33.20	1	-	5/43
Total:	14983	562	7314	251	29.14	10	-	7/75

Bowling against:	Balls	Mdns	Runs	Wkts	Avge	5	10	Best
Queensland	3137	105	1554	58	26.79	2	-	6/65
South Australia	3225	124	1665	51	32.65	4	-	5/33
Tasmania	1977	79	869	42	20.69	1	-	5/54
Victoria	3055	126	1438	46	31.26	1	-	5/68
Western Australia	3589	128	1788	54	33.11	2	-	7/75

Bowling in:	Balls	Mdns	Runs	Wkts	Avge	5	10	Best
First Innings	4666	169	2379	73	32.59	2	-	5/68
Second Innings	5202	184	2478	91	27.23	6	-	6/65
Third Innings	1351	49	673	19	35.42	-	-	3/51
Fourth Innings	3764	160	1784	68	26.24	2	-	7/75

Bowling, by venue:	Balls	Mdns	Runs	Wkts	Avge	5	10	Best
Adelaide	1890	65	1035	24	43.13	2	-	5/125
Brisbane	1573	43	803	32	25.09	1	-	5/93
Devonport	474	14	210	6	35.00	-	-	2/31
Hobart BEL	294	9	151	5	30.20	-	-	3/55
Hobart TCA	249	9	126	7	18.00	-	-	3/74
Melbourne	1315	54	624	17	36.71	-	-	4/49
Newcastle	696	27	414	12	34.50	-	-	3/44
Perth	2616	84	1356	39	34.77	2	-	7/75
St Kilda	204	10	91	3	30.33	-	-	3/91
Sydney	5672	247	2504	106	23.62	5	-	6/65

STATISTICS

Five Wickets in an Innings:

Wkts	Team	Opponent	Venue	Season
5/133	New South Wales	South Australia	Adelaide	1982/83
5/93	New South Wales	Queensland	Brisbane	1982/83
6/65	New South Wales	Queensland	Sydney	1985/86
5/97	New South Wales	South Australia	Sydney	1986/87
5/33	New South Wales	South Australia	Sydney	1987/88
5/68	New South Wales	Victoria	Sydney	1987/88
5/54	New South Wales	Tasmania	Sydney	1987/88
5/125	New South Wales	South Australia	Adelaide	1989/90
7/75	New South Wales	Western Australia	Perth	1991/92
5/43	New South Wales	Western Australia	Perth	1992/93

Batting and Fielding:

* Indicates not out

Season	M	Inn	NO	Runs	HS	0s	Avge	Ct
1980/81	3	2	-	4	3	-	2.00	3
1981/82	5	3	2	4	3*	1	4.00	1
1982/83	10	7	3	38	2	8*	9.50	7
1983/84	3	4	-	16	12	2	4.00	5
1985/86	6	7	3	33	19	2	8.25	1
1986/87	7	7	1	33	19	2	5.50	1
1987/88	8	9	5	21	5*	1	5.25	1
1988/89	10	10	5	48	22*	1	9.60	1
1989/90	7	6	4	24	15*	1	12.00	7
1990/91	6	5	1	32	17	1	8.00	1
1991/92	6	9	2	11	8	5	1.57	-
1992/93	6	5	2	23	9	-	7.67	3
Total:	77	74	28	287	28*	19	6.24	31

Batting against:	M	Inn	NO	Runs	HS	0s	Avge	Ct
Queensland	18	18	6	68	15*	5	5.67	6
South Australia	15	14	7	60	19	2	8.57	8
Tasmania	11	8	1	44	19	1	6.29	6
Victoria	15	12	7	27	9	3	5.40	4
Western Australia	18	22	7	88	28*	8	5.87	7

Batting in:	Inn	NO	Runs	HS	0s	Avge	Ct
First Innings	27	10	104	22*	7	6.12	10
Second Innings	28	12	136	28*	3	8.50	10
Third Innings	12	5	17	8	6	2.43	6
Fourth Innings	7	1	30	19	3	5.00	5

Batting, by venue	M	Inn	NO	Runs	HS	0s	Avge	Ct
Adelaide	8	7	2	34	19	2	6.80	5
Brisbane	7	7	3	21	10*	2	5.25	2
Devonport	2	1	-	6	6	-	6.00	1
Hobart BEL	1	1	1	1	1*	-	-	-
Hobart TCA	2	1	-	0	0	1	0.00	-
Melbourne	7	6	4	14	9	1	7.00	4
Newcastle	5	4	1	5	4	1	1.67	-
Perth	13	18	6	51	22*	7	4.25	6
St Kilda	1	2	1	3	3*	1	3.00	-
Sydney	31	27	10	152	28*	4	8.94	13

Batting, by position	Inn	NO	Runs	HS	0s	Avge
No. 9	1	-	0	0	1	0.00
No. 10	24	8	90	22*	8	5.63
No. 11	49	20	197	28*	10	6.79

Highest Score: 28*   NSW v Western Australia, Sydney, 1982/83

Sheffield Shield Leading Wicket-takers (240 or more):

Bowler	Mat	Balls	Runs	Wkts	Avge	5	10	Best
CV Grimmett (SA, Vic)	79	28465	12796	513	25.29	48	13	9-180
TM Alderman (WA)	97	19288	9299	384	24.21	17	3	7-28
GF Lawson (NSW)	103	20930	8744	367	23.82	12	-	6-31
JR Thomson (NSW, Qld)	84	16939	8591	355	24.20	18	3	7-27
AA Mallett (SA)	77	20906	8173	344	23.76	19	2	7-57
DK Lillee (WA)	75	17814	8086	338	23.92	18	4	7-36
GAR Lock (WA)	63	20107	7210	302	23.87	15	2	7-53
AN Connolly (Vic)	71	18033	7745	297	26.07	12	4	9-67
CG Rackemann (Qld)	77	16845	7520	289	26.02	9	1	7-49
CD Matthews (WA, Tas)	64	14265	6969	279	24.97	18	-	8-101
CJ McDermott (Qld)	60	13140	6700	274	24.45	20	2	8-44
JW Martin (NSW, SA)	77	17078	8703	273	31.87	12	-	8-97
GRJ Matthews (NSW)	87	19958	7594	273	27.81	16	3	8-52
R Benaud (NSW)	73	17948	7174	266	26.96	12	3	7-32
G Dymock (Qld)	75	17110	7223	266	27.15	8	-	6-79
PR Sleep (SA)	127	19467	9893	254	38.94	7	-	8-133
RJ Bright (Vic)	101	22789	8833	252	35.05	10	-	6-61
MR Whitney (NSW)	**77**	**14983**	**7314**	**251**	**29.14**	**10**	**-**	**7-75**
MG Hughes (Vic)	70	15549	7471	251	29.76	9	2	7-81
LO Fleetwood-Smith (Vic)	40	11576	6034	246	24.52	25	8	9-135
AK Davidson (NSW)	62	13423	5195	246	21.11	10	-	7-31
RR Lindwall (NSW, Qld)	66	14084	5518	244	22.61	11	1	7-45
JD Higgs (Vic)	75	14961	7202	240	30.00	12	2	8-66

Sheffield Shield Finals

In 1982/83, the Australian Cricket Board introduced a final to decide the Shield champions. The final is played between the two leading teams after the 30 "home-and-away" matches. The leading team hosts the final, and wins the Shield unless beaten outright.

MR Whitney has appeared in five Shield finals.

Season	Venue	Result	MR Whitney bowling
1982-83	Perth	NSW defeated WA by 54 runs	4-67 & 1-45
1985-86	Sydney	Match Drawn (with Qld)	6-65 & 0-14
1989-90	Sydney	NSW defeated Qld by 345 runs	1-24 & 3-66
1991-92	Perth	WA defeated NSW by 44 runs	2-71 & 7-75
1992-93	Sydney	NSW defeated Qld by 8 wickets	1-55

NSW also reached the Shield final in 1984-85, when Whitney was unavailable due to injury, and in 1990-91, when Whitney did not play as he was in the West Indies with the Australian team.

The best innings' returns by a bowler in a Sheffield Shield final are as follows:

Bowling	Bowler	Final	Season
8-101	CD Matthews	WA v Qld	1987-88
7-41	WJ Holdsworth	NSW v Qld	1992-93
7-75	**MR Whitney**	**NSW v WA**	**1991-92**
7-112	CR Miller	SA v WA	1988-89
6-54	CG Rackemann	Qld v NSW	1984-85
6-65	**MR Whitney**	**NSW v Qld**	**1985-86**

5. NEW SOUTH WALES FIRST-CLASS CRICKET RECORDS

Most Appearances (80 or more):

Matches	Player	Career
115	GF Lawson	1977/78–1991/92
107	SJ Rixon	1974/75–1987/88
103	KD Walters	1962/63–1980/81
101	GRJ Matthews	1982/83–1992/93
94	J Dyson	1975/76–1988/89
93	BC Booth	1954/55–1968/69
93	**MR Whitney**	**1980/81–1992/93**
87	AF Kippax	1918/19–1935/36
86	R Benaud	1948/49–1963/64
83	W Bardsley	1903/04–1925/26
82	WAS Oldfield	1919/20–1937/38
81	CG Macartney	1905/06–1926/27
80	SE Gregory	1889/90–1911/12

Leading Wicket Takers (200 or more):

Bowler	Career	M	Runs	Wkts	Avge	5wi	10m	Best
GF Lawson	1977/78–1991/92	115	9230	395	23.37	13	-	6/31
AA Mailey	1912/13–1929/30	67	9246	334	27.68	28	6	8/81
WJ O'Reilly	1927/28–1945/46	54	5369	325	16.52	26	7	9/41
R Benaud	1948/49–1963/64	86	8376	322	26.01	17	4	7/18
GRJ Matthews	1982/83–1992/93	101	8731	314	27.81	16	3	8/52
MR Whitney	**1980/81–1992/93**	**93**	**8579**	**313**	**27.41**	**13**	**-**	**7/75**
JW Martin	1956/57–1967/68	78	8987	293	30.67	12	-	8/97
AK Davidson	1949/50–1962/63	72	5858	273	21.45	10	-	7/31
CTB Turner	1882/83–1909/10	43	4256	263	16.18	29	11	8/32
MA Noble	1893/94–1919/20	77	5379	230	23.38	13	2	7/44
RG Holland	1978/79–1986/87	68	7215	228	31.64	8	1	9/83
C Kelleway	1907/08–1928/29	57	5137	215	23.89	7	1	7/35
KJ O'Keeffe	1968/69–1979/80	65	5708	211	27.05	12	1	6/49
DJ Colley	1969/70–1977/78	71	6513	203	32.08	6	-	6/30
LS Pascoe	1974/75–1986/87	54	5292	203	26.07	9	2	8/41

6. AUSTRALIAN DOMESTIC LIMITED-OVER CRICKET RECORDS:

Most Appearances (30 or more):

Player	Career	Matches
GM Wood (WA)	1977/78-1991-92	42
DW Hookes (SA)	1975/76-1991/92	38
KH Macleay (WA)	1981/82-1991-92	38
GF Lawson (NSW)	1978/79-1991/92	35
AR Border (NSW, Qld)	1977/78-1992/93	35
TM Alderman (WA)	1974/75-1992/93	35
MR Whitney (NSW)	**1980/81-1992/93**	**34**
DM Jones (Vic)	1981/82-1992/93	34
GRJ Matthews (NSW)	1982/83-1992/93	34
RW Marsh (WA)	1969/70-1983/84	33
WS Andrews (WA)	1982/83-1992/93	33
DC Boon (Tas)	1978/79-1992/93	32
GR Marsh (WA)	1981/82-1992-93	31
MRJ Veletta (WA)	1983/84-1992/93	31
PR Sleep (SA)	1978/79-1992/93	30

Leading Wicket-takers (35 or more):

Bowler	Mat	Balls	Mdns	Runs	Wkts	Avge	Best
KH Macleay (WA)	38	1896	32	1165	53	21.98	5-30
DK Lillee (WA, Tas)	27	1559	32	811	48	16.89	4-21
MR Whitney (NSW)	**34**	**1832**	**36**	**1110**	**40**	**27.75**	**4-30**
G Dymock (Qld)	23	1300	20	749	39	19.21	5-27
GF Lawson (NSW)	35	1811	38	1053	39	27.00	4-31
TM Alderman (WA)	35	1811	34	1169	39	29.97	4-14
CG Rackemann (Qld)	27	1477	31	894	39	22.92	7-34
JR Thomson (NSW, Qld)	28	1449	21	933	37	25.21	6-18
GRJ Matthews (NSW)	34	1584	17	996	35	28.46	3-29